An Introduction to Sentence Structure

An Introduction to English Sentence Structure

Clauses, Markers, Missing Elements

Jon Jonz

SHEFFIELD, UK   BRISTOL, CT

Published by Equinox Publishing Ltd
UK: Unit S3, Kelham House, 3 Lancaster Sreet, Sheffield, S3 8AF
USA: ISD LLC, 70 Enterprise Drive, Suite 2, Bristol, CT 06010
www.equinoxpub.com

First published 2014
© Jon Jonz 2014

British Library Cataloguing-in-Publication Data
A catalogue record for this book is available from the British Library.

ISBN-13 978-1-84553-145-4   (hardback)
        978-1-84553-146-1   (paperback)

Library of Congress Cataloging-in-Publication Data
Jonz, Jon, 1944–
    An introduction to English sentence structure : clauses, markers, missing elements / Jon Jonz
        p. cm. * (Equinox textbooks and surveys in linguistics)
        ISBN-13: 978-1-84553-145-4 (hardback : alk. paper)
        ISBN-10: 1-84553-145-0 (hardback : alk. paper)
        ISBN-13: 978-1-84553-146-1 (paperback : alk. paper)
        ISBN-10: 1-84553-146-9 (paperback : alk. paper)
        1. English language—Clauses. 2. English language—Sentences.
    3. English language—Rhetoric.   I. Title II. Series.
    PE1385.J67 2006
    428.2–dc22
                                2005034645

Designed and typeset by Ben Cracknell Studios | www.benstudios.co.uk
Printed and bound by Lightning Source Inc. (La Vergne, TN),
Lightning Source UK Ltd. (Milton Keynes),
Lightning Source AU Pty. (Scoresby, Victoria)

Contents

Suggested Responses

Frequently Used Charts and Lists (Grouped by Related Topic)

Glossary

References

Index

Preface

You're going to enjoy this book.

In it we develop a viewpoint on English (and language in general) that will help you see through its apparent complexities to the relatively few natural principles that underlie its structure. Regardless of how much you already know about the way English works, there will be something here for you to think about and to take pleasure from. For one thing, you will have the opportunity to read (or reread) parts of one of the most entertaining works in English-language literature, H. G. Wells's *The War of the Worlds*. This classic work is rich in language expression, and it provides an excellent living laboratory for the study of modern English. You may even run into some English-language forms and structures that you have not encountered anywhere else—especially if you have not ever heard or read versions of English other than your own.

You are a humanities student or a teacher in preparation or an aspiring writer or just a plain old language lover—or maybe all of these. And I know that you probably didn't just wander into the bookstore and pick up this book because the cover caught your eye or because you found the title intriguing. Overwhelming odds are that you bought this book as a course requirement. But you will be glad you did. It has been written with you in mind.

Two main things will stick with you after you have finished this book: first, you will have seen how language is shaped to reflect the events in ordinary everyday experience. And second, you will have developed an analytical approach that will give you satisfaction simply through its application and that, as a bonus, will be useful to you not just in your language courses but in all your efforts to understand complex phenomena by first seeing the elegance and simplicity of their top-level organization.

Why 'Clauses, Markers, Missing Elements'? This book is subtitled *Clauses, Markers, Missing Elements* because the secret to having a solid basic understanding of how language works has these three parts:

1 you rely on the relationship between the structure of **clauses** and the structure of ordinary everyday experience;

2 you know about the way that clause complexes are formed, which is signaled by **markers;** and

3 you are aware that language structures very often turn out to be incomplete, to be **missing** significant **elements** of their composition.

Goals As you work your way through this book, you will get good at:

1 identifying the elements of event structure that are reflected in language: the things that happen and the claims that are made, the main characters and the essential props, and the elements of the scenarios;

2 identifying those elements of language that are not related directly to the event structure but that more clearly pertain to interpersonal relationships and discourses;

3 identifying process types, participant roles, and circumstance details;

4 identifying the edges and elements of word groups;

5 recognizing and interpreting beginnings—the leading edge;

6 recognizing and tracking coreference relationships;

7 identifying markers;

8 accounting for missing elements;

9 recognizing and tracking discontinuity; and

10 analyzing subordination, embedding, complementation, and apposition.

Assumptions This book makes two assumptions about you: either (1) you are already interested in language, or (2) you don't have any particularly focused interest in language, but you are open to new ideas.

Approach This book is a descriptive grammar of modern English written on functional principles. It is concerned both with how English is structured and with how it works. However, functional grammars are only rarely as heavily oriented to form as is this one. In fact, dyed-in-the-wool grammarians of the functional persuasion will not be comfortable at all with having this grammar labeled 'functional.' Likewise, structural grammars are only rarely as heavily oriented toward function as is this one. So, dyed-in-the-wool grammarians of the structural persuasion will not embrace this grammar as a full-blooded version of the structuralist breed.

Perhaps the approach taken here is best thought of as a hybrid. It assumes that form matters, and in this sense it is 'structural.' But it also assumes that form follows function, and in this sense it is 'functional.' That's why I call it a 'functional grammar of modern English structure.'

But the book is also completely oriented toward written language. Well, *almost* completely: the last few chapters will give you an opportunity to study written dialog, a second-hand form of speech. However, that's as close as we will get to studying real spoken language. So perhaps a 'functional grammar of modern *written* English structure' would be more accurate.

Payson, Arizona
September 2013

Acknowledgments

This book is based on the ideas of many great contemporary grammarians, and, for better or worse, my interpretation of those ideas.

I gratefully acknowledge all of the following experts, and too many more to name, whose written work has contributed immeasurably to the practice of modern linguistic analysis and language pedagogy and whose ideas— functionalist and otherwise— have helped shape this book: Flor Aarts, Jan Aarts, C. L. Baker, Meriel Bloor, Thomas Bloor, Noel Burton-Roberts, Joan Bybee, Marianne Celce-Murcia, Bernard Comrie, Peter Fries, Tom Givón, Sidney Greenbaum, M. A. K. Halliday, Paul Hopper, Rodney Huddleston, Howard Jackson, Ronald Langacker, Diane Larsen-Freeman, Geoffrey Leech, Graham Lock, Jim McCawley, William Pagliuca, Revere Perkins, Paul Postal, Geoffrey Pullum, Sir Randolph Quirk, Juhani Rudanko, Jan Svartvik, and Geoff Thompson.

I also acknowledge with great appreciation the major contribution made by my friend and colleague Robert Baumgardner and all of his students who worked through several earlier versions of this book, whose patience and support have made this project possible. I am also grateful to Bates Hoffer and a class of his teachers-in-preparation, who provided a critical review of an even earlier version of the book.

Additionally, I acknowledge with great pleasure the sharp eyes of Steve Tharp and Melissa Gantt, two superior grammar students who turned out to be equally fine editors and proofreaders.

The existence of this book owes enormously to the confidence and encouragement shown me by Equinox founder and publisher, Janet Joyce. I am most grateful to her for all the support I have received from Equinox, most especially that from my persistent and dedicated editor, Sandra Margolies, as well as from Ben and Ruth at Ben Cracknell Studios, whose work on design and typesetting has been thoughtful as well as beautiful.

I also want to thank you and the many hundreds of other students of language on whom I have tried out my ideas. You have taught me plenty.

Chapter 1

Language and Events in Experience

Preliminaries

This book is based in approaches to language that assume that sense or meaning is the right place to start if your goal is to understand how language does its work; after all, the main purposes of language are to allow us to think, understand, and express meaning. These approaches are generally known as ***functional***. They begin with big, broad, seemingly unmanageable topics such as event structure and work their way down to the intricacies of individual language expressions. Functional approaches, and there are many (see the References at the back of the book for a sampling), are often contrasted to those approaches that focus attention on the bits and pieces of language and that as a matter of principle don't often venture much beyond that. These latter approaches are usually called ***structural***, since their point of departure and major interest is language structure. In this book we will steer a middle course, keeping one foot planted in the structures of English while taking a step with the other foot in the direction of understanding how language works in everyday life. We will start from the top with event structures, assuming that doing it that way will produce the clearest picture for you. At the same time, however, we will limit ourselves to studying how ***clauses*** and clause combinations work to make ***sentences***, paying only limited attention to segments of language larger than that.

Many other functional approaches take this as a starting point only and assume that knowing about the mechanisms of language necessarily entails studying units larger than clauses and sentences. This book will prepare you for that kind of study should you wish to undertake it, and at the same time it will give you an insight into the structure of English that you can use whatever your goal. Having studied the structure of English from the functional perspective of the clause as representation of events in experience, you will be better able to appreciate both structural and functional analytical orientations.

This book has a distinctly structural orientation because your goals in learning more about English grammar almost certainly include knowing about sentence structure. Perhaps you are studying to be an English teacher, or perhaps you have plans to become a writer. Or you might be planning to specialize in cultural anthropology or even the language acquisition of children. In each of these pursuits and many others, knowing about English-language sentence structure will come in very handy.

For example, if you are going to become an English teacher, you will be expected to develop expert knowledge of the structure of English and the insight necessary to allow you to explain that structure to your students.

If you want to develop your skills as a writer, you will need to draw on the vast potential inherent in the grammar of English sentences as the means by which you express yourself. Having a thorough understanding of the resources available to you will certainly serve you well. This is one reason, by the way, that I selected the sort of language examples for you that I did. More on this later.

If you study cultural anthropology (or a large variety of other topics in the humanities), you will learn quite quickly that language is at the very core of being human. Language plays a focal role in the life of every human being and every human society. In addition to its intrapersonal use in tracking everyday experiences, its structural resources are the common communication currency for every person and every human group.

If you specialize in child language development, you will track the emergence of the various structural resources of language as you study the stages of language acquisition.

In other words, gaining some insight into the way that language structure reflects the components of occurrences in the everyday world will be helpful to you no matter what your reasons for studying language and no matter the specific analytical approach you eventually adopt.

A major advantage to starting with function and working your way to structure is that functional descriptions of structural resources are quite diverse, and each provides its own insight into the nature of the relationship between language and human experience. For example, the account proposed by Talmy Givón simultaneously considers verb type, clause type, participant role and the grammatical roles of subject, object, adverb, and predicate. On the other hand, the account proposed by M. A. K. Halliday involves processes, participants, and circumstances. Halliday's system classifies processes into three big categories reflective of the nature of experience: *material*, *mental*, and *relational* processes. He also proposes three minor categories: *verbal*, *existential*, and *behavioral* processes. The approach we take in this book borrows from both Givón and Halliday (and a few others as well!), and its purpose is to provide you a perspective on language structure that will serve you well, both as an introduction to the wealth of functional grammars and as your foundation for learning about the structure of English sentences.

Some of the terms that have already been used in just these first pages might not be at all familiar, and I am sure that as you read the paragraphs and chapters that follow, a term here or there is going to trip you up. The book's Glossary (pages 262–77) will help you with unfamiliar terms by providing definitions for the expressions that appear in boldface. Additionally, I have tried to use general terms as much as possible; where I have had to introduce special terms, I have defined them in the surrounding context or included a definition.

You will find that some of the book's terms are taken from functional grammars and some from structural grammars. There are a couple of good reasons for doing it this way. On the one hand, I want to use as much familiar terminology as possible, and the odds are that, to the extent that you know any grammatical terminology, you are likely to be most familiar with terms from traditional and structural grammars. On the other hand, after you have enjoyed the insight that a functional approach can afford, you will want to have a new term to tack onto that insight.

For the most part you will be able to understand each chapter's main ideas without worrying too much about unfamiliar terms because, as you read and discuss the ideas in the book, the terms will fall into place for you. However, I know that sometimes you will want further help as you are reading and you won't want to wait for your instructor to clarify things or for ideas simply to fall into place. So, when you need some immediate help, use the Glossary, or if you are really adventurous, look in the Index for the term that is bothering you and find other places in the book where that term appears.

Focus on Language as Representation

Language is central to all of our daily experiences and to our reflection on those experiences. Language and vision are the fundamental media through which we organize and think about our experiences. Vision provides us with an immediate representation of the world around us, and language is the principal medium through which we create the narrative experiences of our everyday lives and share those experiences with others. Language creates a mental record of our everyday lives with which we remember events, make reports, solve problems, and interact with each other about our experiences. We use language, spoken and written, to report on past events, participate in current events, and speculate on future events.

Language reflects three aspects of events in experience. First, language mirrors the *event structure* of experience—that is, the things that happen, the *who's doing what to whom*. Second, language reflects the **relationships** among speakers, and it allows speakers to comment on and manage those relationships. And third, language can reflect the structure of an ongoing **discourse** among speakers; that is, it can be used to manage its own course. This book focuses on the way that language mirrors events; however, before we turn to that central function in earnest, let's make sure that we don't completely overlook the other two functions.

As an example of the third function, that of language managing its own flow, just take a look at the previous paragraph. The words *First*, *Second*, and *And third* are good examples of the way that we employ language to manage itself. These words give some sequentialness to the paragraph that might otherwise be more difficult for you to pick up on. The first three words of the paragraph you are now reading, *As an example,* are themselves a prime example of how language can be employed as its own stage manager. After you read them, you can reasonably expect to read an example. This function of language is referred to as its discourse function.

Now, as an example of the second function of language, the function by which language reflects and comments upon the relationships among speakers in an exchange, consider the immediately preceding paragraph. At the end of the first sentence of that paragraph, you read *just take a look at the previous paragraph.* The only possible relationship that this language can reflect is the one in which the writer makes a gentle suggestion and the reader follows the suggestion. You are, in this case, the grammar teacher's well-known **You understood**. The relationship reflected in the you-understood structure might be called the *one-suggests-and-the-other-pays-attention* relationship. Or perhaps the *one-guides-and-one-gets-guided* relationship.

Whatever expression you might choose to use, it clearly reflects the use of language to steer a relationship. So does the word *clearly* in the previous sentence. By using a relationship unit like *clearly,* I showed that I wanted you to accept what I was saying as being obvious. Check out the fourth sentence of the previous paragraph (*You are . . .*). Do you see a relationship word there? Here's a hint: the same word appears in the immediately preceding question in this very paragraph: *you*. This function of language, the one by which the roles of the parties to the discourse are kept sorted out, is its **relationship function**.

Here are some further examples of relationship and discourse functions of language. First, consider this well-known line from the motion picture *Gone with the Wind*, spoken by Rhett Butler and directed toward Scarlett O'Hara:

> **(1)   Frankly, my dear, I don't give a damn.**

This line reflects at least two aspects of the experience being depicted in the film. The event has to do with one character *not giving a damn* and letting the other character know about this feeling. But what do you make of the word *frankly*? Or of the word group *my dear*? They don't figure directly in the structure of the *give a damn* event; they more clearly relate to the relationship between the characters. *Frankly* has to do with how the speaker wants the listener to consider his remark, in much the same way as *clearly* does in the earlier example. And *my dear* is just like *you* in the previous examples. It names the listener. Neither *frankly* nor *my dear* figures directly in the *give a damn* event. They are examples of the relationship function of language.

Now consider the word *hopefully* in the sentence below:

> **(2)   Hopefully, we will all make it through the lecture.**

What do you think about the status of the word *hopefully*? It doesn't figure directly in the event structure being expressed (*we will all make it through this lecture*). It is more like the word *frankly* in (1). It is relationship material, letting the listener know about an emotional state: the speaker is hopeful and lets the listener know it. Can you also see the relationship function of the word *we* in example (2)? How about the word *hopefully* as it appears at the end of the second sentence of this paragraph? It is performing the discourse function of tying together example (2) and the rest of the paragraph, which is mostly about that example. The word *It* at the beginning of the third, fourth, fifth and eighth sentences of this paragraph also has a discourse function. It ties together all of the sentences of the paragraph that relate directly to *hopefully*.

In short, in addition to its inner-self intrapersonal function of supporting narrative thought and recollection, language is used in interpersonal exchanges to express event structure, manage situations and relationships, and guide discourse. A thorough understanding of how language works has to consider all of these functions. The best way to start is by seeing exactly how language reflects the event structure of everyday experience, how the structure of language matches up with the structure of events. So our focus of attention in this introductory book is mainly on investigating the ways in which event structure is represented in language; we give less attention to the relationship and discourse aspects of language.

Moreover, the language that we will study is English. However, much of what we will have to say about English can be abstracted to apply to many other languages, perhaps even to all languages. This is another advantage of working your way from language structure toward language function: the further you go in the direction of function, the more likely you will be to bump into facts about language that apply universally across languages. If you know another language or other languages, or if you are studying another language, you might want to consider whether the principles that we use in studying English would apply to these other languages as well. By thinking about other languages in the same terms as those we develop for thinking about English, you might be pleasantly surprised by the insights you generate for yourself.

Processes

Everyday experience is made up of events that involve a process that occurs, participants playing various roles in the event, and the circumstances under which the event occurs. Language is structured to reflect, or represent, these essential aspects of experience. A good working understanding of language requires that you arrive at one central insight: the processes, participants, and circumstances of your life are directly reflected in the language that you use, both in your interpersonal social interactions with others and in your own intrapersonal inner life of thinking, planning, rehearsing, and problem-solving.

This is the main point of the book: ordinary experience, the stuff of our lives, provides the model on which language is based. Language structures, at least at the gross level of the clause, are directly related to the events in our everyday lives.

A note about the language examples in this book With only a minor exception here and there, all of the in-text language examples and chapter-end activities are taken from (or adapted from) *The War of the Worlds*, a short and exciting novel written in 1898 by H. G. Wells. *The War of the Worlds* is a pleasure to read, not only for its merits as a well-told story but also for Wells's skillful use of the English language. You will enjoy using this masterwork of English literature as you learn more about the way modern English works.

ACTIVITY **1.1**

To get the flavor of process-participant-circumstance structure, read the narrative below, which is adapted from the opening paragraph of *The War of the Worlds*. As you read, try to imagine yourself as the director of a play by the same title, and as you do, consider these questions:

- What kinds of actions and interactions would you put on the stage?

- Who would the characters be?

- What would the necessary props be?

- How would you have the stage set?

- How would you motivate the action?

- How would the relationships among the characters unfold?

- What tricks would you use to keep the dialog flowing smoothly?

This first activity, and the rest of the chapter for that matter, is intended to help break the ice and get you oriented toward the experience you will have as you use the rest of the book. You will find the three activities that make up the rest of the chapter to be helpful in an introductory, exploratory sense. Don't be too concerned, then, that you are being asked to try out something with which you are not familiar. In order to do a really satisfying job on the activities, you would need to have already mastered the substance of the entire book! In fact, two or three months from now, after you have finished Chapter 10, you might want to come back to these first activities to see how your skills of observing and describing English have grown. If you think you might want to do that, turn right now to Chapter 10 and make yourself a note to revisit this first chapter after you have finished that one—you'll be happy about all you have learned. Now give the activities a try, and don't let the detail bog you down.

This first time you work through the passage, start with the core words in the event structures being related; that is, start by enclosing the processes in square brackets like these: [ ]. I've done several to get you started. Then further on, I have provided some suggested responses for the entire paragraph. It will help a lot if you read the entire paragraph all the way through before you try any bracketing.

> **A note on bracketing conventions** Throughout the book we will use brackets, [ ], to enclose meaningful units, that is, to group together parts of language that belong together. In this chapter, you are going to take a crack at bracketing the processes, then the participants, and then the circumstances in the sample *War of the Worlds* passage. In later chapters we will also try to leave the bracketing at that topmost level as much as possible. However, from time to time, it will be necessary to do some further bracketing (sub-bracketing) just to make reporting our observations clearer. At the end of each of the first few chapters, you will find a short reminder of the few conventions that we will be using for bracketing (and for labeling). Here, for example, in addition to using normal bracketing I have demonstrated the convention that we will use for bracketing constituents that have been interrupted and are therefore discontinuous. This bracketing convention looks something like a squared-off horseshoe (see page 9).

No one [would have believed] in the last years of the nineteenth century that this world [was being watched] keenly and closely by intelligences greater than man's and yet as mortal as his own; that as men [busied] themselves about their various concerns they [were scrutinized] and [studied], perhaps almost as narrowly as a man with a microscope [might scrutinize] the transient creatures that [swarm] and [multiply] in a drop of water. With infinite complacency men went to and fro about their little affairs, serene in their assurance of their empire over matter. It is possible that the infusoria under the microscope do the same. No one gave a thought to the older worlds of space as sources of human danger, or thought of them only to dismiss the idea of life upon them as impossible or improbable. It is curious to recall some of the mental habits of those departed days. At most terrestrial men fancied there might be other men upon Mars, inferior to themselves and ready to welcome a missionary enterprise. Yet across the gulf of space, minds that are to our minds as ours are to those of the beasts that perish, intellects vast and cool and unsympathetic, regarded this earth* with envious eyes, and slowly and surely drew their plans against us. And early in the twentieth century came the great disillusionment.

Now take a look at the Suggested Responses to Activity 1.1 below. I have worked on the same paragraph that you just did, and I have bracketed the most obvious core units, the processes, of most of the event structures. How does your bracketing compare? Don't be concerned that yours might not match this exactly—remember that we are just getting warmed up. And don't be concerned that *infusoria* might be a less than completely familiar word—I told you that you might bump into some unfamiliar language.

In subsequent chapters you can turn to the back of the book to find suggested responses, but for this chapter I am including them right here to help you compare what you are doing to what I might do. Here's something to consider: very often what you will do and what I have done will differ. That will be because there may well be several possible responses, depending on the different interpretations that come to mind. Other times it might be because one of us got off the track. Your instructor will help you determine when your responses are legitimate even if they don't match those provided in the book.

SUGGESTED RESPONSES TO ACTIVITY **1.1**

No one [would have believed] in the last years of the nineteenth century that this world [was being watched] keenly and closely by intelligences greater than man's and yet as mortal as his own; that as men [busied] themselves about their various concerns they [were scrutinized] and [studied], perhaps almost as narrowly as a man with a microscope [might scrutinize] the transient creatures that [swarm] and [multiply] in a drop of water. With infinite complacency men (went) to and fro (about) their little affairs, serene in their assurance of their empire over matter. It [is possible] that the infusoria under the microscope [do] the same. No one [gave] a thought to the older worlds

*Here, and throughout the book, we follow the original *War of the Worlds* text, including UK spelling, and do not capitalize the word *earth*.

of space as sources of human danger, or [thought] of them only to [dismiss] the idea of life upon them as impossible or improbable. It [is curious] to [recall] some of the mental habits of those departed days. At most terrestrial men [fancied] [there might be] other men upon Mars, inferior to themselves and ready to [welcome] a missionary enterprise. Yet across the gulf of space, minds that are to our minds as ours are to those of the beasts that [perish], intellects vast and cool and unsympathetic, [regarded] this earth with envious eyes, and slowly and surely [drew] their plans against us. And early in the twentieth century [came] the great disillusionment.

Processes I have bracketed the following processes: *would have believed, was being watched, busied, were scrutinized, studied, might scrutinize, swarm, multiply, went about, is possible, do, gave, thought, dismiss, is curious, recall, fancied, there might be, welcome, perish, regarded, drew, came*

One thing tends to unite this list. Each process unit includes a verb. Some of the units contain nothing but a verb or verbs. But some of them include additional elements: *went ABOUT, is POSSIBLE, is CURIOUS, and THERE might be.* If you draw the tentative conclusion that expressing the core elements of events in English depends heavily on verbs, but is not limited to verbs, you are on the right trail.

Participants

Now scan the paragraph again. This time bracket the role-players and the necessary props that the role-players might need to use. After you finish, compare your choices to those that are provided below (I've left the processes bracketed for you).

ACTIVITY **1.2**

No one [would have believed] in the last years of the nineteenth century that this world [was being watched] keenly and closely by intelligences greater than man's and yet as mortal as his own; that as men [busied] themselves about their various concerns they [were scrutinized] and [studied], perhaps almost as narrowly as a man with a microscope [might scrutinize] the transient creatures that [swarm] and [multiply] in a drop of water. With infinite complacency men went to and fro about their little affairs, serene in their assurance of their empire over matter. It [is possible] that the infusoria under the microscope [do] the same. No one [gave] a thought to the older worlds of space as sources of human danger, or [thought] of them only to [dismiss] the idea of life upon them as impossible or improbable. It [is curious] to [recall] some of the mental habits of those departed days. At most terrestrial men [fancied] [there might be] other men upon Mars, inferior to themselves and ready to [welcome] a missionary enterprise. Yet across the gulf of space, minds that are to our minds as ours are to those of the beasts that [perish], intellects vast and cool and unsympathetic, [regarded] this earth with envious eyes, and slowly and surely [drew] their plans against us. And early in the twentieth century [came] the great disillusionment.

As before, here is the same paragraph, but this time I have bracketed the participants—the people, things, and ideas that are the role-players or that serve as essential props in the drama. How does your bracketing compare? As before, don't be concerned that yours might not match mine exactly.

SUGGESTED RESPONSES TO ACTIVITY **1.2**

[No one] would have believed in the last years of the nineteenth century that [this world] was being watched keenly and closely [by intelligences greater than man's and yet as mortal as his own]; that as [men] busied [themselves] [about their various concerns] [they] were scrutinized and studied, perhaps almost as narrowly as [a man with a microscope] might scrutinize [the transient creatures that swarm and multiply in a drop of water]. With infinite complacency [men] went to and fro about [their little affairs], serene in their assurance of their empire over matter. It is possible that [the infusoria under the microscope] do [the same]. [No one] gave [a thought] [to the older worlds of space] [as sources of human danger], or thought [of them] only to dismiss [the idea of life upon them] as impossible or improbable. It is curious to recall [some of the mental habits of those departed days]. At most [terrestrial men] fancied there might be [other men upon Mars, inferior to themselves and ready to welcome a missionary enterprise]. Yet across the gulf of space, [minds that are to our minds as ours are to those of the beasts that perish], [intellects vast and cool and unsympathetic], regarded [this earth] [with envious eyes], and slowly and surely drew [their plans against us]. And early in the twentieth century came [the great disillusionment].

Participants I have bracketed the following participants: *no one, this world, by intelligences greater than man's and yet as mortal as his own, men, themselves, about their various concerns, they, a man with a microscope, the transient creatures that swarm and multiply in a drop of water, men, their little affairs, the infusoria under the microscope, the same, no one, a thought, to the older worlds of space, as sources of human danger, of them, the idea of life upon them, some of the mental habits of those departed days, terrestrial men, other men upon Mars, inferior to themselves and ready to welcome a missionary enterprise, minds that are to our minds as ours are to those of the beasts that perish, intellects vast and cool and unsympathetic, this earth, with envious eyes, their plans against us, the great disillusionment*

This list of participants is more remarkable in its consistency than was the list of processes. All of the process units contained, but were not limited to, verbs. Here, however, the list of participants is exclusively **nouns**, **noun groups**, or nounlike words (pronouns) such as *no one, themselves, they,* and *them*—which are a specific sort of **proform**, the general term for stand-in words. In general, that's the way English works. Participants are usually expressed as nouns and the words that form units along with them, or by proforms. For the time being we are ignoring the fact that proforms are not the only acceptable noun-group substitutes. Clauses can be, too. We will take up this matter in some detail later, starting with Chapter 8.

Circumstances

Now scan the paragraph one final time. This time bracket elements of the scenario in which the events occur, that is, the *when, where, why,* and *how* of the events. After you finish, compare your choices to those that I have provided below. I've left the processes and the participants bracketed for you.

ACTIVITY **1.3**

[No one] [would have believed] in the last years of the nineteenth century that [this world] [was being watched] keenly and closely [by intelligences greater than man's and yet as mortal as his own]; that as [men] [busied] [themselves] [about their various concerns] [they] [were scrutinized] and [studied], perhaps almost as narrowly as [a man with a microscope] [might scrutinize] [the transient creatures that [swarm] and [multiply] in a drop of water]. With infinite complacency [men] (went) to and fro (about) [their little affairs], serene in their assurance of their empire over matter. It [is possible] that [the infusoria under the microscope] [do] [the same]. [No one] [gave] [a thought] [to the older worlds of space] [as sources of human danger], or [thought] [of [them] only to [dismiss] the idea of life upon them as impossible or improbable. It [is curious] to [recall] [some of the mental habits of those departed days]. At most [terrestrial men] [fancied] [there might be] [other men upon Mars, inferior to themselves and ready to [welcome] a missionary enterprise]. Yet across the gulf of space, [minds that are to our minds as ours are to those of the beasts that perish], [intellects vast and cool and unsympathetic], [regarded] [this earth] [with envious eyes], and slowly and surely [drew] [their plans against us]. And early in the twentieth century [came] [the great disillusionment].

As before, what follows is the same paragraph, but this time only the elements of the scenario, the circumstances, have been bracketed for you. Compare your own results, and as before don't be too concerned should yours not match mine exactly.

SUGGESTED RESPONSES TO ACTIVITY **1.3**

No one would have believed [in the last years of the nineteenth century] that this world was being watched [keenly] and [closely] by intelligences greater than man's and yet as mortal as his own; that as men busied themselves about their various concerns they were scrutinized and studied, perhaps almost as [narrowly] as a man with a microscope might scrutinize the transient creatures that swarm and multiply in a drop of water. [With infinite complacency] men went [to and fro] about their little affairs, [serene in their assurance of their empire over matter]. It is possible that the infusoria under the microscope do the same. No one gave a thought to the older worlds of space as sources of human danger, or thought of them only to dismiss the idea of life upon them [as impossible or improbable]. It is curious to recall some of the mental habits of those departed days. At most terrestrial men fancied there might be other men upon Mars, inferior to themselves and ready to welcome a missionary enterprise. Yet [across the gulf of space], minds that are to our minds as ours are to those of the beasts that perish, intellects vast and cool and unsympathetic, regarded this earth with envious eyes, and [slowly] and [surely] drew their plans against us. And [early in the twentieth century] came the great disillusionment.

Circumstances I have bracketed the following circumstances: *in the last years of the nineteenth century, keenly, closely, narrowly, With infinite complacency, to and fro, serene in their assurance of their empire over matter, as impossible or improbable, across the gulf of space, slowly, surely, early in the twentieth century*

Recall that a neat and tidy theme appeared to be emerging with regard to processes and participants. That theme was, more or less, that processes were associated with verb-headed groups of words and that participants were associated with noun-headed word groups or noun-group substitutes. With circumstances, however, no clear pattern seems to pop out at you. But let's not jump the gun. Once the whole picture becomes clear, a fairly compact set of possibilities will emerge, and it isn't just that circumstances are adverbs—although some are (*keenly, closely, narrowly, slowly, surely*).

Some Words Left Over

If you have followed along closely, you will have noticed that some words weren't accounted for at all: *that, and, that, as, and, perhaps, almost as . . . as, It, that, or, only to, or, It, to, At most, Yet, and, and,* and *And*. The purpose of most of these words (actually, all of them except *perhaps* and *at most*, which are relationship units) is to signal the beginning of a **subordinate** or an **embedded clause** in a sentence or to put words together into a **compound** (conjoined) unit. We won't have much more to say about these leftovers in this introductory chapter, but by the time we reach Chapter 8, their role in the grammar will become clear.

We will get there; but in the meanwhile, here for the last time is the first paragraph of *The War of the Worlds*, this time with only the leftovers bracketed.

No one would have believed in the last years of the nineteenth century [that] this world was being watched keenly [and] closely by intelligences greater than man's and yet as* mortal as* his own; [that] [as] men busied themselves about their various concerns they were scrutinized [and] studied, [perhaps] almost as narrowly as a man with a microscope might scrutinize the creatures that* swarm and multiply in a drop of water. With infinite complacency men went to and fro about their little affairs, serene in their assurance of their empire over matter. [It] is possible [that] the infusoria under the microscope do the same. No one gave a thought to the older worlds of space as sources of human danger, [or] thought of them [only to] dismiss the idea of life upon them as impossible [or] improbable. [It] is curious [to] recall some of the mental habits of those departed days. [At most] terrestrial men fancied there might be other men upon Mars, inferior to themselves and ready to* welcome a missionary enterprise. [Yet] across the gulf of space, minds that* are to our minds as* ours are to those of the beasts that* perish, intellects vast and cool and unsympathetic, regarded this earth with envious eyes, [and] slowly [and] surely drew their plans against us. [And] early in the twentieth century came the great disillusionment.

This exercise will serve you for the time being as an introduction to doing grammatical analysis by matching up the structures in language with the gross characteristics of events in experience; the processes, participants, and circumstances. The rest of the book will fill in some of the details for you, starting in Chapter 2 with the core of every event: the process. Before you move on to that, though, check out whether some of the ideas have stuck with you, by trying out the Practice with Terminology activity below.

* The words marked with asterisks are also ***markers***, but because we have earlier treated them as parts of other units, I am leaving them alone here. We will have plenty more to say on this matter in chapters to come.

Practice with Terminology

What follows is a preview of the sentences that you will encounter in the Sentences for Analysis in the next chapter (Chapter 2). Certain elements in each sentence have been underscored. Label each underscored element using one or more of the terms shown below (you might not use all of them). Check the Glossary at the back of the book if you are not certain about the definition of any of the terms.

Circumstance	Noun	Pronoun
Compound (conjoined)	Participant	Verb
Discontinuous constituent	Process	You understood

1   The curate talked wildly to me under the hedge.
2   The fugitives streamed over Westminster Bridge.
3   The Martians resumed the offensive.
4   The majority of the men remained busy with preparations.
5   Three Martians came out about eight o'clock.
6   They advanced slowly and cautiously.

7 These Martians communicated <u>with one another</u> by means of sirenlike howls.

8 We <u>heard</u> a howling and firing of the guns at Ripley and St. George's Hill.

9 The Ripley gunners were unseasoned artillery <u>volunteers</u>.

10 They fired <u>one wild, premature, ineffectual volley</u>, and bolted on horse.

11 The Martians walked <u>serenely</u> over their guns.

12 The St. George's Hill men <u>were hidden</u> near a pine wood.

13 <u>They</u> remained undetected.

14 The Martians <u>were very near to them</u>.

15 Artillery shells flashed <u>all round them</u>.

16 They advanced <u>a few paces</u>, staggered, and went down.

17 Everybody <u>yelled</u> together.

18 The guns <u>were reloaded</u> in frantic haste.

19 The whole second <u>volley</u> flew wide of the Martian on the ground.

20 Both of his companions aimed their Heat-Rays <u>on the men</u>.

21 The ammunition dump <u>blew up</u>.

22 <u>The pine trees all about the guns</u> flashed into fire.

23 <u>After this</u> the Martians halted.

24 An overthrown Martian crawled <u>tediously</u> out of his hood.

25 <u>He</u> was a small brown figure.

26 He <u>resembled a speck of blight</u>.

27 The Martian <u>repaired</u> his support.

28 <u>About nine</u> he had finished.

29 <u>There were</u> four more Martians on the other side of the hill.

30 Each carried <u>a thick black tube</u>.

31 <u>A dozen rockets</u> sprang out of the hills.

32 At the same time four of their fighting machines <u>crossed</u> the river.

33 At this sight the curate cried faintly in his <u>throat</u>.

34 <u>The occasional howling of the Martians</u> had ceased.

35 They <u>took up</u> their positions in absolute silence.

36 The night <u>was lit only by the slender moon</u>.

37 <u>There were</u> no stars out.

38 <u>The guns</u> were waiting.

39 The signal rockets burst and rained <u>their sparks</u>.

40 <u>The spirit of all those watching batteries</u> rose to a tense expectation.

41   The Martians <u>advanced</u> into the line of fire.

42   A hundred <u>questions</u> struggled together in my mind.

43   Then there was <u>a sound like the distant concussion of a gun</u>.

44   The Martian beside us <u>raised</u> his tube and discharged it.

45   There was <u>no flash and no smoke</u>.

46   <u>In my excitement</u> I forgot my personal safety.

47   A big projectile hurtled overhead <u>towards Hounslow</u>.

48   <u>I</u> expected smoke or fire, or some such evidence of its work.

49   I saw <u>only the deep blue sky above</u>.

50   <u>There had been</u> no crash, no answering explosion.

Chapter 2

Clauses: Processes

Preliminaries

In the previous chapter we showed that the elements of the event structure, the processes, the participants, and the circumstances, accounted for most of the language in a short segment of written English. Once we accounted for these elements of event structure, we were left with only three kinds of items: (1) units that reflected the structure of the ongoing discourse, (2) units that reflected the relationships among the parties to the discourse, and (3) markers of such language structures as conjunction, subordination, embedding, and discontinuity. In this chapter and the next, we will push this idea just a little bit further by outlining the basic resources that English employs in building clauses. First, in this chapter we take a look at processes; then in Chapter 3 we fill out the picture by considering participants and circumstances.

A note about the subtitle *Clauses, Markers, Missing Elements* The subtitle of the book reflects the assumption that developing a comfortable sense of how English sentences work requires you to consider three things. First, clauses are built from the top down—out of the components of events: processes, participants, and circumstances. Second, clauses are combined to form sentences, and these combinations are marked for recognition. And third, leaving things unsaid but taken for granted (like *You understood*) is a major structural resource that all language users exploit. In this chapter and the next four, we go to work in earnest on the first task, seeing how clauses are built. The second task, seeing how clauses combine, forms the substance of the remainder of the book, starting with Chapter 7. The final task, becoming aware of missing elements, is something we will work on all along. For example, check out item 18 in the Sentences for Analysis at the end of this chapter. Isn't there something about the event structure that is just taken for granted and left unexpressed in this sentence? (Hint: Are all of the entailed participant roles expressed?)

Clauses as Models of Everyday Events

Processes, participants, and circumstances are not merely randomly distributed throughout paragraphs of written language or in face-to-face **dialogs** among individuals. As language users we can engage in sensible exchanges chiefly because we share a set of conventions that govern the ways in which the elements of event structure can be expressed. The central conventionalized language unit into which we compress event structure is the clause.

Not surprisingly, the nature of events, that is, the structure of what happens, is mirrored directly in this main structural unit of language, the clause. The structure of events and the structure of clauses match up solidly in two very important ways. First, just as everyday life itself is a succession of process-based events, so are the clauses in a discourse a series of process-based units. Process, or change, is the central feature of experience. Likewise, the process is the focal structural feature of the clause, which is itself the central experiential unit of language.

Second, just as everyday life can be seen as an unfolding drama, so can we treat clauses as little self-contained dramas in which the process dictates the number and type of participant roles, and in which we as language users are able to comment on features of the scenarios in which the dramas evolve. I've summarized these ideas in Chart 2.1.

Here is a clause-size example of a mini-drama (adapted from *The War of the Worlds*):

(1) **That night another invisible missile started on its way to the earth from Mars, just a second or so under twenty-four hours after the first one.**

Chart 2.1 *Processes in Events and Clauses*

Events	Clauses
Events are dynamic, process-based combinations of doing, thinking, feeling, and relating.	The focal element of a clause, the process, is an expression of doing, thinking, feeling, or relating.
Events are narrative: they are constituted of action, thought, emotion, and the relationships among participating characters in a specific setting over time.	Clauses are mini-narratives: they are constituted of processes, role-playing participants, circumstances, and the relationships among speakers within broader discourses.

This clause relates the narrative of *another invisible missile* (a participant) that *started* (the process) *on its way to the earth from Mars* (a part of the scenario having to do with place) *just a second or so under twenty-four hours after the first one* (a part of the scenario having to do with time), and states that it happened *that night* (another part of the scenario having to do with time). Of course, this clause is as rare in *The War of the Worlds* as it would be in most normal human interaction, because it stands alone as a separate sentence. The nature of events, and of our language-based references to them, is that events are complex, involving a number of processes interacting with one another. Only rarely do we find any exchanges, either in writing or in speech, that involve sentences made up of only one clause. Usually sentences look more like this one, a ***clause complex***:

> (2) **Why the shots ceased after the tenth no one on earth has attempted to explain.**

Here we have a complex of events involving at least: *cease, attempt,* and *explain* (three processes), *the shots, no one on earth* (two obvious participants), and the timeframe (circumstance) *after the tenth.* There is even a bit more lurking just beyond what we can fairly readily account for here. That part of the account has to wait for a while.

Initially, for the sake of simplicity, we will try to see how individual stand-alone clauses are structured, but our ultimate goal, of course, is to develop a way of understanding how normal English, with all of its complexities and potentials, works.

In this chapter and the next two we work with two main ideas. The first, the substance of the present chapter and the next, is that clauses reflect event structure in a remarkably direct and transparent manner by focusing on event-structure processes, their participant roles and attendant circumstances. The second, to be taken up in Chapter 4, is that clauses are themselves built up of units, called *word groups,* that have their own focal elements, which, like magnets, attract their own satellites.

Processes

We can make one central observation about the nature of events that comprise our everyday experience: some events involve two or more participants—or to be more exact, two or more participant *roles*—and some involve only one participant role. The number and type of required participant roles are implicit in the context-specific meaning of a process and, except for *be,* are basically dictated by the verb. Here are some examples, adapted from *The War of the Worlds:*

(3) Great intelligences watched this world closely.

(4) Mars is older than our earth.

(5) It was 40,000,000 miles from us.

(6) There might be other men upon Mars.

(7) All that time the Martians must have been getting ready.

(8) Intelligent life might have developed there.

Of these examples, the process *watched* in example (3) is the only one that requires more than one participant role (*Great intelligences* and *this world*). The rest require only one: (4) *being old*, (5) *being 40 million miles away*, (6) *there being (men on Mars)*, (7) *getting ready*, (8) *developing*.

Moreover, as you probably guessed, these examples were not selected at random. Taken as a group, they represent all of the common process types in English (summarized in List 2.1, along with the abbreviations that we'll use for them throughout the book).

Our potential for observation and expression is essentially boundless, as is the potential for variety in the experiences that we build from our lives. However, we are constrained in English to interpret our environment in the broad terms represented by the following event types. (a) Aside from the weather and the time, events entail exactly one directly expressible participant role, or they involve two or more such roles; here we call these two categories **other-than-transitive** and **transitive** respectively. (b) Things exist, and existence is most frequently expressed in English by *there* plus *be* (*there* + *be*). And (c) we can assign **attributes** and **locations** to participants, using *be* plus attribute (*be* + Att), linking verb plus attribute (LV +

List 2.1 *Six Process Types*

Transitive	Other-than-transitive	
a Any process that entails at least two directly expressible participant roles is a transitive process (Trans)	**b** *be* plus attribute (*be* + Att)	
	c *be* plus location (*be* + Loc)	
	d *there* plus *be* (*there* + *be*) (and certain other verbs of existence)	
	e linking verb plus attribute (LV + Att)	
	f intransitive (Intrans) (including *be* + Ø)	

Att), and *be* plus location (*be* + Loc) process types. This is the basic inventory from which an infinity of observations can be expressed. Here again are examples (3) to (8), this time with appropriate process-type labels.

Trans
(9) **Great intelligences [watched] this world closely.**

be + Att
(10) **Mars [is older than our earth].**

be + Loc
(11) **It [was 40,000,000 miles from us].**

there + *be*
(12) **[There might be] other men upon Mars.**

LV + Att
(13) **All that time the Martians [must have been getting ready].**

Intrans
(14) **Intelligent life [might have developed] there.**

Transitive and other-than-transitive

Trans
(15) **Great intelligences [watched] this world closely.**

The number of directly expressible entailed participant roles determines whether a process is considered transitive or other-than-transitive. Transitive processes always entail two or more directly expressible participant roles. Processes that are other-than-transitive entail only one such participant role.

In a transitive process entailing two roles, both roles are expressed directly; that is, they do not require a role-specifying preposition group. However, some transitive processes, such as *put*, for example, entail three roles, and only two can be directly expressed: *I put the books on the shelf.* Here two roles (the put*er* and the put*ee*) are directly expressed. The third entailed role, the *location*, is expressed obliquely with the role-specifying **preposition group** *on*. Other transitive processes, *give*, for example, allow three directly expressed participants: *I gave Mary the book.* (There is more on this in Chapter 3.)

Regardless of the total number of overtly expressed roles, transitive processes always have at least two directly expressible, entailed, participant roles, and other-than-transitive processes have only one. However, we should keep two things in mind: (a) all processes, even other-than-transitive processes, can optionally involve additional, non-entailed roles—especially client, beneficiary or associate roles, and (b) no role has to be overtly stated (participants can be missing elements). (More on this, too, in Chapter 3.)

In examples (9) to (14), only (9), repeated above as (15), is transitive, entailing more than one participant role (watch*er* and watch*ee*). All of the others are other-than-transitive.

Here are some additional examples of transitive processes with the directly expressed, entailed role-players underscored:

> Trans
> (16) <u>We</u> [might have seen] <u>the gathering trouble</u> far back in the nineteenth century.

>   Trans
> (17) <u>English readers</u> [heard of] <u>it</u> first in the issue of *Nature* dated August 2.

>   Trans
> (18) <u>He</u> [compared] <u>it</u> to a colossal puff of flame.

Be plus attribute (*be* + Att)

>   be + Att
> (19) Mars [is older than our earth].

To ascribe qualities, states, and characteristics to a participant, we can associate the quality, state, or characteristic with the participant, without embellishment, using a form of the verb *be*.

We might note that example (10), repeated above as (19), could easily be expressed *Mars older than our earth*, omitting *is* (the form of *be*). The sense would still be there; it just wouldn't sound like English. In this sense, *be* is almost always a helper in the expression of a process rather than the real core of the event structure. Used by itself, *be* rarely ever means anything directly related to the structure of an event, except to Shakespearean characters (*To be or not to be . . .*) and heavy-duty philosophers (*I think; therefore I am*). For more on this point see the section '*Be* + Ø (intransitive *be*)' below.

If the attribute in a *be*-plus-attribute (*be* + Att) process is an ***adjective group***, the main ***adjective*** has traditionally been called a ***predicate adjective***. Likewise, if the attribute in a *be*-plus-attribute process is a noun group, the main noun has traditionally been called a ***predicate noun***. And sometimes predicate adjectives and predicate nouns have been jointly referred to as ***subject complements***. We'll stick to the one term, ***attribute***. Here are some further examples of *be*-plus-attribute processes:

be + Att
(20) **Their mathematical learning [is far in excess of ours].**

be + Att
(21) **For countless centuries Mars [has been the star of war].**

be + Att
(22) **It [might be hollow].**

Be plus location (be + Loc)

be + Loc
(23) **It [was 40,000,000 miles from us].**

Locations can likewise be associated with participants when we use a form of the word *be*. This isn't the only way to do the job, of course, just as *be* + Att is not the only way to associate characteristics with participants. It's just the most basic way. Example (11), repeated above as (23), just as with (10), could easily be understood without *was*, the form of *be*, but *It 40,000,000 miles from us* just wouldn't sound quite right. The form of *be* is required for the sentence to sound right, but it doesn't add anything meaningful. Here are additional examples of *be*-plus-location (*be* + Loc) processes:

be + Loc
(24) **The first missile then [could scarcely have been 10,000,000 miles away].**

be + Loc
(25) **[All around it was] the unfathomable darkness of empty space.**

be + Loc
(26) **I [was at home] at that hour and writing in my study.**

There plus be (there + be)

there + be
(27) **[There might be] other men upon Mars.**

This structure, the ***existential there clause***, is a narrator's stock-in-trade and is sometimes a writing teacher's target for disdain. The narrator loves it (and the writing teacher often disparages it) because it is a neutral way of expressing existence in the most broad and unspecified way. Neither *there* nor *be* by itself has any independent sense in this existential-*there* process type. Only the combination has a meaning. That is one reason why *there* in *there* + *be* is called an ***expletive***. In this combination, *there* doesn't really have an independent event-structure meaning; it contributes its sense only by virtue of its combination with *be*.

Nothing except the fact of existence is implied when we use *there + be* in English. Compare it to another combination with the expletive 'there', *there + appear*, as in *There appeared before my eyes a miraculous form*. Here we have gone beyond just plain old existence and we have added a sense of *coming into* existence. That's no longer neutral. Example (12), repeated above as (27), makes no claim except that Martian men might exist. This could be why a writing teacher might advise against using *there + be*. It's not specific. On the other hand, H. G. Wells relies on it for just that very reason, so go figure. Here are some additional examples of *there + be* processes:

there + be
(28) [There was] nothing of this in the papers.

there + be
(29) That night, too, [there was] another jetting out of gas from the distant planet.

there + be
(30) [There were] lights in the upper windows of the houses.

Be plus Ø (intransitive *be; be* + Ø)

We will see the word *be* (and its variants, *am, is, are, was,* and *were*) doing many different jobs, but only rarely will it mean *exist*. To express existence, as a process, we almost always use *there + be*. However, when we use *be* alone, we call it **intransitive be**. Here are some of the rare examples of intransitive *be* (*be* + Ø) from *The War of the Worlds*:

be + Ø
(31) Such things, I told myself, [could not be].

be + Ø
(32) One on the extreme left, the remotest that [is], flourished
       a huge case high in the air . . .

be + Ø
(33) To their intelligence, it [may be], the giant was even such another as
       themselves.

Linking verb plus attribute (LV + Att)

LV + Att
(34) All that time the Martians [must have been getting ready].

When it comes to connecting participants and attributes, we very often embellish the **attributive** process, most basically expressed using *be*-plus-attribute, with some additional comment or information. The difference between *we are ready* and *we are* *getting ready* has more to do with the process of *becoming* something than it does with *being* something. *Being* something happens out there at the end of *becoming* something. Different emphasis. The process of attribution is still central, but something has been overlaid upon it. Example (13), repeated above as (34), seems to have an especially sinister, premeditated sense about it that probably would be impossible to express with *must have* BEEN *ready* rather than *must have been* GETTING *ready*. The premeditation is implicit in the preparation. This is the kind of implication that distinguishes the linking-verb-plus-attribute (LV + Att) process from the more neutral *be*-plus-attribute (*be* + Att) process. Other grammars often include *be* among the linking verbs, but because the two categories are distinct in the kind of meaning each conveys, we treat them here as separate.

As was the case in *be* + Att processes, if the attribute in a LV + Att process is an adjective group, the main adjective is sometimes called a *predicate adjective*. Similarly, if the attribute in a linking verb + attribute process is a noun group, the main noun is sometimes called a *predicate noun*. Sometimes predicate adjectives and predicate nouns are jointly referred to as *subject complements*. Here are some additional examples of LV + Att processes:

LV + Att
(35)　It [seemed such a little thing], so bright and small and still.

LV + Att
(36)　At the same time a faint hissing sound [became audible].

LV + Att
(37)　Their figures [grew misty] and then flashed into clearness again.

Intransitive (Intrans)

Intrans
(38)　Intelligent life [might have developed] there.

All processes in which only one entailed role is directly expressible and which are not primarily either attributive or **locative** get the generic label **intransitive** (Intrans). Depending upon the specific application, the 'same' verb can be either transitive or intransitive. Consider example (14), repeated above as (38). Here the word *developed* means something like *grew* or *came into existence* or *evolved* or *matured*. However, it isn't much of a stretch to see that *developed* can mean something quite different: consider *The government developed a plan for combating terrorists*. Here the process involves two directly expressed participant roles, *the government* (the develop*er*) and *a plan for combating terrorists* (the develop*ee*). I put the word *same* into quotation marks earlier to indicate that perhaps we should be looking for the differences between the words in their transitive and intransitive environments without being distracted by the similarities. Here are some processes that appear as intransitives in the first chapter of *The War of the Worlds*. In other applications they could very well be transitive.

Intrans
(39) The transient creatures [multiplied] in a drop of water.

Intrans
(40) Its oceans [have shrunk] until they cover but a third of its surface.

Intrans
(41) It [was dropping off] in flakes and raining down upon the sand.

Zero-participant processes

Zero-participant
(42) It [was a warm night].

Zero-participant
(43) It [was glaringly hot, not a cloud in the sky nor a breath of wind].

Zero-participant
(44) It [was then about a quarter past five].

Some processes, especially time and weather expressions, don't require explicit participants in English. So, to the six common process types in English we add this seventh, a type that has no required participant roles. Note that English sentences, except for imperatives, need to have something overt contributing the grammatical subject function. In zero-participant clauses we use *it*, an expletive like *there*, to perform the subject function, which is in this case a ***nonreferential***, strictly grammatical, function.

The paragraph that follows is the second of *The War of the Worlds*. In it some of its processes have been bracketed. Below the paragraph, I have identified the selected processes by labeling them according to List 2.1 (Six Process Types). As you look over the paragraph, you will notice that not all parts of it have bracketed processes. Some things need to be left to deal with later; so, here and elsewhere throughout the book, for simplicity's sake, we will be selective in the examples that we present. We will come back to examples from time to time to upgrade our observations as we fill in additional background. I have chosen to do this so that you can be looking at examples from a real and coherent context.

(45) The planet Mars, I scarcely [need remind] the reader, [revolves] about the sun at a mean distance of 140,000,000 miles, and the light and heat it [receives] from the sun [is barely half of that received by this world]. It must be, if the nebular hypothesis has any truth, older than our world; and long before this earth ceased to be molten, life upon its surface [must have begun] its course. The fact that it [is scarcely one-seventh of the volume of the earth] [must have accelerated] its cooling to the temperature at which life could begin. It has air and water and all that [is necessary] for the support of animated existence.

The process *need remind* in the first line is transitive (Trans) because it entails two or more directly expressed participant roles: (a) the one doing the reminding, *I*, (b) the one being reminded, *the reader*, and (c) the content of the reminder, *the planet Mars revolves about the sun at a mean distance of 140,000,000 miles*.

The next bracketed process, *revolve*, is intransitive (Intrans) because it strictly entails only one participant role, the participant doing the revolving, *the planet Mars*.

On the other hand, the process *receive*, like *remind*, entails at least two directly expressible participant roles and is therefore transitive (Trans). It involves two such directly expressed roles, (a) the receiver, *it*, and (b) the thing being transferred, *light and heat*. It additionally involves one obliquely expressed role, (c) the source, *from the sun*.

The next selected process, *is barely half of that received by this world*, entails only one participant role, the entity to which the quality or state is being attributed, in this case, *light and heat*. It is a *be*-plus-attribute (*be* + Att) process. All attributive processes have one entailed participant role.

And by continuing to follow the Six Process Types chart, we can come to the following conclusions: (a) *must have begun* is transitive (Trans); (b) *is scarcely one-seventh of the volume of the earth* is a *be*-plus-attribute (*be* + Att) process; (c) *must have accelerated* is transitive (Trans); and (d) *is necessary* is a *be*-plus-attribute (*be* + Att) process.

Practice with Terminology

What follows is a preview of the sentences that you will encounter in this chapter's Sentences for Analysis section. Certain elements in each sentence have been underscored. Label each underscored element using one or more of the terms shown below. Check the Glossary at the back of the book if you are not certain about the definition of any of the terms.

Be	Intransitive verb	Subject complement
Expletive	Linking verb	Transitive process
Existential-*there* sentence	Nonreferential	Transitive verb
Intransitive *be*	Predicate adjective	
Intransitive process	Predicate noun	

1   The curate <u>talked</u> wildly to me under the hedge.

2   The fugitives <u>streamed</u> over Westminster Bridge.

3   The Martians <u>resumed</u> the offensive.

4   The majority of the men <u>remained</u> busy with preparations.

5   Three Martians <u>came out</u> about eight o'clock.

6   They <u>advanced</u> slowly and cautiously.

7   These Martians <u>communicated</u> with one another by means of sirenlike howls.

8   We <u>heard</u> a howling and firing of the guns at Ripley and St. George's Hill.

9   The Ripley gunners were <u>unseasoned artillery volunteers</u>.

10   They <u>fired</u> one wild, premature, ineffectual volley, and bolted on horse.

11   The Martians <u>walked</u> serenely over their guns.

12   The St. George's Hill men were <u>hidden</u> near a pine wood.

13   They <u>remained</u> undetected.

14   The Martians <u>were</u> very near to them.

15   Artillery shells <u>flashed</u> all round them.

16   They <u>advanced</u> a few paces, staggered, and went down.

17   Everybody <u>yelled</u> together.

18   The guns were <u>reloaded</u> in frantic haste.

19   The whole second volley <u>flew wide</u> of the Martian on the ground.

20   Both of his companions <u>aimed</u> their Heat-Rays on the men.

21   The ammunition dump <u>blew up</u>.

22   The pine trees all about the guns <u>flashed</u> into fire.

23   After this the Martians <u>halted</u>.

24   An overthrown Martian <u>crawled</u> tediously out of his hood.

25   He was <u>a small brown figure</u>.

26   He resembled <u>a speck of blight</u>.

27   The Martian <u>repaired</u> his support.

28   About nine he had <u>finished</u>.

29   <u>There were four more Martians on the other side of the hill</u>.

30   Each <u>carried</u> a thick black tube.

31   A dozen rockets <u>sprang</u> out of the hills.

32   At the same time four of their fighting machines <u>crossed</u> the river.

33   At this sight the curate <u>cried</u> faintly in his throat.

34   The occasional howling of the Martians had <u>ceased</u>.

35   They <u>took up</u> their positions in absolute silence.

36   The night was <u>lit only by the slender moon</u>.

37   <u>There</u> were no stars out.

38   The guns <u>were</u> waiting.

39   The signal rockets <u>burst</u> and rained their sparks.

40   The spirit of all those watching batteries <u>rose</u> to a tense expectation.

41   The Martians <u>advanced</u> into the line of fire.

42   A hundred questions <u>struggled</u> together in my mind.

43   Then <u>there</u> was a sound like the distant concussion of a gun.

44   The Martian beside us <u>raised</u> his tube and discharged it.

45   <u>There was no flash and no smoke</u>.

46   In my excitement I <u>forgot</u> my personal safety.

47   A big projectile <u>hurtled</u> overhead towards Hounslow.

48   I <u>expected</u> smoke or fire, or some such evidence of its work.

49   I <u>saw</u> only the deep blue sky above.

50   There had <u>been</u> no crash, no answering explosion.

Some Bracketing and Labeling Conventions

The reporting style that we use throughout the book is as simple as possible while doing the required job. We use minimal bracketing to isolate clause-level word groups, and starting in Chapter 8 we apply the ***triangle convention*** for reporting clause complexes. To work on the Sentences for Analysis section (below), you will need some or all of the following devices.

Brackets Use square brackets to delineate the left- and right-hand ***edges*** of processes.

(46) The storm [burst] upon us six years ago now.

(47) He [compared] it to a colossal puff of flame.

Discontinuous constituent Sometimes a unit will be interrupted by another unit. In such a case, the interrupted unit is wrapped around the interrupting unit through use of a squared-off connector:

(48) He ⌐Intrans⌐ had ⌐ at once ⌐ resorted ⌐ to the spectroscope.

(49) ⌐LV + Att (Inverted Order)⌐ A singularly appropriate phrase ⌐ it ⌐ proved.

Function label The process type (taken from List 2.1) of each bracketed process is indicated above the bracketed unit.

(50) The storm [burst]^{Intrans} upon us six years ago now.

(51) He [compared]^{Trans} it to a colossal puff of flame.

Missing elements Missing elements are indicated by parentheses and the proposed element itself is expressed in capital letters.

(52) '(YOU) Come into the house,' I said.

(53) The scouts (WHO) (WERE) watching them remained absolutely stationary for the next half hour.

Continued unit Should one line of a report run beyond the margins of the paper, a pair of arrows should be used, one at the end of the first line and one at the beginning of the next, to indicate the continuity.

(54) Peculiar markings were seen near the site during the next two ↪
      → oppositions.

(55) A huge outbreak of incandescent gas had occurred towards ↪
      → midnight of the 12th.

Sentences for Analysis

In the following sentences, adapted from *The War of the Worlds*, bracket and identify processes by type (see List 2.1), as shown in the example.

Trans
(56) This world [was being watched] closely by great intelligences.

* 1   The curate talked wildly to me under the hedge.
   2   The fugitives streamed over Westminster Bridge.
   3   The Martians resumed the offensive.
   4   The majority of the men remained busy with preparations.
   5   Three Martians came out about eight o'clock.
   6   They advanced slowly and cautiously.
   7   These Martians communicated with one another by means of sirenlike howls.
   8   We heard a howling and firing of the guns at Ripley and St. George's Hill.
* 9   The Ripley gunners were unseasoned artillery volunteers.
  10   They fired one wild, premature, ineffectual volley, and bolted on horse.
  11   The Martians walked serenely over their guns.
  12   The St. George's Hill men were hidden near a pine wood.
  13   They remained undetected.
* 14   The Martians were very near to them.
  15   Artillery shells flashed all round them.
  16   They advanced a few paces, staggered, and went down.
  17   Everybody yelled together.
  18   The guns were reloaded in frantic haste.
  19   The whole second volley flew wide of the Martian on the ground.
* 20   Both of his companions aimed their Heat-Rays on the men.
  21   The ammunition dump blew up.
  22   The pine trees all about the guns flashed into fire.
  23   After this the Martians halted.
  24   An overthrown Martian crawled tediously out of his hood.
  25   He was a small brown figure.
* 26   He resembled a speck of blight.
  27   The Martian repaired his support.
  28   About nine he had finished.

29 There were four more Martians on the other side of the hill.

30 Each carried a thick black tube.

✱ 31 A dozen rockets sprang out of the hills.

32 At the same time four of their fighting machines crossed the river.

33 At this sight the curate cried faintly in his throat.

34 The occasional howling of the Martians had ceased.

35 They took up their positions in absolute silence.

✱ 36 The night was lit only by the slender moon.

37 There were no stars out.

38 The guns were waiting.

39 The signal rockets burst and rained their sparks.

40 The spirit of all those watching batteries rose to a tense expectation.

41 The Martians advanced into the line of fire.

✱ 42 A hundred questions struggled together in my mind.

43 Then there was a sound like the distant concussion of a gun.

44 The Martian beside us raised his tube and discharged it.

45 There was no flash and no smoke.

✱ 46 In my excitement I forgot my personal safety.

47 A big projectile hurtled overhead towards Hounslow.

48 I expected smoke or fire, or some such evidence of its work.

49 I saw only the deep blue sky above.

✱ 50 There had been no crash, no answering explosion.

Note: Suggested responses for the sentences marked by an asterisk (✱) are given at the back of the book. As a way of getting started on this activity, you might want to work first on those items. Where your responses and the suggested ones differ, you will want to get advice from your instructor. Very often, several interpretations might be appropriate.

Chapter 3

Clauses: Participants and Circumstances

Preliminaries

So far we have said that the main structural unit of English, the clause, reflects the actions, thoughts, emotions, and states of affairs that we experience. Clauses are organized around a core unit, the process, whose very nature sets up expectations regarding role-players and essential props. Language users can also pack into clauses information about the circumstances under which events occur.

In Chapter 2 we had some practice identifying processes; now it's time to learn more about the role-players, essential props, and circumstances.

Participants

Participant roles and participant role-players Every process entails specific participant roles. We categorize a process by considering the number of participant roles that are entailed. Transitive processes entail two or more directly expressible participant roles. Other-than-transitive processes entail only one.

However, both the *number of roles* and the *number of role-players* in a process that are overtly expressed in a clause will often be very different from the number of entailed participant roles themselves.

For one thing, participants can be missing elements. Consider, for example, the event that is represented by the process *carry*, in its transitive sense of transporting items from one place to another. When used in this sense, *carry* entails two specific participant roles, carry*er* and carry*ee*; it may additionally involve an optional instrument. For example, in *They carried their suitcases into the airport with their own hands, they* plays the carry*er* role, *their suitcases* plays the carry*ee* role, and *with their own hands* is an instrument.

However, bearing in mind that the number of roles actually expressed in a clause can vary from the total number of entailed and optional participant roles in the event represented by the clause, let's take another look at the *carry* event. As we just showed, *carry* entails two roles, and it can include a third, maybe even more. However, tally the role-players expressed in this clause: *The suitcases were carried into the airport*. Only one, right? *The suitcases*. Nonetheless, the number of participant roles involved in *carrying* is still at least two. After all, someone has to carry the suitcases. That is to say, even though *carrying* entails two participant roles and permits even more, only one role-player (the carry*ee*) is expressed in *The suitcases were carried into the airport*, and the others (the carry*er* and perhaps an instrument) are simply assumed; they are missing elements. Most transitive processes have the same potential as *carry*. One or more of the participant roles can go unexpressed (for more on this, see 'Voice' in Chapter 5).

Similarly, *carry* and many other processes (transitive and otherwise) can represent requests or demands. For example: *Carry your own suitcase!* In clauses such as these, just as in *The suitcases were carried into the airport*, only one of the entailed roles is overtly expressed. The other is the missing element, *You understood* (for more on this, see 'Direct Requests' in Chapter 6).

Moreover, it is also frequently the case that multiple role-players are expressed for each participant role, as is the case with *They carried their suitcases into the airport with their own hands*. Even though carry*er* is just one role, it is being played by several individuals, represented by *they*. Likewise, *suitcases* (the carry*ee*) involves more than one suitcase, and *with their own hands* involves a number of hands. Consider, as an additional example, *Several gamblers played their cards*. In this case, *played* entails exactly two participant roles, the play*er* role and the play*ee* role. However, you will notice that the play*er* role is being fulfilled by *several gamblers*, and the play*ee* role by *their cards*. In each of these cases, each participant role is being executed by multiple players.

List 3.1 *Some Generic Participant Roles*

Affected, Agent, Associate, Beneficiary, Causer, Client, Experiencer, Goal, Instrument, Location, Patient, Recipient, Result, among others

Generic participant roles Many different generic participant roles can be identified. In the earlier examples, we identified the participant roles as carry*er*, carry*ee*, instrument, play*er*, and play*ee*, but we could just as well have adopted a slightly more abstract set of labels—***agent*, *patient*, and *instrument***—chosen from generics such as those in List 3.1 (previous page).

List 3.1 isn't exhaustive; you might also read about *behavers, carriers, phenomena, sayers, sensers, targets, themes,* and more, depending upon whose grammar you are studying. When we are interested in discovering the comparatively small set of resources available to a language user, and especially when we are interested in comparing the resources of one language with those of another, a set of generics is very handy. Here are some examples from *The War of the Worlds*:

(1) **Affected** (the participant affected by or undergoing the process)
     <u>Something</u> was crushed under the rolling wheels.

(2) **Agent** (the participant performing an action)
     <u>My wife</u> pointed out to me the brightness of the signal lights.

(3) **Associate** (the participant with whom an action is carried out)
     He invited me up to take a turn <u>with him</u> that night in a scrutiny of the red planet.

(4) **Beneficiary** (the participant for whose benefit an action is undertaken; compare **client** and recipient)
     He remained standing at the edge of the pit that the Thing had made <u>for itself.</u>

(5) **Causer** (the participant causing an **affected** to undergo a process)
     Something was crushed under <u>the rolling wheels.</u>

(6) **Client** (the participant on whose behalf an action is undertaken; compare **beneficiary**)
     Markham was jubilant at securing a new photograph of the planet <u>for the illustrated paper he edited in those days.</u>

(7) **Experiencer** (the participant who is affected by mental phenomena such as feeling, liking, thinking, wanting)
     Had our instruments permitted it, <u>we</u> might have seen the gathering trouble far back in the nineteenth century.

(8) **Goal** (the participant toward whom an action is directed; compare **patient**)
     My wife pointed out to me <u>the brightness of the signal lights.</u>

(9) **Instrument** (the participant with which an actor accomplishes an action)
     They rapped on the scaly burnt metal with <u>a stick.</u>

(10) **Location** (the participant that designates the place of the state or action)
     The early editions of the evening papers had startled <u>London</u> with enormous headlines.

(11) **Patient** (the participant that undergoes an action; compare **goal**)
A leg of the tripod had been smashed by one of the shells.

(12) **Recipient** (the participant to whom a **patient** is transferred)
It was this, as much as anything, that gave people courage.

(13) **Result** (the participant that is the outcome of a process)
We rebuilt the church only three years ago.

However, for our immediate purposes here, specifics such as carry*er* and carry*ee* are probably more immediately relevant and easily understood than the more abstract agent and patient. But even so we may from time to time find it handy to refer to generic labels such as those listed.

Participant functions Participant roles in a process are played either by the subject or by an object. These are traditional grammatical terms, and we will employ them, even though they don't always do a good job: the subject is *not always necessarily what a clause is about* and an object is *not always a thing*. These two terms, however, are very handy, so let's define them, using very much the same approach that we did with *transitive* and *other-than-transitive*. Here goes: (a) the first-named participant in an ordinary, canonically (default) ordered clause is called the ***subject***, and (b) all other participants are called ***objects***. This definition holds even in cases such as (14), in which the ordinary, expected order of things is completely reversed:

(14) **Now, you I like!**

You is an object, and *I* is the subject. That is because the ***canonical*** order that this clause would take is *I like you*. It is rearranged for effect, and it gets that effect partly because of the unusual arrangement.

With regard to objects we will diverge slightly from more traditional terminology. Traditionally, only two types of objects have been recognized: ***direct*** and ***indirect objects***. However, for our purposes these labels don't go quite far enough.

Here's an example of what I mean. Consider the event structure in which a train and a car collide. Almost all observers will agree that in this sort of event, two participant roles are evident: the collid*er* and the collid*ee*. That such is the case can be demonstrated by the two ways in which the event might be viewed:

(15) **The car collided with the train.**

(16) **The train collided with the car.**

In (15), the train was at the crossing first, and the driver of the car ran the vehicle right into the side of the train. In (15), then, the car is the collid*er* and the train is the collid*ee*. The car ran into the train. On the other hand, in (16), the car was in the crossing first, and it didn't get out of the path of the train. In (16) the roles switch: the train is the collid*er* and the car is the collid*ee*. The train ran into the car.

As evidence for these participant roles being an integral part of the *collide* event structure, notice how strange (18) is. Strange, that is, unless you are trying to convince the police officer that you really are a good driver, all appearances to the contrary.

(17) **The car collided with the tree.**   (collider/collidee)

(18) **The tree collided with the car.**   (collider?/collidee?)

However, in traditional terminology, only one of the participants in any of these examples (15–18) gets a participant-role label: the subject. The other participant has usually been called a **comitative adverb** or the **object of the preposition**, or even the **object of a prepositional verb**. To accommodate this sort of problem, we will add the term **oblique object** (meaning *participant introduced by a preposition group*) to the traditional three-item constellation of subject, direct object, and indirect object, to make available four participant terms: *subject, direct object, oblique object,* and *indirect object*.

Doing this will enable us to define *indirect object* very succinctly in terms of the other two. Here goes:

a The *subject* (Subj) in a canonically ordered clause is the first-named participant and cannot be introduced by a preposition group.

b A *direct object* (DirObj) is any participant, other than the subject, that cannot be introduced by a preposition group.

c An *oblique object* (OblObj) is any participant that must be introduced by a preposition group, and

d An *indirect object* (IndObj) is any participant, other than the subject, that may appear as either an oblique object (introduced by a preposition group) or a direct object (no preposition group) without altering its participant role.

For example:

(19) My curiosity gave me courage.

(20) My curiosity gave courage to me.

In the following examples the participants in (19) and (20) are labeled in the two ways permitted by the specifications in the previous paragraph.

       Subj   DirObj DirObj

(21) [**My curiosity**] gave [**me**] [**courage**].

       Subj   DirObj   OblObj

(22) [**My curiosity**] gave [**courage**] [**to me**].

Now, because *me* can appear either as a directly expressed object as in (21) or as an obliquely expressed object as in (22), in either case it could be called an *indirect object*, as in both (23) and (24):

       Subj   IndObj DirObj

(23) [**My curiosity**] gave [**me**] [**courage**].

       Subj   DirObj   IndObj

(24) [**My curiosity**] gave [**courage**] [**to me**].

Notice that neither (25) nor (26) below can work.

(25) My curiosity gave courage *me.

(To work, the indirect object *me* would need to include *to*.)

(26) My curiosity gave me *for courage.

(A direct object, such as *courage*, cannot include a preposition group.)

The reason that (25) and (26) do not work can be explained only in terms of participant roles: the giv*ee*, the *courage*, cannot be introduced with a preposition group; it is one of the two requisite directly expressible roles. The recipient of the *courage*, *me*, can, although it need not be. That's the way English works. A certain limited number of object participant roles in transitive processes (recipient, client, and beneficiary) can be expressed either with or without a preposition group. That's what an *indirect object* is: it can be expressed either way.

List 3.2 is a condensed version of what we've just said, and (27) to (30) are examples of ***participant functions*** (adapted from *The War of the Worlds*).

List 3.2 *Participant Functions*

Subject	The first-named participant of a clause is called the subject.
Object	All participants other than the subject are called objects.
Direct object	A direct object is never introduced by a preposition group.
Oblique object	An oblique object is always introduced by a preposition group.
Indirect object	An indirect object must be capable of appearing both with and without a preposition group; an indirect object usually plays the role of recipient (to whom things are transferred), or beneficiary (for whose benefit an action is undertaken), or client (at whose behest an action is undertaken).

Subjects

        Subj
(27) [The thunderstorm] had passed.

       Subj
[The pine trees near the Oriental College] had gone.

       Subj
[The common about the sand pits] was visible.

Direct objects (DirObj)

              DirObj
(28) The fire threw [a red reflection] upon the clouds above.

             DirObj
A haze of smoke hid [the Martian shapes].

             DirObj
I could not recognize [the black objects].

Oblique objects (OblObj)

              OblObj
(29) The pine trees were lit [by a vivid red glare].

            OblObj
The fire threw a red reflection [upon the clouds above].

                OblObj
I could distinguish no people at all, though I peered intently [for them].

Indirect objects (IndObj)

IndObj
(30) **The water gave [me] my best chance of escape.**

IndObj
The Thing had made a pit [for itself].

IndObj
The fugitives offered enormous sums of money [to steamboat owners].

ACTIVITY **3.1**

What follows are the first two paragraphs of *The War of the Worlds* (you've seen them both in earlier examples) with some of the participants bracketed. Give some thought to the roles that are being played and to the participant function labels (from List 3.2) that each might receive. Try to fill in the table that follows—I have sprinkled some hints here and there, and responses for the whole thing appear at the back of the book.

[No one] would have believed in the last years of the nineteenth century that [this world] was being watched keenly and closely [by intelligences greater than man's and yet as mortal as his own]; that as men busied [themselves] about their various concerns [they] were scrutinized and studied, perhaps almost as narrowly as [a man with a microscope] might scrutinize [the transient creatures that swarm and multiply in a drop of water]. With infinite complacency men went to and fro over this globe about their little affairs, serene in their assurance of their empire over matter. It is possible that [the infusoria under the microscope] do the same. No one gave a thought [to the older worlds of space] as sources of human danger, or thought [of them] only to dismiss the idea of life upon them as impossible or improbable. It is curious to recall [some of the mental habits of those departed days]. At most terrestrial men fancied there might be [other men upon Mars, perhaps inferior to themselves and ready to welcome a missionary enterprise]. Yet across the gulf of space, minds that are to our minds as ours are to those of the beasts that perish, intellects vast and cool and unsympathetic, regarded [this earth] [with envious eyes], and slowly and surely drew their plans against us. And early in the twentieth century came [the great disillusionment].

　　The planet Mars, I scarcely need remind the reader, revolves about the sun at a mean distance of 140,000,000 miles, and [the light and heat it receives from the sun] is barely half of that received by this world. It must be, if the nebular hypothesis has any truth, older than our world; and long before [this earth] ceased to be molten, [life upon its surface] must have begun [its course]. The fact that it is scarcely one-seventh of the volume of the earth must have accelerated [its cooling] to the temperature at which life could begin. It has air and water and all that is necessary for the support of animated existence.

Participant	Participant role	Participant function
No one		subject
this world	watchee	
by intelligences greater than man's . . .	watcher	oblique object
themselves		
they		
a man with a microscope	scrutinizer	
the transient creatures that swarm . . .		direct object
the infusoria under the microscope		
to the older worlds of space		indirect object
of them	thinkee	
some of the mental habits of . . .		
other men upon Mars . . .	exister	
this earth		
with envious eyes	tool for regarding	
the great disillusionment		
the light and heat . . .		
this earth		
life upon its surface		subject
its course		
its cooling		

Circumstances

Circumstances provide contextual or situational information about when, where, why, and how an event occurs. Circumstances build the environment and the setting, adding elements that describe the scenario in which events take place. List 3.3 describes the main types of circumstance.

List 3.3 *Circumstance Types*

Circumstance of Time
Sets the timeframe, frequency, or duration of a process

Circumstance of Place
Tells the locations, positions, directions, or distances at which
a process occurs

Circumstance of Reason
Gives the reasons, contingencies, or the purposes for which
a process occurs

Circumstance of Means
Tells about the resources through which a process occurs

Circumstance of Manner
Specifies the way in which a process occurs or the degree or extent to which it occurs

Circumstance of Condition
Specifies the qualifying factors under which a process occurs
or the outcomes or results of a process

Here are some examples (adapted from *The War of the Worlds*), with labels in use.

Circumstances of time (Time)

Time
(31) **I asked myself [for the first time in my life] how an ironclad or a steam
engine would seem to an intelligent lower animal.**

Circumstances of place (Place)

Place
(32) **[Over the smoke of the burning land] the little fading pinpoint of Mars was
dropping into the west.**

Circumstances of reason (Reason)

Reason
(33) **The gun he drove had been unlimbered near Horsell, [in order to command
the sand pits].**

Circumstances of means (Means)

Means

(34) Martians were crawling slowly towards their second cylinder [under cover of a metal shield].

Circumstances of manner (Manner)

Manner

(35) I leaned out of the window [eagerly].

Circumstances of condition (Condition)

Condition

(36) [If the gun had been unlimbered near Horsell], it would have precipitated the action.

ACTIVITY **3.2**

Here are the first four paragraphs of *The War of the Worlds* (you have already seen the first two) with some of the circumstance units bracketed. Try to decide what type each highlighted circumstance represents. As before, some hints are provided following the paragraphs, and responses can be found at the back of the book.

No one would have believed [in the last years of the nineteenth century] that this world was being watched [keenly] and closely by intelligences greater than man's and yet as mortal as his own; that as men busied themselves about their various concerns they were scrutinized and studied, perhaps almost as narrowly as a man with a microscope might scrutinize the transient creatures that swarm and multiply in a drop of water. [With infinite complacency] men went [to and fro] over this globe about their little affairs, serene in their assurance of their empire over matter. It is possible that the infusoria under the microscope do the same. No one gave a thought to the older worlds of space as sources of human danger, or thought of them only to dismiss the idea of life upon them as impossible or improbable. It is curious to recall some of the mental habits of those departed days. At most terrestrial men fancied there might be other men upon Mars, perhaps inferior to themselves and ready to welcome a missionary enterprise. Yet [across the gulf of space], minds that are to our minds as ours are to those of the beasts that perish, intellects vast and cool and unsympathetic, regarded this earth with envious eyes, and [slowly and surely] drew their plans against us. And [early in the twentieth century] came the great disillusionment.

The planet Mars, I scarcely need remind the reader, revolves about the sun [at a mean distance of 140,000,000 miles], and the light and heat it receives from the sun is barely half of that received by this world. It must be, [if the nebular hypothesis has any truth], older than our world; and long before this earth ceased to be molten, life upon its surface must have begun its course. The fact that it is scarcely one-seventh of the volume of the earth must have accelerated its cooling to the temperature at which life could begin. It has air and water and all that is necessary for the support of animated existence.

Yet so vain is man, and so blinded by his vanity, that no writer, [up to the very end of the nineteenth century], expressed any idea that intelligent life might have developed there [far, or indeed at all, beyond its earthly level]. Nor was it generally understood that since Mars is older than our earth, with scarcely a quarter of the superficial area and remoter from the sun, it necessarily follows that it is not only more distant from time's beginning but nearer its end.

The secular cooling that must someday overtake our planet has already gone far indeed with our neighbour. Its physical condition is still largely a mystery, but we know now that [even in its equatorial region] the midday temperature barely approaches that of our coldest winter. Its air is much more attenuated than ours, its oceans have shrunk until they cover but a third of its surface, and as its slow seasons change huge snowcaps gather and melt [about either pole] and periodically inundate its temperate zones. That last stage of exhaustion, which to us is still incredibly remote, has become a present-day problem for the inhabitants of Mars. The immediate pressure of necessity has brightened their intellects, enlarged their powers, and hardened their hearts. And looking [across space] with instruments, and intelligences such as we have scarcely dreamed of, they see, at its nearest distance only 35,000,000 of miles sunward of them, a morning star of hope, our own warmer planet, green with vegetation and grey with water, with a cloudy atmosphere eloquent of fertility, with glimpses through its drifting cloud wisps of broad stretches of populous country and narrow, navy-crowded seas.

Circumstance	Circumstance type
in the last years of the nineteenth century	time or place
keenly	
With infinite complacency	manner
to and fro	
across the gulf of space	
slowly and surely	
early in the twentieth century	
at a mean distance of 140,000,000 miles	
if the nebular hypothesis has any truth	condition
up to the very end of the nineteenth century	
far, or indeed at all, beyond its earthly level	
even in its equatorial region	
about either pole	
across space	

A note about the difference between participants and circumstances
Sometimes determining whether a clause constituent is performing the function of a participant or that of a circumstance is a tricky business. Often the context of the surrounding discourse will make it clear, but at other times you will find yourself pulled in both directions. That is not unusual. All language has ambiguity as a built-in resource, and English is no exception. See below for an example.

Consider examples (37), (38), and (39) below. Pay particular attention to the functions that are being performed by the elements introduced by the word *with*.

(37) I went for a walk [with my wife].

(38) Some of those who saw its flight say it travelled [with a hissing sound].

(39) At once, [with a quick mental leap], he linked the Thing [with the flash upon Mars].

In (37), I would say that *with my wife* expresses an associate role, and it is therefore a participant (an oblique object). In (38), on the other hand, *with a hissing sound* expresses the manner in which the traveling was done, so I would call it a ***circumstance of manner***.

ACTIVITY **3.3**

How would you categorize *with a quick mental leap* and *with the flash upon Mars* in (39)? Participants? Circumstances? One of each? One possible response is discussed at the back of the book. Now consider (40).

> (40) **Even at this first encounter, this first glimpse, I was overcome** [**with disgust and dread**].

Couldn't one view *with disgust and dread* as either an oblique object (the thing that overcame me) or a ***circumstance of reason*** (the reason that I felt overcome)? Both ways seem to make sense, and it would probably be necessary for us to search the text of *The War of the Worlds* to find some justification to prefer one interpretation over the other. A close textual analysis would very likely, though not necessarily, reveal the most appropriate interpretation. However, in isolation from bigger contexts, one interpretation is as sensible as the other.

Practice with Terminology

What follows is a preview of the sentences that you will encounter in this chapter's Sentences for Analysis. Certain elements in the sentences have been underscored. Label each underscored element using one or more of the terms shown below. Check the Glossary if you are not certain about the definition of any of the terms.

Terms related to *Participants*	Terms related to *Circumstances*
Direct object	Condition
Indirect object	Manner
Oblique object	Means
Preposition group	Place
Subject	Preposition group
	Reason
	Time

1 Men busied <u>themselves</u> about their various concerns.
2 A man with a microscope scrutinized <u>the transient creatures</u>.

3   The creatures swarm <u>in</u> a drop of water.

4   <u>The men</u> went about their little affairs.

5   <u>They</u> were serene.

6   <u>No one</u> gave a thought to the older worlds of space.

7   There might be <u>other men</u> upon Mars.

8   Other minds regarded this earth <u>with envious eyes</u>.

9   The creatures drew their plans <u>against us</u>.

10   Early in the twentieth century came <u>the great disillusionment</u>.

11   Men on this earth are alien and lowly <u>to</u> them.

12   <u>Life</u> is an incessant struggle for existence.

13   <u>This world</u> is still crowded with life.

14   Generation after generation the destruction creeps <u>upon them</u>.

15   We should not judge <u>of them</u> too harshly.

16   <u>Our species</u> has wrought ruthless and utter destruction upon animals.

17   European immigrants waged a war of extermination <u>against</u> the Tasmanians.

18   The Martians calculated their descent <u>with amazing subtlety</u>.

19   <u>Their mathematical learning</u> is far in excess of ours.

20   We might have seen <u>the gathering trouble</u> far back in the nineteenth century.

21   <u>For countless centuries</u> Mars has been the star of war.

22   <u>The Martians</u> must have been getting ready.

23   A great light was seen <u>on the illuminated part of the disk</u>.

24   English readers heard of it <u>first</u> in the issue of *Nature* dated August 2.

25   <u>This blaze</u> may have been the casting of the huge gun.

26   Peculiar markings were seen near the site <u>during</u> the next two oppositions.

27   The storm burst <u>upon us</u> six years ago now.

28   A huge outbreak of gas had occurred <u>towards midnight of the 12th</u>.

29   He had at once resorted <u>to the spectroscope</u>.

30   His investigations had indicated <u>a mass of flaming gas</u>.

31   The mass was moving <u>with</u> an enormous velocity towards this earth.

32   This jet of fire became invisible <u>about a quarter past twelve</u>.

33   He compared <u>it</u> to a colossal puff of flame.

34   Flaming gases <u>suddenly and violently</u> squirted out of the planet.

35   A singularly appropriate phrase <u>it</u> proved.

36   <u>The next day</u> there was nothing of this in the papers.

37   Ogilvy, the well-known astronomer, was immensely excited <u>at the news</u>.

38   I took a turn that night <u>with him</u> in a scrutiny of the red planet.

39   I still remember that vigil <u>very distinctly</u>.

40   The shadowed lantern threw a feeble glow <u>upon</u> the floor in the corner.

41   <u>Through the telescope</u> one saw a circle of deep blue.

42   <u>It</u> seemed such a little thing.

43   <u>The planet</u> grew larger and smaller.

44   Forty millions of miles <u>it</u> was from us.

45   <u>Few people</u> realize the immensity of the material universe.

46   Near it in the field were <u>three faint points of light</u>.

47   <u>In a telescope</u> it seems far profounder.

48   <u>No one on earth</u> dreamed of that unerring missile.

49   <u>That night</u> there was another jetting out of gas from the distant planet.

50   I saw a reddish flash at the edge <u>right at midnight</u>.

Analyzing and Reporting Clause Elements

Here in this section we introduce a system for analyzing grammatical structures and reporting your results. Near the end of the next few chapters, a section like this one will be available to you to help guide your work.

Step 1: *Identifying processes* Bracket and label the process type above the bracket.

                        Trans
  (41)   **Through the telescope one** [**saw**] **a circle of deep blue.**

Step 2: *Identifying participants* By referring to your own personal experience, determine the number of participant roles that the process requires. In the clause find the role-players; bracket them and label participant functions above the bracketed elements. Be aware that sometimes required participant roles are expressed by understood (missing) elements. Two possibilities come to mind for (41), given in (42) and (43).

                      Subj   Trans DirObj
  (42)   **Through the telescope** [**one**] [**saw**] [**a circle of deep blue**].

      OblObj   Subj   Trans DirObj
  (43)   [**Through the telescope**] [**one**] [**saw**] [**a circle of deep blue**].

In (42), the analysis proposes only two participants: *one*, playing the role of see*er*; and *a circle of deep blue*, playing the role of see*ee*. *Through the telescope* is left to be analyzed (see 44). However, in (43), three participants are proposed: *one*, playing the role of see*er*, *a circle of deep blue*, playing the role of see*ee*, and *through the telescope*, playing the role of instrument.

Step 3: *Identifying circumstances* All of the remaining clause-level bracketable elements are circumstances. Bracket and label them by type.

> Means   Subj   Trans   DirObj
> (44)   [Through the telescope] [one] [saw] [a circle of deep blue].

Step 4: *Taking stock* Our conclusion is that the clause chosen for the example could be interpreted and analyzed in two ways:

> OblObj   Subj   Trans   DirObj
> (45)   [Through the telescope] [one] [saw] [a circle of deep blue].

> Means   Subj   Trans   DirObj
> (46)   [Through the telescope] [one] [saw] [a circle of deep blue].

Some Bracketing and Labeling Conventions

The reporting style used throughout this book is as simple as possible while doing the required job. Minimal bracketing is used to isolate clause-level word groups, and starting in Chapter 8, the triangle convention is applied for reporting clause complexes. To complete the Sentences for Analysis that follow, you will need some or all of the following devices.

Brackets Use square brackets to delineate the left- and right-hand edges of clause-level constituents:

> (47)   [The storm] [burst] [upon us] [six years ago now].

> (48)   [He] [compared] [it] [to a colossal puff of flame].

Discontinuous constituent Sometimes a unit will be interrupted by another unit. In such a case, the interrupted unit wraps around the interrupting unit using a squared-off connector:

> Intrans
> (48)   [He] had [at once] resorted [to the spectroscope].

> LV + Att (Inverted Order)
> (49)   A singularly appropriate phrase [it] proved.

Function label The grammatical function of each bracketed unit is indicated at the top of the bracketed unit.

       Subj   Intrans Place   Time

(51) [The storm] [burst] [upon us] [six years ago now].

       Subj Trans   DirObj OblObj

(52) [He] [compared] [it] [to a colossal puff of flame].

Missing elements Missing elements are indicated by parentheses and the proposed element itself is expressed in capital letters.

(53) '(YOU) Come into the house,' I said.

(54) The scouts (WHO) (WERE) watching them remained absolutely stationary for the next half hour.

Continued unit Should one line of a report run beyond the margins of the paper, a pair of arrows should be used, one at the end of the first line and one at the beginning of the next, to indicate the continuity.

(55) Peculiar markings were seen near the site during the next two ⟳
→ oppositions.

(56) A huge outbreak of incandescent gas had occurred towards ⟳
→ midnight of the 12th.

Sentences for Analysis

In the following sentences, adapted from *The War of the Worlds*, bracket and identify processes, participants, and circumstances by function, as shown in this example:

       Subj   Trans   Manner   OblObj

(57) [This world] [was being watched] [closely] [by great intelligences].

1 Men busied themselves about their various concerns.
2 A man with a microscope scrutinized the transient creatures.
3 The creatures swarm in a drop of water.
4 The men went about their little affairs.
* 5 They were serene.
6 No one gave a thought to the older worlds of space.
7 There might be other men upon Mars.
* 8 Other minds regarded this earth with envious eyes.
9 The creatures drew their plans against us.

10   Early in the twentieth century came the great disillusionment.

11   Men on this earth are alien and lowly to them.

12   Life is an incessant struggle for existence.

13   This world is still crowded with life.

∗ 14   Generation after generation the destruction creeps upon them.

15   We should not judge of them too harshly.

16   Our species has wrought ruthless and utter destruction upon animals.

∗ 17   European immigrants waged a war of extermination against the Tasmanians.

18   The Martians calculated their descent with amazing subtlety.

19   Their mathematical learning is far in excess of ours.

∗ 20   We might have seen the gathering trouble far back in the nineteenth century.

21   For countless centuries Mars has been the star of war.

22   The Martians must have been getting ready.

∗ 23   A great light was seen on the illuminated part of the disk.

24   English readers heard of it first in the issue of *Nature* dated August 2.

25   This blaze may have been the casting of the huge gun.

26   Peculiar markings were seen near the site during the next two oppositions.

27   The storm burst upon us six years ago now.

28   A huge outbreak of gas had occurred towards midnight of the 12th.

29   He had at once resorted to the spectroscope.

30   His investigations had indicated a mass of flaming gas.

31   The mass was moving with an enormous velocity towards this earth.

∗ 32   This jet of fire became invisible about a quarter past twelve.

33   He compared it to a colossal puff of flame.

34   Flaming gases suddenly and violently squirted out of the planet.

35   A singularly appropriate phrase it proved.

36   The next day there was nothing of this in the papers.

∗ 37   Ogilvy, the well-known astronomer, was immensely excited at the news.

38   I took a turn that night with him in a scrutiny of the red planet.

39   I still remember that vigil very distinctly.

40   The shadowed lantern threw a feeble glow upon the floor in the corner.

∗ 41   Through the telescope one saw a circle of deep blue.

42   It seemed such a little thing.

43   The planet grew larger and smaller.

44   Forty millions of miles it was from us.

45　Few people realize the immensity of the material universe.

46　Near it in the field were three faint points of light.

✻ 47　In a telescope it seems far profounder.

48　No one on earth dreamed of that unerring missile.

49　That night there was another jetting out of gas from the distant planet.

50　I saw a reddish flash at the edge right at midnight.

> **Note:** Suggested responses for the sentences marked by an asterisk (✻) are given at the back of the book. As a way of getting started on this activity, you might want to work first on those items. Where your responses and the suggested ones differ, you will want to get advice from your instructor. Very often, several interpretations might be appropriate.

Chapter 4

Word Groups and Phrases

Preliminaries

Part of the job that you had to accomplish by the end of the last chapter was to group together words that belonged together and then tag your groupings with an appropriate label according to whether the group functioned as process, participant, or circumstance. You have probably done a very good job of this task of word grouping even though we offered nothing by way of direct instruction for the task. I counted on your intuitions as a user of the language. Now we'll start building on those intuitions. In this chapter we will initiate a discussion about the constituent structure of word groupings, and this discussion will continue throughout the remainder of the book.

In the final analysis, once you have a sense of how event structure is reflected in the content of clauses, understanding the internal workings of English amounts to sorting out the dynamics of word groups. This book puts special emphasis on noun groups and **verb groups**. Verb groups (Chapter 5) are of special interest because they serve in the core unit, the process, of every English-language clause; in addition, the configuration of their elements determines whether clauses are statements, requests, or questions (Chapter 6).

Noun groups (Chapter 7), on the other hand, are especially important not only because they typically serve as home to participants but also because they serve as our key to understanding how English-language clauses are joined into clause complexes (Chapters 8, 9, and 10). In this chapter we will get a sense of what the term **word group** means, and we will contrast word groups with phrases. Then we will put that knowledge to work by looking in some detail into the elements of adjective groups, adverb groups, and prepositional phrases.

Word Groups

Word groups function in clauses as participants, processes, and circumstances. If they do not directly perform one of these event-structure functions, they form part of a larger unit that does, such as another word group, or a phrase, or even a clause.

Word groups can also function outside clauses as either relationship units or discourse units, but as we have mentioned, our focus in this book is on the mechanisms inside clauses. An occasional look outside the clause, at the relationship and discourse aspects of language, is about all we will have space for. However, one very important outcome of knowing more about how clauses operate internally is that you will be able to put that knowledge to work, as you pursue your other academic interests, on the complex task of understanding the subtleties and complexities of language in its relationship and discourse functions.

The main point of this chapter is that word groups have **heads** and edges. They are built up around **main words** (heads) that occupy the focal position in the group. The first and last elements in word groups are at the edges of the group. (*Note:* Word groups are named for their main words.)

Inside the boundaries of a word group all internally contained word groups, phrases, and clauses pertain directly to the main word. Put another way, every word in a word group, except the main word, modifies or complements the main word in some way—and if it does not do so directly, it belongs to a word group, phrase, or clause that does.

At the risk of insulting you by pointing out something painfully obvious here, I want to make sure you notice that a clause can fit inside a word group (Chart 4.1). It is common to rank words, word groups, phrases, clauses, and clause complexes in that order, but no rules operate to prohibit items at the upper end of the scale from becoming embedded in items at the lower end. The key to the enormous productive potential of any language is that higher-ranking units such as clauses or clause complexes can fit into lower-ranking units such as word groups. Moreover, these lower-ranking units, which might be hosting higher-ranking units within, can themselves fit inside an even lower-ranking unit that might itself be part of a higher-ranking unit that is in turn part of a lower-ranking unit, and so forth.

Chart 4.1 *The Word Group: Finite Resources, Infinite Potential*

Left-hand edge	Precentral space	Central Word	Postcentral space	Right-hand edge
Words* Word groups Phrases Clauses	Words* Word groups Phrases Clauses	**Main word**	Words* Word groups Phrases Clauses	Words* Word groups Phrases Clauses

* Except when we want to emphasize their function as the head word in a word group, individual words will be treated as single-word word groups and the group label will normally be applied.

In this very important sense, words, word groups, phrases, and clauses are similar to nested boxes or nested dolls: you can open up one, only to find another tucked away inside. This principle, called **recursion**, is one very significant factor in the extraordinary creativity of language. Think about it: a good deal of what you say, hear, write, and read, you have never said, heard, written, or read before. Nor are you likely to encounter exactly the same thing in exactly the same form ever again. You owe this ability, to some very large extent, to the recursive nature of word groups, phrases, and clauses.

To help make this point more tangible, here are some sample noun groups from the first few paragraphs of *The War of the Worlds*, with their main words underscored:

(1) the transient <u>creatures</u> that swarm and multiply in a drop of water

(2) the <u>infusoria</u> under the microscope

(3) other <u>men</u> upon Mars, perhaps inferior to themselves and ready to welcome a missionary enterprise

In example (1), repeated below as (4), a higher-ranking unit, the clause '(CREATURES) *swarm and multiply in a drop of water*,' is just one part of the word group that is built up around the word *creatures*. The whole word group is made up of four units—two units in front of and one behind the main word:

     1   2   3   4

(4) the transient creatures that swarm and multiply in a drop of water

    1 = *the* [a **determiner** (Det)]
    2 = *transient* [an **adjective group** (AdjG)]
    3 = *creatures* [the **main noun** (MN)]
    4 = (CREATURES) *swarm and multiply in a drop of water* [a **clause**]

You might have noticed two peculiarities about this account. One item, *that*, is not included in the list, and another, (CREATURES), is added. The first item, *that*, is not included because it is a marker and not a part of the event structure. The second item, (CREATURES), is added because it is a missing element, an understood part of the event structure of its clause. The word is printed in upper-case letters and enclosed in parentheses to indicate that it is an understood and not overtly expressed element of the clause. If this explanation seems a bit dense, I have good news and bad news for you. The bad news is that it's going to take a few more chapters to do a good job of making it all clear. The good news is that when we get to that stage, we'll pretty much be finished introducing all three of the main ideas of this book: clauses, markers, and missing elements.

In example (2), repeated as (5), the higher-ranking unit, the phrase *under the microscope* is just one unit in the word group that is built around *infusoria*. The whole word group is made up of three units.

       1   2   3

(5) the infusoria under the microscope

> 1 = **the** [a determiner]
> 2 = **infusoria** [the main noun]
> 3 = **under the microscope** [a **prepositional phrase** (PP)]

Similarly, example (3), repeated as (6), which is headed by the word *men*, has a higher-ranking unit, a clause (I've underscored it for you), inside a lower-ranking unit, the word group headed by *ready*. This word group is itself combined with another word group (headed by *inferior*) to form a compound unit that is within the lower-ranking unit, the word group headed by *men*. In the word group headed by *men*, then, we find five units (overlooking for the moment the words *perhaps* and *and*).

        1   2   3   4

(6) other men upon Mars, perhaps inferior to themselves ↩

                       5

→ **and ready *to welcome a missionary enterprise***

> 1 = **other** (a determiner)
> 2 = **men** (the main noun)
> 3 = **upon Mars** (a prepositional phrase)
> 4 = **inferior to themselves** (an adjective group)
> 5 = **ready *to welcome a missionary enterprise*** (an adjective group with embedded clause)

You might be wondering what the upper limit is for the size and configuration of the ultimate word group. No need to try to calculate the total number of possible combinations and configurations. Its only limit, for practical purposes, is whatever we can put up with. That's the creative power of human language.

> **A note about charts** The charts in this book put concepts into a graphic form, but they share one major defect: each gives the impression of a static, closed-end state of affairs. Chart 4.1, for example, appears to limit the size of the word-group to exactly five subcomponents: left-hand edge, precentral, central, postcentral, and right-hand edge. However, the intent of the chart is to show (a) that word groups have a main word (core element) that acts as a magnet for the satellites that **modify** or complement it, (b) that a word group is bounded— that is, it has edges, and (c) that some elements appear between the elements on the edges and the central word itself. Moreover, it should be clear that the satellites can be single words, word groups, phrases, or clauses. It will come in handy to refer to the edges of word groups and to the satellites that appear between the edges and the central word. I use the terms *left-hand edge* and *right-hand edge* simply for convenience. This book is mostly about written English, which reads from left to right. I could just as easily use *leading edge* or *front edge* and *trailing edge* or *back edge*. At any rate, all that is implied in the headings for the columns in the chart is that word groups are headed, that the heads attract satellites, and that there are sequential constraints to the order in which the elements of the group occur.

Four (or five) major word types English is usually said to have four major word-group types and a whole rash of minor types (Chart 4.2). In the traditional treatment, prepositions are dealt with as a minor group, but there is nothing minor about the work they do in English. They are due for a promotion, so in this chapter we will treat them with more respect.

The chapter points out some facts about three of the major types: adjectives, adverbs, and prepositions. Then Chapters 5, 6, and 7 work on the other two: verbs and nouns. The present chapter also touches on the minor groups.

Adjective groups You will find adjective groups performing two primary functions: (a) as modifiers or complements within noun groups, either in front of or behind the main noun, and (b) as the attribute in *be*-plus-attribute or linking verb-plus-attribute processes.

Chart 4.2 *Identifying Word Types*

Nouns

Inflections	Nouns can often be made plural. Noun groups can be made possessive.
Derivational endings	-(i)an, -age, -al, -ant, -ation, -dom, -ee, -er, -ery, -ese, -ess, -ette, -ful, -hood, -ing, -ism, -ist, -ite, -ity, -ment, -ness, -or, -ship, -ster
Syntax	Nouns fit into the main noun position in a noun group; therefore, they can be preceded by a determiner.

Verbs

Inflections	Verbs can be inflected for present tense, past tense, progressive, perfect, and passive participles.
Derivational endings	-ate, -en, -ify (-fy), ize
Syntax	Verbs fit into the main verb position in a verb group; therefore, they can be preceded by a modal, a semiauxiliary, or a core auxiliary.

Adjectives

Inflections	Adjectives often have comparative and superlative forms.
Derivational endings	-able, -al, -ed, -esque, -ful, -ic, -ish, -ive, -less, -like, -ly, -ous, -y
Syntax	Adjectives can appear in processes as attributes (but so can nouns). Adjectives can often be compared, using *more/most* or *less/least*, and emphasized, using *very* (but so can adverbs).

Adverbs

Inflections	None
Derivational endings	-ly (if the part to which -ly is added is an adjective), -ward, -wise
Syntax	Adverbs can appear alone as circumstance (but so can nouns). Adverbs can often be compared, using *more/most* or *less/least*, and emphasized, using *very* (but so can adjectives).

Other categories Determiners, modals, markers, prepositions, and pronouns are in ***closed classes***, that is, they do not easily admit new members. Since they are in closed classes, they can be gathered into lists, as has been done throughout this book.

Here are some adjective-group examples from *The War of the Worlds*. The adjective groups are underscored.

(7) its <u>slow</u> seasons

(8) our own <u>warmer</u> planet, <u>green with vegetation</u> and <u>grey with water</u>

(9) a <u>singularly appropriate</u> phrase

(10) such a <u>little</u> thing, <u>so bright and small and still</u>

(11) It seems to me now <u>almost incredibly wonderful</u>

Example (7), repeated below as (12), shows *slow* to be a single-item adjective group (AdjG) within a noun group (NG), occurring in front of the main noun (MN):

(12) [its slow seasons]
      Det AdjG   MN
      └──────────────┘
            NG

However, example (8), repeated below as (13), in addition to displaying a similar model in *warmer*, also has two multiword adjective groups—*green with vegetation* and *grey with water*—both of which follow the main noun *planet*:

(13) [our own warmer planet, green with vegetation and grey with water]
           AdjG   MAdj   PP   MAdj   PP
                          └──────────────┘   └──────────────┘
                                AdjG   AdjG

Example (9) includes an adjective group, *singularly appropriate*, made up of a main adjective, *appropriate*, and an ***intensifier***, *singularly*. The adjective groups in example (10) appear both in front of (*little*) and behind (*so bright and small and still*) the main noun. Example (11) shows an adjective group, *almost incredibly wonderful*, that is the attribute in a linking verb-plus-attribute process. This adjective group, which is a part of the process unit, has as one of its constituents an adverb group, *almost incredibly*, functioning as an intensifier of the main adjective *wonderful*. Main adjectives can even be preceded by adjective groups (*luminescent* blue) or noun groups (*gunmetal* grey), and are often followed by entire clauses (quite unable *to do anything*). All of these possibilities are summarized in Chart 4.3.

How can you tell when you have found an adjective in a clause? One way has traditionally been to say that adjectives modify nouns; they might appear in front of or behind the main noun of a noun group or they might appear in a *be*-plus-attribute or linking verb-plus-attribute process. Fair enough. But this description also fits at least one other category of word group, namely noun group. Moreover, prepositional

Chart 4.3 *The Adjective Group*

Left-hand edge	Precentral space	Central Word Main adjective	Postcentral space	Right-hand edge
Intensifier*	Adverb group Adjective group Noun group		*indeed*	Prepositional phrase Clause

* Some common intensifiers for adjective groups (same as adverb group intensifiers): a bit, a little, absolutely, all, almost, at all, barely, completely, extremely, fully, hardly, kind of, mildly, nearly, quite, really, scarcely, slightly, so, sort of, such, totally, utterly, very

phrases and clauses can also appear as modifiers within noun groups or as attributes in attributive processes. In other words, adjectives do not own the exclusive rights to modifying nouns, so identifying adjectives by seeing where they show up in clauses will get you only part of the way to knowing you have an adjective on your hands.

There are a couple of other tricks, too. First, you might be able to recognize an adjective by its ending. For example, words that end in *-able* or *-ible* are adjectives (for example, break*able*, not*able*, mail*able*, incred*ible*, ed*ible* . . .). Other word endings that might tip you off to the identity of an adjective are *-al, -ed, -esque, -ful, -ic, -ish, -ive, -less, -like, -ly, -ous,* and *-y,* as in these examples:

(14)   ment*al*, navy-crowd*ed*, grot*esque*, power*ful*, telescop*ic*, redd*ish*, repuls*ive*, count*less*, man*like*, earth*ly*, envi*ous*, cloud*y*

Additionally, adjectives can often be used in comparisons by using *more, most, less,* and *least* or by adding *-er* or *-est* to the basic adjective, and they can be intensified using *very*. However, very often one category can share characteristics with another; for example, adverbs can also be compared by using *more, most, less,* and *least,* and they can be intensified using *very*. It usually takes an accumulation of evidence to make a determination.

> **A note about intensifiers.** We have been using the term *intensifier* here to refer to the class of items that function in much the same way as the volume control on an electronic device. So it is handy to think of intensifiers as **extent expressions** that are used to increase or decrease the volume on adjectives, adjective groups, adverbs, adverb groups, nouns, noun groups, prepositions, preposition groups, prepositional phrases, verbs, verb groups, and even clauses.

Here's a summary of tests for identifying adjectives.

Inflections	Adjectives often have **comparative** and **superlative** forms.
Derivational endings	-able, -al, -ed, -esque, -ful, -ic, -ish, -ive, -less, -like, -ly, -ous, -y
Syntax	Adjectives can appear in processes as attributes (but so can nouns). Adjectives can often be compared, using *more/most* or *less/least*, and emphasized, using *very* (but so can adverbs).

ACTIVITY **4.1**

There follow several paragraphs of *The War of the Worlds,* with the first few adjective groups underscored. See whether you can identify the rest—there are twenty-five, more or less (you can check your work at the back of the book).

The Martians seem to have calculated their descent with <u>amazing</u> subtlety— their <u>mathematical</u> learning is evidently far in excess of ours—and to have carried out their preparations with a <u>well-nigh perfect</u> unanimity. Had our instruments permitted it, we might have seen the gathering trouble far back in the nineteenth century. Men like Schiaparelli watched the red planet—it is odd, by-the-bye, that for countless centuries Mars has been the star of war—but failed to interpret the fluctuating appearances of the markings they mapped so well. All that time the Martians must have been getting ready.

During the opposition of 1894 a great light was seen on the illuminated part of the disk, first at the Lick Observatory, then by Perrotin of Nice, and then by other observers. English readers heard of it first in the issue of *Nature* dated August 2. I am inclined to think that this blaze may have been the casting of the huge gun, in the vast pit sunk into their planet, from which their shots were fired at us. Peculiar markings, as yet unexplained, were seen near the site of that outbreak during the next two oppositions.

The storm burst upon us six years ago now. As Mars approached opposition, Lavelle of Java set the wires of the astronomical exchange palpitating with the amazing intelligence of a huge outbreak of incandescent gas upon the planet. It had occurred towards midnight of the twelfth; and the spectroscope, to which he had at once resorted, indicated a mass of flaming gas, chiefly hydrogen, moving with an enormous velocity towards this earth. This jet of fire had become invisible about a quarter past twelve. He compared it to a colossal puff of flame suddenly and violently squirted out of the planet, 'as flaming gases rushed out of a gun.'

Adverb groups When you find adverb groups at the level of the clause, they will be providing situational information in event structures, or they will be intensifying the entire clause. In other words, adverb groups can appear as circumstances in an event structure, or they can be intensifiers that have the entire clause in their scope. However, as was just mentioned, adverb groups can also appear within adjective groups, and given that many of the words and word groups that we are calling *intensifiers* are themselves adverbs, it can be argued that adverbs can appear with essentially *any* type of word group, phrase, or even clause. For example, here's an intensifier (an adverb) at work within a noun group:

(15) She got [*quite* [a deal]] on her new car.

The traditional way of defining the category *adverb* is to say that adverbs modify verbs, adjectives, and other adverbs. That's OK as far as it goes, but, as (15) shows, it doesn't go far enough. And as will become clear in later chapters, it only scratches the surface.

Here are some examples from *The War of the Worlds* of adverb groups working as circumstance. Main adverbs are underscored. In these examples, you can see something of the variety of situational or circumstantial information that adverb groups can provide. Example (16) provides a timeframe, and (17) gives information about manner, as does (18). Example (19) gives a location in space, and (20) shows an adverb that has an entire clause (*to crush the opposition*) in its scope (more on this in Chapters 9 and 10).

(16) far <u>back</u> in the nineteenth century

(17) so <u>well</u>

(18) very <u>distinctly</u>

(19) not <u>far</u> from the sand pits

(20) they did not wish to destroy the country but <u>only</u> to crush the opposition

In addition to these clause-level (event-structure) and intensification applications, an adverb group can also serve as a discourse unit (as in 21) or a relationship unit (as in 22).

(21) a great light was seen on the illuminated part of the disk, <u>first</u> at the Lick Observatory, <u>then</u> by Perrotin of Nice, and <u>then</u> by other observers.

(22) it <u>necessarily</u> follows that it is not only more distant from time's beginning but nearer its end.

Chart 4.4 *The Adverb Group*

	Central Word	
Left-hand edge	**Main adverb**	Right-hand edge
Intensifiers*		*indeed* Prepositional phrase

*Some common intensifiers for adverb groups (same as for adjective groups): a bit, a little, absolutely, all, almost, at all, barely, completely, extremely, fully, hardly, kind of, mildly, nearly, quite, really, scarcely, slightly, so, sort of, such, totally, utterly, very

Adverb groups are capable of carrying information at several levels: (a) they can be used to express clause-level circumstance, (b) they can be relationship-level comment—usually on the content of an entire clause, or (c) they can be discourse organizers.

Note: The words that we are calling intensifiers are themselves usually classified as adverbs.

Example (21) uses adverb groups to provide chronological sequence to a series of events in the discourse. Example (22) conveys the author's conclusion that *anybody* ought to be able to see how one thing leads to another logically.

As Chart 4.4 shows, a main adverb is modified and complemented in much the same way as are all other word types. Our examples demonstrate some of the ways in which intensifiers such as *far* in (16), *so* in (17), and *very* in (18) can adjust the volume of the adverb. And you can see that prepositional phrases add information in the adverb groups shown in (16)—*in the nineteenth century*—and in (19)—*from the sand pits.*

We can identify adverb groups by virtue of their providing information about the when, where, how, and why of a scenario in which an event takes place. However, this is not a sure-fire way to identify adverb groups because several other kinds of units can also do the same kind of work: noun groups, prepositional phrases, and clauses, for example. As was the case with adjectives, adverbs share their main workload with other kinds of word groups. They do not own the exclusive rights to modifying verbs, adjectives, and other adverbs, as is frequently claimed.

Sometimes you can recognize an adverb because of its ending. Some adverbs end with *-ward* or *-wise*, and they can also end with *-ly*, provided that the unit to which the *-ly* is added qualifies as an adjective.

You can also make comparisons by using adverb groups that include the words *more, most, less,* and *least,* much the way you can with adjective groups. Like adjectives, adverbs are often applied in comparisons by adding *-er* or *-est*: earli*er*, lat*er*, near*er*, and farth*er*, for example. Also like adjectives, adverbs can be emphasized using *very*. Here's a summary of tests for identifying adverbs.

Inflections	None
Derivational endings	-ly (if the part to which -ly is added is an adjective), -ward, -wise
Syntax	Adverbs can appear alone as circumstance (but so can nouns). Adverbs can often be compared, using *more/most* or *less/least*, and emphasized by using *very* (but so can adjectives).

ACTIVITY **4.2**

Look through the paragraphs of *The War of the Worlds* that follow, and list all of the adverb groups that you can, including those that are intensifiers; otherwise, you'll find the pickings mighty slim. The first few are underscored for you here, and the whole segment is reproduced at the back of the book, with the adverbs, about thirty, give or take, highlighted for you.

A <u>singularly</u> appropriate phrase it proved. Yet the next day there was nothing of this in the papers except a little note in the *Daily Telegraph*, and the world went in ignorance of one of the gravest dangers that <u>ever</u> threatened the human race. I might not have heard of the eruption <u>at all</u> had I not met Ogilvy, the well-known astronomer, at Ottershaw. He was <u>immensely</u> excited at the news, and in the excess of his feelings invited me up to take a turn with him that night in a scrutiny of the red planet.

In spite of all that has happened since, I still remember that vigil very distinctly: the black and silent observatory, the shadowed lantern throwing a feeble glow upon the floor in the corner, the steady ticking of the clockwork of the telescope, the little slit in the roof—an oblong profundity with the stardust streaked across it. Ogilvy moved about, invisible but audible. Looking through the telescope, one saw a circle of deep blue and the little round planet swimming in the field. It seemed such a little thing, so bright and small and still, faintly marked with transverse stripes, and slightly flattened from the perfect round. But so little it was, so silvery warm—a pin's-head of light! It was as if it quivered, but really this was the telescope vibrating with the activity of the clockwork that kept the planet in view.

As I watched, the planet seemed to grow larger and smaller and to advance and recede, but that was simply that my eye was tired. Forty millions of miles it was from us—more than forty millions of miles of void. Few people realize the immensity of vacancy in which the dust of the material universe swims.

Near it in the field, I remember, were three faint points of light, three telescopic stars infinitely remote, and all around it was the unfathomable darkness of empty space. You know how that blackness looks on a frosty starlight night. In a telescope it seems far profounder. And invisible to me because it was so remote and small, flying swiftly and steadily towards me across that incredible distance, drawing nearer every minute by so many thousands of miles, came the Thing they were sending us, the Thing that was to bring so much struggle and calamity and death to the earth. I never dreamed of it then as I watched; no one on earth dreamed of that unerring missile.

Minor word groups In this book you will find charts that describe five kinds of major word group: verb, noun, adjective, adverb, preposition. This might leave the impression that verbs, nouns, adjectives, adverbs, and prepositions are the only kinds of words that attract satellites and form larger units, becoming the main word in the larger unit. However, in principle, every word can be the main word of its own group. That goes for **conjunctions** (both **coordinate** and **correlative**), determiners, intensifiers, and every other imaginable class of word.

Phrases

Phrases are assemblies of word groups, other phrases, and clauses. In this regard, phrases are very much like word groups. However, they differ from word groups in one significant respect: phrases do not have main words upon which they are built. Phrases are not head-plus-satellite units. At a minimum, a phrase contains two word groups; that is, a phrase incorporates at least two head-plus-satellite units. And it could have a whole lot more.

A note about terminology The analytical approach taken in this book varies in significant ways from traditional analyses; and because it does, we cannot avoid some minor, but crucial, disagreements about terms. For the most part, we leave traditional terms to do their work. Nouns are nouns, verbs are verbs, adjectives are adjectives, and so forth. In addition to the more familiar traditional terms, however, we do use some contemporary terms (for example, *process*, *participant*, and *circumstance*). We will also need to deviate from traditional thinking a little bit in the matter of naming all of the working units of the analysis, such as clauses, clause complexes, phrases, and word groups. Take for example the very next section, in which we consider the phrase. Traditionally, the term *phrase* has referred roughly to any collection of words that is bigger than one word but smaller than a clause. Moreover, use of the term *phrase* by many contemporary grammarians also includes clauses. Here and throughout the book we will carve up the territory just a bit differently. *Clause* will designate a process-based unit that reflects event structure, *group* will designate a unit made up of a head word (minimally) and satellites (possibly), and *phrase* will designate a unit made up of at least two word groups, neither of which is embedded in the other, and (perhaps) other phrases and even clauses.

Subject and predicate Traditionally, one kind of phrase has figured centrally in grammatical analysis: the predicate. The predicate is most readily understood to be everything in a clause that is left over if the subject is taken away, that is, the process, the object(s), and the circumstance(s). Historically, grammars have very often broken clauses up into two subparts this way, into subjects (the first-named participant) and predicates (everything else). Contemporary grammars often refer to the predicate as a *verb phrase*. (Sorry, but I did warn you about the terminology thing. Don't make too much of it.) For example:

(23)

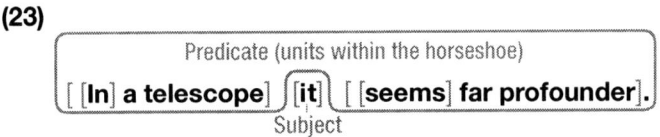

Here in (23), the predicate (*In a telescope . . . seems far profounder*) is made up of a prepositional phrase (*In a telescope*), a verb group (*seems*), and an adjective group (*far profounder*). In this book, however, we initially break clauses up into three (as opposed to two) kinds of functional units: processes, participants, and circumstances—so instead of referring to the subject and the predicate, we would say that the clause (the event structure) in (23) is comprised of a circumstance of place or manner (*In a telescope*), a participant (*it*), and a process (*seems far profounder*):

<pre>
       Place   Subj   LV + Att
</pre>
(24) [[In] a telescope] [it] [[seems] far profounder].

Therefore, subjects figure fairly centrally in our analysis because a subject is the first-named participant. The predicate, as a category, however, doesn't figure as significantly here because we pay specific attention to the kinds of things that go to make up a predicate—namely, the process, all participants except the subject, and all circumstances. Nonetheless, the word *predicate* does occasionally come in handy, especially when we talk about constructing conjoined units, so we will have occasion to use it.

Other clause-level phrases Some other clause-level units are also phrases by our definition. For example, all of the other-than-transitive processes, except the intransitive category, will be called *phrases* here because they are all aggregates of more than one headed group. All have (a) a verb group, headed either by *be* or by a linking verb, and (b) another unit, either an attribute (a noun group, an adjective group, a prepositional phrase, or a clause), or a location (a noun group, an adverb group, a prepositional phrase, or a clause), or an expletive *there*.

For example, *seems far profounder* is a phrase because it is made up of two word groups: a verb group (*seems*) and an adjective group (*far profounder*).

<pre>
        LV + Att
</pre>
(25) [[seems] far profounder]
<pre>
        VG   AdjG
</pre>

Equally important, we will consider one additional kind of phrase as absolutely essential to understanding how English works: the prepositional phrase.

Prepositional phrases All ***prepositional phrases*** are made up of two units: a preposition group and a complementary unit, sometimes called the *object of the preposition*, which is either a noun group, a pronoun group, a clause, or an adverb group. List 4.1 catalogs common—and not-so-common—prepositions, and later Chart 4.5 illustrates the structure of the prepositional phrase.

List 4.1 *Some Common (and Not-So-Common) Prepositions*

Single-word Prepositions: about, above, across, after, against, along, among, around, as, at, atop, barring, before, behind, below, beneath, beside, between, beyond, but, by, concerning, considering, despite, down, during, except, excepting, excluding, following, for, from, given, granted, in, including, inside, into, less, like, minus, near (to), notwithstanding, of, off, on, onto, opposite, out, outside, over, past, pending, plus, regarding, respecting, save, since, through, throughout, times, to, toward(s), under, underneath, unlike, until, up, upon, versus, with, within, without, . . .

Multiple-word Prepositions: according to, ahead of, along with, as far as, as for, as to, away from, because of, but for, by means of, by way of, close to, contrary to, due to, except for, followed by, for the sake of, in addition to, in back of, in case of, in common with, in contact with, in favor of, in front of, in line with, in place of, in return for, in spite of, inside of, instead of, near to, next to, on account of, on behalf of, on top of, out of, outside of, owing to, prior to, regardless of, thanks to, up against, up to, with the exception of, . . .

Prepositional phrases have two main event-structure (clause-level) functions: (a) oblique and indirect objects, in which the preposition group marks the participant role, and (b) circumstance. As we have previously noted, prepositional phrases can also perform other functions, at levels below the event structure, within clauses. For example, they can be attributes in attributive processes, they can be locations in locative processes, and they can be satellites modifying or complementing main nouns within noun groups, among other things. Prepositional phrases can also work outside of clauses as carriers of discourse functions (for example, *for example*).

Here are some examples of prepositional phrases from *The War of the Worlds*.

Complement in a NG

(26) No one would have believed in [the last years of the nineteenth century]

(27) It is possible that [the infusoria under the microscope] do the same.

Complement in an AdjG

(28) . . . then came the silhouette of Maybury Hill, with its treetops and roofs [black and sharp against the red].

(29) I was bruised, weary, [wet to the skin], deafened and blinded by the storm.

Chart 4.5 *The Prepositional Phrase (a Preposition Group and Its Complement)*

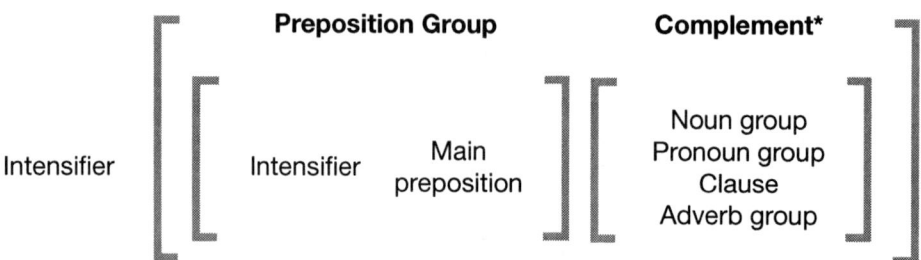

*The complement of the preposition group in a prepositional phrase is often called the *object of the preposition*.

Some common intensifiers for prepositional phrases (the same ones can be found with the preposition group itself): all, almost, close, completely, directly, exactly, far, just, more or less, nearly, only, partly, really, right, somewhat, soon, straight, very, way, well, . . .

Some preposition groups that can be followed by an adverb group: after (after today), at (at last), before (before long), by (by tomorrow), for (for later), from (from now on), since (since then), until (until tonight)

Complement in an AdvG

(30) He had eaten no food since midday, he told me [early in his narrative].

(31) But there was practically nothing more to tell people until [late in the afternoon].

Oblique object

(32) . . . the horse had an hour's rest while I took supper [with my cousins].

(33) I saw that the driving clouds had been pierced as it were [by a thread of green fire].

Circumstance of time

(34) My wife was curiously silent [throughout the drive].

(35) I struggled to my feet [at last].

Circumstance of place

(36) The heavy firing that had broken out while we were driving [down Maybury Hill] ceased as abruptly.

(37) Something very like the war fever that occasionally runs [through a civilized community] had got into my blood.

Circumstance of reason

(38) So much I saw then, all vaguely [for the flickering of the lightning], in blinding highlights and dense black shadows.

(39) They could not stop in Edgware [because of the growing traffic through the place].

Circumstance of means

(40) For some minutes I lay there in the rain and darkness watching, [by the intermittent light], these monstrous beings of metal moving about in the distance over the hedge tops.

(41) The Martians are able to discharge enormous clouds of a black and poisonous vapour [by means of rockets].

Circumstance of manner

(42) We got to Leatherhead [without misadventure] about nine o'clock.

(43) She answered only [in monosyllables].

Circumstance of condition

(44) I got up presently, walked perhaps half a mile [without meeting a soul].

(45) At the sight of the sea, Mrs. Elphinstone, [in spite of the assurances of her sister-in-law], gave way to panic.

Attribute in a be-*plus-attribute process*

(46) But they [were in no hurry].

(47) The situation [was of the strangest and gravest description].

Location in a be-*plus-location process*

(48) The scent of hay [was in the air through the lush meadows beyond Pyrford].

(49) . . . and in another minute it [was with its companion].

A note about *of* The preposition group *of* is most frequently seen *within* a noun group introducing a relationship between the main noun and the complement of the preposition group (see example 50). Although it can have other functions, these are rare by comparison (see examples 51–54).

The preposition group *of* occurs several times in example (50):

(50) **The most extraordinary thing to my mind, <u>of</u> all the strange and wonderful things that happened upon that Friday, was the dovetailing <u>of</u> the commonplace habits <u>of</u> our social order with the first beginnings <u>of</u> the series <u>of</u> events that <u>was</u> to topple that social order headlong.**

Less frequently does *of* appear in an adjective group (51), or introduce a participant (52), or a relationship unit (53), or an attribute (54).

(51) **My muscles and nerves seemed [drained <u>of</u> their strength].**

(52) **I began to comfort her and myself by repeating all that Ogilvy had told me [of the impossibility of the Martians establishing themselves on the earth].**

(53) **Many people had heard of the cylinder, [of course], and talked about it in their leisure, but it certainly did not make the sensation that an ultimatum to Germany would have done.**

(54) **My neighbour [was of the opinion that the troops would be able to capture or to destroy the Martians during the day].**

Practice with Terminology

What follows is a preview of the sentences that you will encounter in this chapter's Sentences for Analysis. Certain elements in each sentence have been underscored. Label each underscored element, using one or more of the terms shown below. Check the Glossary if you are not certain about the definition of any of the terms.

Clause	Main word (specify type)	Prepositional phrase
Complement	Modifier	Recursion
Discourse unit	Phrase (specify type)	Relationship unit
Intensifier	Predicate	Word group (specify type)

1 I sat <u>on the table</u> there in the darkness.

2 Patches of <u>green</u> and crimson swam before my eyes.

3 I little suspected <u>the meaning of the minute gleam</u>.

4 It would presently bring me <u>trouble</u>.

5 At 1:00 <u>Ogilvy</u> gave it up.

6 <u>Down below in the darkness</u> were Ottershaw and Chertsey.

7 He was <u>full of speculation</u> that night.

8 He scoffed at the <u>vulgar</u> idea of inhabitants on Mars.

9 Meteorites might be falling <u>in a heavy shower</u> upon the planet.

10 <u>A huge volcanic explosion</u> was in progress.

11 Organic evolution had not taken the same direction <u>in the two adjacent planets</u>.

12   The chances against anything manlike on Mars are a million to one.

13   Hundreds of observers saw the flame that night and the night after.

14   Dense clouds of smoke were visible through a powerful telescope on earth.

15   Even the daily papers woke up to the disturbances at last.

16   Popular notes appeared here, there, and everywhere.

17   Those Martian missiles drew earthward through the empty gulf of space.

18   Men went about their petty concerns.

19   Markham secured a new photograph of the planet for an illustrated paper.

20   People in these latter times scarcely realize the abundance and enterprise of our nineteenth-century papers.

21   The first missile then could scarcely have been 10,000,000 miles away.

22   I went for a walk with my wife.

23   I explained the signs of the zodiac to her.

24   It was a warm night.

25   A party of excursionists from Chertsey or Isleworth passed us.

26   There were lights in the upper windows of the houses.

27   From the railway station in the distance came the sound of shunting trains.

28   Their ringing and rumbling was softened almost into melody by the distance.

29   My wife pointed out to me the brightness of the signal lights.

30   It seemed so safe and tranquil.

31   Then came the night of the first falling star.

32   It was seen early in the morning.

33   It left a greenish streak behind it.

34   The height of its first appearance was about ninety or one hundred miles.

35   I was at home at that hour.

36   The blind was up.

37   This strangest of all things should have been visible to me.

38   No one looked for the fallen mass that night.

39   Find it he did, soon after dawn, and not far from the sand pits.

40   An enormous hole had been made by the impact of the projectile.

41   The sand and gravel had been flung violently in every direction over the heath.

42   The heaps were visible a mile and a half away.

43   The heather was on fire eastward.

44   The Thing itself lay almost entirely buried in sand amidst the scattered splinters of a fir tree.

45 The uncovered part <u>had</u> the appearance of a huge cylinder.

46 Its outline was softened <u>by a thick scaly dun-coloured encrustation</u>.

47 It <u>had</u> a diameter of about thirty yards.

48 He <u>was surprised</u> at the size and more so at the shape of the mass.

49 It was still <u>tremendously</u> hot from its flight through the air.

50 He remained <u>at the edge of the pit</u>.

Analyzing and Reporting Word Groups and Phrases

Step 1: *Identifying processes* Bracket and label the process type above the bracket.

> Trans
> (55)   Markham [secured] a new photograph of the planet ↻
> → **for an illustrated paper last night**

Step 2: *Identifying participants* By referring to your own personal experience, determine the number of participant roles that the process requires. In the clause find the role-players; bracket them and label participant functions above the bracketed elements. Be aware that required participant roles are sometimes expressed by understood (missing) elements.

> Subj   Trans   DirObj
> (56)   [Markham] [secured] [a new photograph of the planet] ↻
> IndObj
> → [[for] an illustrated paper] last night

In (56), the analysis proposes three participants: *Markham,* playing the role of secur*er*, *a new photograph of the planet,* playing the role of secur*ee*, and *for an illustrated paper*, playing the role of client.

Step 3: *Identifying circumstances* All of the remaining clause-level bracketable elements are circumstances. Bracket and label them by type.

> Subj   Trans   DirObj
> (57)   [Markham] [secured] [a new photograph of the planet] ↻
> IndObj   Time
> → [[for] an illustrated paper] [last night]

Example (57) demonstrates that the clause has a circumstance unit expressing time.

Step 4: *Labeling the main word for each bracketed word group* If any clause-level bracketed unit is a phrase, sub-bracket all component word groups except one (we will assume that the remaining elements form a group). Label the main word for each sub-bracketed group (the main word of a single-element group gets the group label).

Step 5: *Labeling adjective groups, adverb groups, and prepositional phrases, and taking stock* Here is our final report:

Some Bracketing and Labeling Conventions

To work on the Sentences for Analysis on pages 77–9, you will need some or all of the following devices.

Brackets Use square brackets to delineate the left- and right-hand edges of clause-level constituents; sub-bracket as necessary to isolate word groups within clause-level constituents:

(60) [The storm] [burst] [[upon] us] [six years ago now].

(61) [He] [compared] [it] [[to] a colossal puff of flame].

Discontinuous constituent Sometimes a unit is interrupted by another unit. In such a case, the interrupted unit is wrapped around the interrupting unit using a squared-off connector:

(62) [He] had [at once] resorted [to the spectroscope].
         Intrans

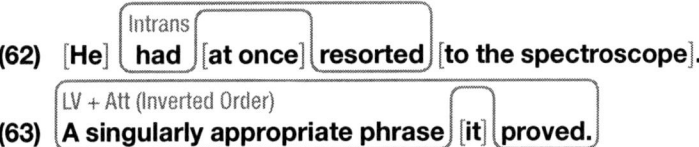
(63) A singularly appropriate phrase [it] proved.
         LV + Att (Inverted Order)

A note on reporting conventions We normally leave our bracketing at a *minimal*, essentially event-structure, level. Our goal is to make sure that we bracket the processes, participants and circumstances into group-size units. This means that we bracket prepositional phrases and then sub-bracket them into their preposition groups and complements. Likewise we sub-bracket 'be + . . .' and 'LV + . . .' process types to isolate the verb group from the rest of the phrase. We normally do not use *maximal* bracketing, except as might be required for emphasis or clarity. Here's why.

Even a *nearly* maximal bracketing approach (one in which not even each individual word is bracketed), if applied to the circumstance of place in example 75 from this chapter's Sentences for Analysis, might look something like the monstrosity in (64), with the bracket pairs resized for added clarity in (65) and detailed in (66).

(64)   [[on] [its way [[to] [the earth]]]]

(65)   [[on] [its way [[to] [the earth]]]]

(66)   [[on] [its way [[to] [the earth]]]]
      MP   Det MN   PG Det   MN
                                  PP
     PG   NG
           Prepositional Phrase

'on its way to the earth'

This level of bracketing provides a lot of detail and makes us engage in a further level of analytical thinking, but for our purposes such detail might overshadow the basic ideas. We will leave it at the minimal level needed whenever possible.

Function label The grammatical function of each bracketed unit is indicated at the top of the bracketed unit.

      Subj   Intrans   Place   Time
(67)   [The storm] [burst] [[upon] us] [six years ago now].

      Subj Trans   DirObj OblObj
(68)   [He] [compared] [it] [[to] a colossal puff of flame].

Element label The word category of the main word of each bracketed unit is indicated at the bottom of the bracketed unit. By convention, single-element groups are given group designations, their highest rank.

(69) [The blind] [[was] up].
       MN   VG AdvG

(70) [It] [[had] a diameter of about thirty yards].
    ProG   VG   MN

Missing elements Missing elements are indicated by parentheses and the proposed element itself is expressed in capital letters.

(71) '(YOU) Come into the house,' I said.

(72) The scouts (WHO) (WERE) watching them remained absolutely stationary for the next half hour.

Continued unit Should one line of a report run beyond the margins of the paper, a pair of arrows should be used, one at the end of the first line and one at the beginning of the next, to indicate the continuity.

(73) Peculiar markings were seen near the site during the next two ↺
   → oppositions.

(74) A huge outbreak of incandescent gas had occurred towards ↺
   → midnight of the 12th.

Sentences for Analysis

The following sentences are adapted from *The War of the Worlds*. Analyze them and report your results as shown in the example below. Make certain that your analyses have the following features:

a Bracket processes, participants, and circumstances and label them by function above the bracket.
b Sub-bracket as necessary, observing minimal bracketing conventions.
c Label the main word in each bracketed word group directly below its position in the group. Single-element groups are normally given the group label.
d Label adjective groups and adverb groups, sub-bracketing where necessary. Additionally, identify and label embedded prepositional phrases.

       Time   Subj   Intrans   Place
(75) [That night] [another invisible missile] [started] [[on] its way to the earth]
         MN   AdjG   MN   VG   PG   MN   PP

1 I sat on the table there in the darkness.

2 Patches of green and crimson swam before my eyes.

3 I little suspected the meaning of the minute gleam.

4 It would presently bring me trouble.

5 At 1:00 Ogilvy gave it up.

＊6 Down below in the darkness were Ottershaw and Chertsey.

7 He was full of speculation that night.

8 He scoffed at the vulgar idea of inhabitants on Mars.

9 Meteorites might be falling in a heavy shower upon the planet.

10 A huge volcanic explosion was in progress.

11 Organic evolution had not taken the same direction in the two adjacent planets.

＊12 The chances against anything manlike on Mars are a million to one.

13 Hundreds of observers saw the flame that night and the night after.

14 Dense clouds of smoke were visible through a powerful telescope on earth.

15 Even the daily papers woke up to the disturbances at last.

＊16 Popular notes appeared here, there, and everywhere.

17 Those Martian missiles drew earthward through the empty gulf of space.

18 Men went about their petty concerns.

19 Markham secured a new photograph of the planet for an illustrated paper.

＊20 People in these latter times scarcely realize the abundance and enterprise of our nineteenth-century papers.

21 The first missile then could scarcely have been 10,000,000 miles away.

22 I went for a walk with my wife.

23 I explained the signs of the zodiac to her.

24 It was a warm night.

25 A party of excursionists from Chertsey or Isleworth passed us.

＊26 There were lights in the upper windows of the houses.

27 From the railway station in the distance came the sound of shunting trains.

28 Their ringing and rumbling was softened almost into melody by the distance.

29 My wife pointed out to me the brightness of the signal lights.

＊30 It seemed so safe and tranquil.

31 Then came the night of the first falling star.

32 It was seen early in the morning.

33 It left a greenish streak behind it.

34 The height of its first appearance was about ninety or one hundred miles.

＊35 I was at home at that hour.

36 The blind was up.

37   This strangest of all things should have been visible to me.

38   No one looked for the fallen mass that night.

39   Find it he did, soon after dawn, and not far from the sand pits.

✳ 40   An enormous hole had been made by the impact of the projectile.

41   The sand and gravel had been flung violently in every direction over the heath.

42   The heaps were visible a mile and a half away.

43   The heather was on fire eastward.

✳ 44   The Thing itself lay almost entirely buried in sand amidst the scattered splinters of a fir tree.

45   The uncovered part had the appearance of a huge cylinder.

46   Its outline was softened by a thick scaly dun-coloured encrustation.

47   It had a diameter of about thirty yards.

48   He was surprised at the size and more so at the shape of the mass.

49   It was still tremendously hot from its flight through the air.

✳ 50   He remained at the edge of the pit.

Note: Suggested responses for the sentences marked by an asterisk (✳) are given at the back of the book. As a way of getting started on this activity, you might want to work first on those items. Where your responses and the suggested ones differ, you will want to get advice from your instructor. Very often, several interpretations might be appropriate.

Chapter 5

Verb Groups

Preliminaries

Here's the story so far: language reflects events in everyday life. Those events are narrative in nature, with plots, characters, and settings. The structure of language matches up nicely with the narrative structure of events in that the nature of both involves getting the who's-doing-what-to-whom straight. Events are made up of processes, participants, and circumstances, and so are clauses. In representing event structure, it's the process that has the central role, in language structure just as in the events that it represents.

ACTIVITY **5.1**

Without the process unit, it is very difficult, often impossible, to make sense of a clause. Here are some examples; try to figure out the missing process units before you check the completed sentences at the back of the book.

(1) The fact that it ___1___ ___2___ its cooling to the temperature at which life ___3___ .

(2) The secular cooling that ___4___ our planet ___5___ with our neighbour.

(3) Its physical condition ___6___ , but we ___7___ now that even in its equatorial region the midday temperature ___8___ that of our coldest winter.

(4) Its air ___9___ , its oceans ___10___ until they ___11___ but a third of its surface, and as its slow seasons ___12___ huge snowcaps ___13___ and ___14___ about either pole and periodically ___15___ its temperate zones.

The main point of this chapter and the next is that, because the process unit figures so centrally in the representation of event structures, it can be expected to have some special structural characteristics that other units do not share. In this chapter we will consider the special features of English-language verb groups—remember, all process units in English must have a verb group. Then, in Chapter 6, we will consider several functions of English-language clauses, each of which depends on features of the verb group.

Verb Groups

Two peculiarities distinguish verb groups from other kinds of word groups. First, a verb group cannot consist of just an individual unaccompanied *uninflected* main word. In this regard, verb groups are unlike all other word groups. All the others— noun, adjective, adverb (including intensifiers), preposition, determiner, conjunction, etc.—can consist of just a single uninflected word, although they often consist of many. Not so with the verb group. The verb group must contain at least two elements: a main verb and a second element. This second element is always the element at the left-hand edge of the verb group or, in the case of tense, included with that element. This element at the left-hand edge must be selected from a short menu: (a) *tense*, which must be marked on a verb, (b) a *modal auxiliary*, or (c) a *nonfinite clause marker*. No mixing is allowed—just one of these possibilities in any verb group:

Tense (in this case, Past):

(5) Men [busied] themselves about their various concerns.

Modal (here, might*):*

(6) There [might be] other men upon Mars.

Nonfinite clause marker (shown here, to*):*

(7) . . . ready [to welcome] a missionary enterprise

The second peculiarity of the verb group is that this element on its left-hand edge— whether it is tense or modal or nonfinite clause marker—is used to provide essential structural cues about whether the clause is a statement, a contingency, a question, or some direct form of request. Here's how the system works:

a Plain statements, sometimes called *indicative* clauses, contain neutral, normal verb groups in which the element on the left-hand edge is either past or present tense.

b Statements expressing contingencies, sometimes called **conditional** clauses, contain a modal.

    c Questions, sometimes called *interrogative* clauses, can contain either tense or modal, but the verb group itself will be discontinuous, looping around the subject of the clause so that its left-hand edge becomes the very first element in the whole clause.

    d Direct requests, sometimes called *imperative* clauses, start at the left-hand edge of the verb group because the subject of the clause, which must be *you,* is a missing element.

In the rest of this chapter and the next, we will fill in some of the details about these special structural characteristics of verb groups. This chapter concentrates on the elements of verb groups themselves, and Chapter 6 provides detail about the role of the verb group's left-hand edge in creating clause types. These chapters show that the beginnings of clauses in general hold powerful potential for guiding language users in establishing and maintaining interpersonal relationships and in making sense of the narrative events that language represents. The left-hand edge of the verb group itself always figures crucially in these functions.

Most of the discussion about verbs, verb groups, and clause types in this chapter and the next makes three main assumptions:

    a You can identify verbs.

    b You feel comfortable about breaking clauses up into their event-structure parts (processes, participants, circumstances).

    c You recognize that clauses are not simply ordered strings of individual words but rather that words cluster together into larger units, such as word groups and phrases.

The first assumption (which underlies the other two) will now become the focus of attention.

You are probably able to recognize verbs because they have been a part of your English classes since your days in elementary school. It might also be that you recognize verbs by some of their word endings, such as *-ate, -en, -ify (-fy),* or *-ize.* For example:

    (8) exterminate, darken, justify, realize

Here are a few more ideas about picking out verbs.

A summary of tests for identifying verbs	
Inflections	Verbs can be inflected for present tense, past tense, progressive, perfect, and passive participles (see below).
Derivational endings	-ate, -en, -ify (-fy), ize
Syntax	Verbs fit into the main verb position in a verb group and can be preceded by a modal, or a semiauxiliary, or a core auxiliary.

To this we can also add the idea that verbs and verb groups figure prominently in the process units of event structures; so if you understand event structure, finding the verb follows right along with finding the process.

Chart 5.1 summarizes the elements of the verb group. We have already said that a verb group must have at its left-hand edge either tense, or a modal, or a nonfinite clause marker. Between this element at the left-hand edge and the main verb itself might be found either a **semiauxiliary**, a **core auxiliary**, or some combination of the two (see Chart 5.1). In the event that there is no modal, no semiauxiliary, and no **primary auxiliary** (*be* or *have*) to use in making a question or negating a clause (more on this in Chapter 6), then the **periphrastic auxiliary** verb (**dummy do**) will pop up. I've included the periphrastic auxiliary on the chart, but because it relates very closely to the power of beginnings, it will not be more fully explored until the next chapter.

Main verb Every word group has a head word. All of the clauses, phrases, word groups, and other words embedded within the boundaries of the word group modify or complement the head word. In a verb group, the main verb (MV) is the head of the group, and you should expect it to be the last verb in the group. Very often, the main verb carries the central sense of the process. However, in attributive or locative processes that use either a linking verb or some form of *be*, it would be an error to say that the sense of the process resides in the verb group. In such processes, the main sense derives more from the attribute or the location. For example, in (11) think about which part you could more readily do without, the form of *be* or the attribute. That is, which of these has more content, *Mars . . . older than our earth* or *Mars is . . . ?*

The verb groups in examples (9), (10), and (11) each contain just tense at the left-hand edge.

Intrans

(9) Early in the twentieth century [came] the great disillusionment.

Past MV

Chart 5.1 *The Verb Group*

Left-hand edge	Precentral space	Central Word	Right-hand edge
Tense (either present or past) or Modal or Nonfinite clause marker	Semiauxiliaries and core auxiliaries or The periphrastic auxiliary verb (dummy *do*) for Q or NEG if no modal or other auxiliary is present (see Chapter 6)	Main verb	Postposed particles (verb particles)
			Idiomatic elements

Note: Intensifiers can fit in almost anywhere.

Modals (can't be tensed)	can, could, dare, had best, had better, may, might, must, need, ought (to), shall, should, used to, will, would, would rather, would sooner, Ø (zero)	**Nonfinite clause markers**	infinitive to; infinitive (to); free *-ing*; poss . . . free *-ing*
Semiauxiliaries (can be tensed)	appear to, be (un)able to, be about to, be (dis)inclined to, be liable to, be supposed to, be bound to, be fixin' to, be going to, be to, be (un)willing to, come to, dare (to), fail to, get to, happen to, have (got) to, need to, seem to, tend to, turn out to . . .	**Core auxiliaries**	*have + -ed/-en* (perfective aspect); *be + -ing* (progressive aspect); *be + -ed/-en* (passive voice) *Note:* Occasionally *get* substitutes for *be* to form either progressive aspect or passive voice.
		Periphrastic auxiliary	dummy *do*

                      Trans

(10)   . . . no writer . . . [expressed] any idea . . .

               Past MV

        be + Att

(11)   **Mars [[is] older than our earth].**

       Pres MV

In example (9), the verb group is *came*. This group, while comprised of only a single word, nonetheless has two elements. The first element is past tense, marked on the second element, the main verb *come*. Tense is said to be at the left-hand edge, not because it appears first but because it is marked on the verb that does appear first.

The reason for doing this is to make it clear that tense competes with **modality** and nonfinite clause marking for a place in the verb group and that these other two elements *do* appear first in the verb group. We also want to avoid saying that tense appears at the end of the main verb, because it often does not—as is demonstrated in the main verb in example (9), *came*, where it is represented by a change in the vowel when compared to its basic form, *come*. Where is tense located in the word *came*? Is it in the letter *a*? Check out the main verb in example (11), *is*. Where is tense located in the word *is*? We won't get into these issues of word form (**morphology**) here—although your instructor might want to do so. We'll just leave it at this: (a) tense competes with modality and nonfinite clause marking for the prime location at the left-hand edge of the verb group, and (b) tense gets marked on the first verb in the verb group, whether that verb is the main verb or an auxiliary verb.

Tense and time reference English has two tenses, present and past, and there really isn't much to forming either one. To create the past tense, all **regular verbs** add only -*ed* to the **basic** verb form, and all regular verbs add Ø (zero) to the basic verb form to create the present tense in almost all cases. That is, when the subject of the clause is *I, you, we, you all* (or *you guys*), and *they*, English present-tense verbs look just like the basic form. The form changes only when the subject of the clause is *he, she,* or *it* (or can be replaced by one of these). Then English adds an -*s* or -*es* to the basic form.

Furthermore, English does not have a future tense form even in the minimal way that it has present and past tense forms. Events that are to occur in some future timeframe (from a reference point in the present) are expressed in English with either the present tense (He <u>leaves</u> for Paris in the morning), with the present tense plus progressive **aspect** (He <u>is leaving</u> for Paris in the morning), or with a modal (He <u>will leave</u> for Paris in the morning).

It should also be pointed out that the timeframe in which events occur, or in which they are likely to occur, is not always directly reflected by the past or present tense marked on the element at the left-hand edge of the verb group. In English, we can make a very wide variety of timeframe references using either the present or past tense in combination with various modalities, semiauxiliaries, and progressive and perfective aspects. For example, in (12), the tense expressed at the left-hand edge of the three verb groups, *has brightened, (HAS) enlarged*, and *(HAS) hardened*, is present, but the timeframe in which the events occurred is not. It is more like something that has already happened and has just recently been finished. (See further examples in the 'Modality,' 'Aspect,' and 'Semiauxiliary' sections, which follow.)

> (12)   **The immediate pressure of necessity <u>has brightened</u> their intellects, <u>enlarged</u> their powers, and <u>hardened</u> their hearts.**

Tense is just one of several resources in English used in representing the timeframe of events. This resource does its job by changing slightly the forms that a verb can take and contributes information about the timeframe in which events occur by interacting with other verb-group and clause-level elements. In (12) tense interacts with aspect (discussion follows) to produce a sense of past acts coming to fruition. In the earlier example (*He leaves for Paris in the morning*) the present tense interacts with circumstance (*in the morning*) to produce a sense of action that is yet to take place. When we say *He goes to Paris every year*, what timeframe have we evoked with the combination of present tense and the circumstance *every year*? Has he gone to Paris in the past? Yes. Is he going right now? Could be. Will he go again next year? Probably.

Modality   The modal auxiliary verbs are *can, could, dare, had best, had better, may, might, must, need, ought (to), shall, should, used to, will, would, would rather, would sooner*, and, as we will suggest in Chapter 6, Ø (zero). We have settled on this list by applying two criteria. First, the word must appear at the left-hand edge of the verb group but not as a main verb, even if similar words have main-verb potential. In this list the words *can, dare, need*, and *will* are potentially main verbs. When they are, of course, they have very different senses: *can* sometimes means *preserve foodstuffs, dare* can mean *challenge, need* can mean *require*, and *will* can mean *bequeath. May*, when capitalized, can also refer to a month of the year, a noun. When these items are applied in these senses, they might best be considered different words.

Our second criterion is related to the first. Modals cannot be tensed. When the word *can* is used with tense, as in *I canned five bushels of tomatoes from my garden this year*, it is a main verb, not a modal. Modals compete with tense for the spot at the left-hand edge of the verb group, and in this clause, past tense appears (the *-ed* of *canned*).

If we were to check with a language historian, we would find out that some modal auxiliary pairs relate to one another: years ago *could* was a past-tense form of a main verb *can*, from which the modal auxiliary *can* has evolved. But that is history. Far in the past, *would* was a past-tense form of *will, should* was a past-tense form of *shall,* and *might* was a past-tense form of *may,* just as *could* was a past-tense form of *can.* In the past. Not in present-day English.

Modals might also be seen as relationship units that are worked into the clause structure instead of being tacked on to a clause, as *frankly* or *hopefully* might be. After all, when we use modals, we are frequently expressing observations about necessity, certainty, or obligation, and these observations often get intermixed with the elements of the event structure. Some modals contribute to the representation of an event, as well as to the maintenance of interspeaker relationships, by adding to the process this sense of necessity, certainty, or obligation, as with *must, need, should, ought* (*to*), and so forth. The modals in (13) and (14) seem more on the relationship side to me, whereas those in (15) and (16) seem more on the representational side. What do you think?

(13) All that time the Martians <u>must</u> have been getting ready.

(14) The planet Mars, I scarcely <u>need</u> remind the reader, revolves about the sun at a mean distance of 140,000,000 miles.

(15) At the time it did not seem to me nearly so urgent that the landlord <u>should</u> leave his.

(16) 'Blow yer trenches! You always want trenches; you <u>ought to</u> ha' been born a rabbit, Snippy.'

Modals can also contribute to the representation of an event by adding a sense of permission or possibility, as with *can, could, may,* and *might.*

(17) Those who have never seen a living Martian <u>can</u> scarcely imagine the strange horror of its appearance.

(18) One night (the first missile then <u>could</u> scarcely have been 10,000,000 miles away) I went for a walk with my wife.

(19) It <u>may</u> be the gases of the firing caused the Martians inconvenience.

(20) Had our instruments permitted it, we <u>might</u> have seen the gathering trouble far back in the nineteenth century.

Modals can contribute to the representation of an event by adding a sense of probability or volition, as *will, would,* and *shall* all do.

(21) 'A shell in the pit,' said I, 'if the worst comes to the worst <u>will</u> kill them all.'

(22) A Martian, therefore, <u>would</u> weigh three times more than on Mars, albeit his muscular strength would be the same.

(23) 'I <u>shall</u> go on,' he said.

Modals also interact with other verb-group elements to provide a timeframe for an event. For example, look back at (13), (16), (18), and (20) to see how a sense of certainty (13), obligation (16), probability (18), and possibility (20) are set into past timeframes by the interaction of the modal element with the core auxiliary *have* + *-ed/-en*, called the **perfective aspect** (discussion below). Here are some further examples:

> (24) **None of the telegrams <u>could</u> have been written by an eyewitness of their advance.**

Compare *None of the telegrams <u>have</u> been written by an eyewitness of their advance* (present tense) or *None of the telegrams <u>had</u> been written by an eyewitness of their advance* (past tense), which are without the sense of likeliness in a past timeframe that the modal *could* adds to the clause when combined with perfective aspect.

> (25) **This <u>might</u> have happened by a handling-machine escaping from the guidance of its Martian.**

Compare *This <u>has</u> happened by a handling-machine escaping from the guidance of its Martian* (present tense) or *This <u>had</u> happened by a handling-machine escaping from the guidance of its Martian* (past tense), without the sense of past-timeframe possibility contributed by the modal and perfective aspect.

Finally, the modal <u>used to</u> is employed in the verb group to provide a sense of repetitive action or habit.

> (26) **All these—the sort of people that lived in these houses, and all those damn little clerks that <u>used to</u> live down that way—they'd be no good.**
>
> (27) **They just <u>used to</u> skedaddle off to work.**

Nonfinite clause markers We will postpone detailed treatment of the nonfinite clause markers until Chapter 9, where we will have a chance to spend more time with them in the proper context. Nonfinite verb groups get their name (*nonfinite*) from the fact that they cannot help establish a timeframe. **Finite** is the name given to those verb groups with tense or modality, which do have a timeframe.

For now, we will just say that the word *to*, when it marks (signals) a nonfinite clause, displaces both tense and modality and occupies the left-hand edge of the verb group. The same goes for the nonfinite clause marker, **free** *-ing*. Therefore, the nonfinite verb groups are those in which the left-hand edge is occupied by either *to* or free *-ing*. Free *-ing*, like tense, gets amalgamated with a verb form, producing a one-word unit.

The label *free -ing*, by the way, derives from the fact that this *-ing* is only remotely and indirectly related to the expression of progressive aspect. For that, English uses *be + -ing* (more on this below). So free *-ing* gets its name because it is not bound to (is free of) a necessary relationship with *be*. Here are a number of examples with the nonfinite verb groups underscored:

(28) . . . thought of them only <u>to dismiss</u> the idea of life upon them as impossible or improbable.

(29) And <u>looking</u> across space with instruments, and intelligences such as we have scarcely dreamed of.

(30) <u>To carry</u> warfare sunward is, indeed, their only escape.

(31) . . . the spectroscope, to which he had at once resorted, indicated a mass of flaming gas, chiefly hydrogen, <u>moving</u> with an enormous velocity towards this earth.

(32) . . . and in the excess of his feelings invited me up <u>to take a turn</u> with him that night in a scrutiny of the red planet.

(33) I still remember that vigil very distinctly: the black and silent observatory, the shadowed lantern <u>throwing</u> a feeble glow upon the floor in the corner.

(34) <u>Looking</u> through the telescope, one saw a circle of deep blue and the little round planet swimming in the field.

(35) I wished I had a light <u>to smoke</u> by.

An additional note about *-ing* Several kinds of words end in the sequence *-ing*. Here we have just noted that *-ing* might be attached to the element on the left-hand edge of the verb group. When it is, it is known as a *nonfinite clause marker*. In the next section we will show that *-ing* might be a part of the two-part core auxiliary, *be + -ing*, known as **progressive aspect**. Similarly, *-ing* might be the last part of a noun (a meet*ing*, for example) or an adjective (for example, a charm*ing* person). You will also see words that end with *-ing* in which the *-ing* is not a separate unit at all (br*ing*, for example). It is handy to think of all of these occurrences as separate and unrelated to one another because each signals a different meaning and each has a different function.

For this reason, we use the label *free -ing* to refer to the nonfinite clause marker and *be + -ing* to refer to progressive aspect—even though the sequence *-ing* is an element of both. The nonfinite clause marker signals a relationship between one clause and another. The progressive aspect, on the other hand, is part of the system by which speakers of English place events into a timeframe. We will take up nonfinite clause markers in considerable detail in Chapter 9.

Core auxiliaries At its left-hand edge a verb group can have only one tense (either past or present), *or* one modal (although some varieties of English do sometimes permit two or even three), *or* one nonfinite clause marker. However, in the space between its left-hand edge and its main verb (which is always the last verb in the group), a verb group might have up to three core auxiliaries, one each from perfective aspect (*have + -ed/-en*), progressive aspect (*be + -ing*), and passive voice (*be + -ed/-en*). Moreover, if a verb group also has a semiauxiliary that contains the **verb particle** *to*, another set of three core auxiliaries are then sanctioned (more on this in 'Semiauxiliaries' later in the chapter). In the following example three core auxiliaries are evident in the bracketed verb group. It's an example that I invented. H. G. Wells found no use for such things in *The War of the Worlds*, and the rest of us don't say or write things like this very often either. Nonetheless, the potential is there.

(36)   **The dog [had been being given] free run of the house.**

The three core auxiliaries (perfective aspect, progressive aspect, passive voice) are discontinuous constituents. English often exploits discontinuity as an expressive resource: in the next chapter we will run across one sort of discontinuous verb group in which the discontinuity helps cue an interrogative clause, and in later chapters we will have occasion to discuss other types of discontinuous constituents as well. Here, however, we consider a simple, short-range discontinuity. We will return to example (36) in a bit, but for now, let's look at a sample from *The War of the Worlds*. The thing to notice is that the perfective aspect, *have + -ed/-en*, is wrapped around the main verb *begin*. When this happens, *begin* and the *-ed/-en* form one unit, *begun*. In this regard, the *-ed/-en* part of the perfective aspect is like tense: it attaches to its host. Units like these that append themselves to other units are usually called **inflections**. In this case, the resultant amalgamated unit, *begun*, is called a **past participle** or **perfect participle**.

Trans

(37)   **... life upon its surface [must have begun] its course.**
          Modal   MV
                have + -ed/-en

Here is a second example from *The War of the Worlds*. This time, two core auxiliaries appear:

LV + Att

(38)   **All that time the Martians [[must have been getting] ready].**
          Modal   MV
                have + -ed/-en be + -ing

The verb group in (38) is made up of four constituents broken up into six elements; two of the constituents are discontinuous, as shown below.

a At the left-hand edge is a modal: ***must***

b Then comes the first part of the perfective aspect: must ***have***

c Next comes the first part of the progressive aspect: must have ***be***

d Then the last part of the perfective aspect (*-ed/-en*) appears: must have be***en***

e Then the main verb occurs: must have been ***get***

f Finally, the last part of the progressive aspect (*-ing*) shows up, forming a present participle or ***progressive participle***: must have been gett***ing***

All together, it looks like this:

h   (a)   (b)   (c+d)   (e+f)
must + have + be-en + get-ing
Modal   MV
have + -ed/-en   be + -ing

ACTIVITY **5.2**

Look back now at the example at (36). That verb group has three discontinuous core auxiliaries. See if you can produce a sketch of it that resembles the one right above here in (38). Then check your sketch with the one suggested at the back of the book.

Aspect   As we have mentioned, perfective and progressive aspects interact with tense and with other elements of a clause to produce a timeframe for the event that the clause represents. We noted above (in 'Modality') that perfective aspect (*have + -ed/-en*) can combine with modality to produce a sense of possibility, probability, or obligation in a past timeframe. Here we need to add that the perfective and progressive aspects can team up with tense, and with each other, to produce a wide variety of timeframes. Here are some examples.

(39)   **Something within the cylinder [was unscrewing] the top!**

Here past tense and progressive aspect team up to indicate a timeframe of a current event in the past, a sense of present-in-the-past.

(40)   **The pinnacle of the mosque [had vanished].**

In this example the past tense and the perfective aspect indicate a sense of a past event in the past, a past-in-the-past timeframe.

(41) **Presently the Martians [will be coming] this way again.**

This example, on the other hand, has a timeframe in which an event is likely to be ongoing at some point in the future, what might be considered a present-in-the-future timeframe that is the product of modality (*will*) and progressive aspect (*be* + *-ing*).

(42) **... the thread of life that has begun here [will have streamed out and caught] our sister planet within its toils.**

Allowing modality (*will*) to interact with perfective aspect (*have* + *-ed/-en*) emphasizes that an event is likely to have already occurred at some future point, a past-in-the-future timeframe.

(43) **And this was the little world in which I [had been living] securely for years.**

In this final example, the past tense interacts with both perfective and progressive aspects to provide a timeframe in which, from the vantage point of some past time, some event had begun even earlier and was continuing, a present-in-the-past-from-a-past-point-of-view perspective.

These examples do not exhaust the possibilities, but the point should be clear by now: English can make reference to events from the perspective of past, present, and future timeframes, whether those events have already occurred, are just occurring, or are expected to occur later with respect to those past, present, or future perspectives. Our tools for getting the job done are tense, modality, and aspect.

Voice Passive voice (*be* + *-ed/-en*) has the main purpose of allowing a speaker to rearrange the order of the role-players from the canonical order (***active voice***). The do*ee* role can be put first in the clause and the do*er* role can be put last (or omitted completely). Here's an example:

(44) **... in the last years of the nineteenth century ... this world was being watched keenly and closely by intelligences ...**

In (44) the watch*er* role, usually given first billing as subject, is slipped into an oblique object spot, introduced with *by*, following the process, while the watch*ee* role, usually appearing as direct object, is boosted to the subject spot at the head of the clause. The passive voice, which is made up of the core auxiliary *be* + *-ed/-en* in the verb group and a shift in placement of expected participant roles, has two main purposes. First, it allows us to focus attention on a participant role by changing its normal position from object to subject. Second, it allows us to omit one participant altogether; the do*er* can become a missing element. Here's the clause from example (44) again, more or less, with its participants shifted around. First they appear in normal run-of-the-mill expected active-voice order (45), then in passive voice (46), then in passive voice with the do*er* left out (47), and then finally in normal active voice with the do*er* role omitted for comparison, just to show that while you can get away with omitting the doer in passive voice (47), you can't get away with it in active voice (48).

(45) . . . intelligences were watching this world keenly and closely . . .

(46) . . . this world was being watched keenly and closely by intelligences . . .

(47) . . . this world was being watched keenly and closely . . .

(48) . . . (Ø) were watching this world keenly and closely . . . (not English)

Just as the *-ed/-en* form of the verb in perfective aspect (*have* + *-ed/-en*) is sometimes referred to as the *perfect participle*, the *-ed/-en* form of the verb in passive voice (*be* + *-ed/-en*) is sometimes referred to as the **passive participle**. Traditionally, the *-ed/-en* form of the verb in any application has been called the *past participle*, just as the *-ing* form has been called the **present participle**, but the reasons for referring to these forms in this way are mighty obscure. We will use the more modern terminology.

Additionally, just as *get* sometimes substitutes for *be* in *be*-plus-attribute and *be*-plus-location processes, *get* can also substitute for *be* to form either progressive aspect (usually with an emphasis on starting) or passive voice (often with the sense that the subject of the clause somehow bears responsibility for what happens).

(49) **We got going early last night.** (No examples in *The War of the Worlds*)

(50) **'You'll get eaten!' 'We're the beast-tamers!'**

Some additional ways to express progressive aspect In addition to noticing that *get* + *-ing* is a progressive aspect that emphasizes that a process is just getting underway or just beginning, you might keep an eye out for further ways that *-ing* teams up with other verbs to express a number of variations on progressive aspect. You can find it being used with *come, go, keep, continue, stop,* (or *cease*) and perhaps even others:

(51) **A boy came running towards me.**

(52) **I went stretching my legs clumsily and feeling my way in the darkness.**

(53) Mrs. Elphinstone would listen to no reasoning, and <u>kept</u> <u>calling</u> upon 'George.'

(54) The little vessel <u>continued</u> <u>beating</u> its way seaward.

(55) As they grew hungry, the rights of property <u>ceased</u> <u>being</u> regarded.

Such expressions could also be seen as clause complexes, involving two separate clause structures, the second being a free *-ing* nonfinite clause. More about this when we take up such matters in Chapter 9. Here it is worth remembering that finding the best analysis will not always be completely straightforward. Choosing among competing analyses is often hard, and variation in interpretation is to be expected.

Verbs with unusual forms Normal verbs have five forms. All verbs except *be* behave normally with respect to the present-tense form; just add Ø (zero) to the basic form when the subject is *I, you, we, you all* (or *you guys*), and *they*. When the subject is *he, she,* or *it,* add *-s* or *-es* to the basic form. All verbs including *be* behave normally with respect to the *-ing* form; just add *-ing* to the basic form:

The basic form	jump	
The present-tense form	jump*s*	(add *-s* or *-es* to the basic form)
The past-tense form	jump*ed*	(add *-ed* to the basic form)
The *-ed/-en* form	jump*ed*	(add *-ed* to the basic form)
The *-ing* form	jump*ing*	(add *-ing* to the basic form)

However, many verbs have unusual past tense or *-ed/-en* forms; these verbs are often referred to as **irregular verbs**. List 5.1 details the prizewinner for unusual forms, the verb *be*. Then List 5.2 gives you some examples of other irregular verbs, those with unusual past tense or *-ed/-en* forms.

List 5.1 *The Many Unusual Forms of Be (Am, Are, Is, Was, Were, Been)*

Present tense	I **am** you **are** he **is**, she **is**, it **is**	we **are** you (all) **are** they **are**
Past tense	I **was** you **were** he **was**, she **was**, it **was**	we **were** you (all) **were**
-ed/-en	**been**	they **were**

Semiauxiliaries Core auxiliaries can sometimes share the space between the left-hand edge and the main verb of a verb group. When they do, the category of item that appears there we will call a **semiauxiliary**. Here is a partial list of items that can count as semiauxiliaries:

appear to, be (un)able to, be about to, be bound to, be fixin' to, be going to, be (dis)inclined to, be liable to, be supposed to, be to, be (un)willing to, come to, dare (to), fail to, get to, happen to, have (got) to, need to, seem to, tend to, turn out to, . . .

Some semiauxiliaries have been referred to as **modal idioms** (as in **idiomatic expression**) because they often have the same sense that the central modals such as *can* or *should* have—compare *can* with *be able to*, and *should* with *have (got) to*. Some of them might be called **catenatives**, or *chaining verbs*, because they look something like multiword verbs (see below) in that they are a string of words that mean something only when they are taken as a unit. Here we use *semiauxiliary* as a catchall label for the range of possibilities.

Some semiauxiliaries are even a little like the perfective and progressive aspects in that they team up with other verb group elements to fix a timeframe for an event. *Be about to, be fixin' to, be going to, be supposed to, be to,* and *turn out to* seem to be especially clear possibilities in this regard.

(56) I told the curate I *was going to* seek food, and felt my way towards the pantry.

(57) There was no question that he personally *was to* capture and fight the great machine.

Even though they often overlap with modals both in sense and in function, semiauxiliaries differ from modals in two ways: first, they can be tensed, whereas modals compete with tense for the spot at the left-hand edge of the verb group; second, you can have more than just one in a verb group. Whereas in most varieties of English only one (and sometimes a second) modal is normally used in a verb group, you can use as many semiauxiliaries as you can stand:

(58) He was about to be able to be willing to dare to . . .

And because you can have more than one semiauxiliary per verb group, they all have the effect of sanctioning a second pass through the entire set of core auxiliaries as well.

List 5.2 *Some Verbs with Unusual Past-tense and -ed/-en Forms*

Basic form	Past tense	-ed/-en form
arise	arose	arisen
awake	awoke	awoke *or* awaked
be	was, were	been
bear	bore	borne
beat	beat	beaten
become	became	become
begin	began	begun
bend	bent	bent
bid	bad(e) *or* bid	bade, bid, *or* bidden
bite	bit	bitten
bleed	bled	bled
blow	blew	blown
break	broke	broken
build	built	built
burst	burst	burst
choose	chose	chosen
come	came	come
cost	cost	cost
creep	crept	crept
cut	cut	cut
deal	dealt	dealt
dig	dug	dug
dive	dived *or* dove	dived
do	did	done
draw	drew	drawn
drink	drank	drunk

Basic form	Past tense	-ed/-en form
drive	drove	driven
eat	ate	eaten
fall	fell	fallen
feed	fed	fed
feel	felt	felt
fight	fought	fought
find	found	found
fit	fit	fitted *or* fit
fly	flew	flown
forget	forgot	forgotten *or* forgot
forgive	forgave	forgiven
freeze	froze	frozen
get	got	gotten
give	gave	given
go	went	gone
grow	grew	grown
hang	hung *or* hanged	hung *or* hanged
have	had	had
hear	heard	heard
hide	hid	hidden
hit	hit	hit
hurt	hurt	hurt
keep	kept	kept
kneel	knelt *or* kneeled	knelt *or* kneeled
know	knew	known
lay	laid	laid

List 5.2 *continued*

Basic form	Past tense	-ed/-en form
lead	led	led
lend	lent	lent
let	let	let
lie	lay	lain
lose	lost	lost
mistake	mistook	mistaken
mow	mowed	mown *or* mowed
pay	paid	paid
prove	proved	proven *or* proved
put	put	put
quit	quit *or* quitted	quit *or* quitted
read	read	read
ride	rode	ridden
ring	rang	rung
rise	rose	risen
say	said	said
see	saw	seen
sell	sold	sold
send	sent	sent
set	set	set
sew	sewed	sewed *or* sown
shake	shook	shaken
shave	shaved	shaved *or* shaven
shine	shone *or* shined	shone *or* shined

Basic form	Past tense	-ed/-en form
show	showed	showed *or* shown
shrink	shrank	shrunk
shut	shut	shut
slay	slew	slain
sleep	slept	slept
slide	slid	slid
speak	spoke	spoken
speed	sped	sped
spend	spent	spent
spin	spun	spun
split	split	split
spread	spread	spread
steal	stole	stolen
string	strung	strung
swear	swore	sworn
sweep	swept	swept
swell	swelled	swelled *or* swollen
swim	swam	swum
teach	taught	taught
tear	tore	torn
thrust	thrust	thrust
wake	woke	woken
wear	wore	worn
wed	wedded *or* wed	wedded *or* wed
weep	wept	wept

You probably won't find the term *semiauxiliary* (or, for that matter, the concept that it represents) in most popular school grammars, but we adopt it here because it does a good job of accounting for a very common English-language constituent, and in the bargain, it could also get you thinking about one of the ways that language develops over time. Here's what I mean.

Semiauxiliaries might be seen as a spot in English clauses where formerly full-blown nonfinite clauses (introduced with *to*) are being taken into the verb group as auxiliaries as time goes by. If such is the case, it could explain the obligatory presence of the verb particle *to* in all but one of the semiauxiliaries: *dare (to)*. Note that two present-tense forms, *dares to* and just plain *dares*, are both possible semiauxiliaries, but none of the other semiauxiliaries can work without *to*.

If semiauxiliaries are constructions that include *to*-marked nonfinite clauses on their way, over time, to being modals, this might also account for the fact that following a semiauxiliary, you can take additional trips through the core auxiliaries. Core auxiliaries are normally distributed just one per clause, but if semiauxiliaries are transitional forms incorporating a clause remnant, then the permissible additional passes through the core auxiliaries don't seem so peculiar. We will return to nonfinite clauses in detail in the final two chapters of the book.

Here are some additional examples of semiauxiliaries from *The War of the Worlds*.

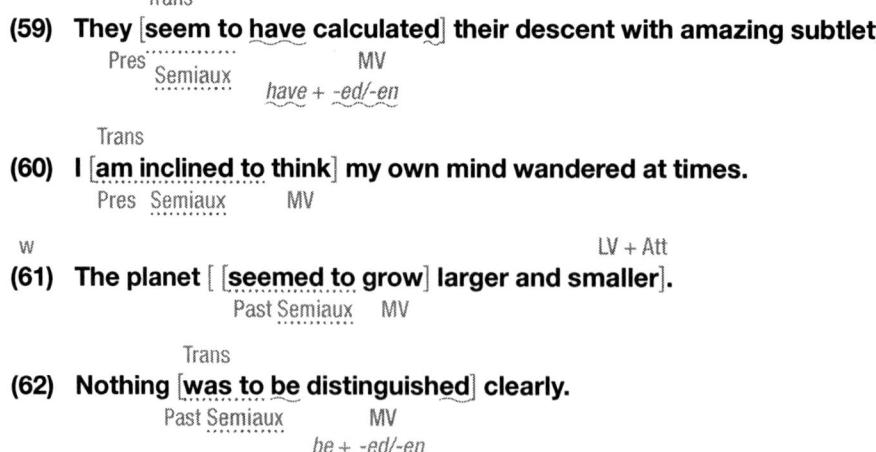

(59) They [seem to have calculated] their descent with amazing subtlety.

(60) I [am inclined to think] my own mind wandered at times.

(61) The planet [[seemed to grow] larger and smaller].

(62) Nothing [was to be distinguished] clearly.

Intensifiers Almost every word group comes equipped with a volume knob (or a brightness knob or a contrast knob—choose your own analogy), and verb groups are no exception. We have adopted the term *intensifier* to apply to all of the words that we use to tweak the knob, even though some of these words actually diminish the impact of the affected word group. For example, *barely* or *scarcely* are intensifiers that turn the volume down rather than up. In (63) the word *scarcely* is a good example of this toning-down effect that intensifiers can have.

                       Intrans
(63) **'They [can scarcely move],' I said.**
            Modal   AdvG   MV
                  (Intens)

Multiword verbs Main verbs often depend upon an additional word or two to complete their meaning, for example, *blow up, bring up, catch on, come across, get by, get up, look into, look up, put off, put out,* and lots of others. These verbal units are multiword verbs or **phrasal verbs**. The additional words that these verbs require are called **postposed particles**, *verb particles*, or simply **particles**.

The best way to decide whether a particle belongs in the process with the verb group or if it might be a preposition group that belongs with a participant or a circumstance that follows is to consider all of the possibilities. For example, think about the meanings of examples (64) and (65):

    (64) . . . it had not <u>occurred to him</u> that it might be hollow.

    (65) He <u>pointed out to me</u> how unlikely it was.

In (64), the word *to* might be a part of a unit *to him* or a part of a unit *occurred to.* To decide, ask yourself whether *occurred* and *occurred to* mean different things, the way that, say, *get* and *get by* mean different things, or that *look* and *look into* do. When something occurs, doesn't it have to occur *to* someone or something? In other words, isn't the idea of *occurred to* subsumed by *occurred*? I would say that it is. Therefore, in my estimation, *to* belongs with the next unit, *to him,* an oblique object, the occur*ee,* if you will. Some verbs might even require an oblique object: for example, *cope* (*with*) or *care* (*for*). Because the preposition groups, such as *with* and *for*, are required to introduce the second participant, the verbs that require them are sometimes called **prepositional verbs** and the participant is called the *object of a prepositional verb.*

However, let's apply the same test to *point* and *point out* in (65). Here we get a far different sense of what the process is. We don't feel quite the emphasis with *point* that we do with *point out. Point* might mean something like *direct* or *aim* whereas *point out* might mean *urge specific attention.* Here *out* belongs to the unit *point out,* a main verb-plus-particle combination, a multiword verb.

ACTIVITY 5.3

Try your hand at applying this 'prepositional verb' test to examples (66) to (70) to determine whether the underscored units are prepositional verbs (verb-plus-particle units) or simply verbs with oblique objects following. Then check out the suggested responses at the back of the book.

(66) . . . no one on earth <u>dreamed of</u> that unerring missile.

(67) I loved in those days to <u>look up</u> at the night sky.

(68) He approached the mass, <u>surprised at</u> the size.

(69) . . . the ashy encrustation that covered the meteorite, was <u>falling off</u> the circular edge of the end.

(70) . . . then turned, <u>scrambled out of</u> the pit, and <u>set off</u> running wildly into Woking.

Very often multiword verbs are discontinuous, with the particle at the right-hand edge displaced further down the clause to the right. Sometimes this sort of discontinuity is optional, and sometimes, often when the direct object consists of a pronoun group, it is obligatory. For example:

(71) He was immensely excited at the news, and in the excess of his feelings <u>invited</u> me <u>up</u> to take a turn with him that night in a scrutiny of the red planet.

(72) At that I gripped my wife's arm, and without ceremony <u>ran</u> her <u>out</u> into the road.

In (71) the direct object is the pronoun *me,* and the multiword verb, *invite up,* wraps around it. *He invited up me* doesn't work, whereas *He invited up the cleric* might. Similarly, in (72) the direct object is the pronoun *her,* with the multiword verb *ran out* wrapped around it. *He ran out her into the street* is just as peculiar as *He invited up me.*

On the other hand, if you contrast (73) and (74), you might at first imagine (74) to be the same as (73), but with the particle *over* displaced to the right, forming a discontinuous constituent, something like (71) or (72).

(73) There was debris in the road, and the car <u>ran over</u> it.

(74) There was debris in the road, and the car <u>ran it over.</u>

Why then does (74) sound sort of peculiar?

A closer examination reveals that the processes in the two clauses might be different; they can mean different things. Think of it this way: in (73), the process is not a multiword unit but is simply *run*, and *over it* is an oblique object; in (74), however, the process is *run over*. You might be able to tell the two apart because the process *run over* often implies some intentionality, even some malice, and that doesn't fit the context in (73), in which the driver of the car, one assumes, bore no malice toward the debris. That's why it sounds a little odd. *Run* and *run over* are different things for sure, so *run over* ought to be considered a unit. However, as (73) shows, not every time the two words are next to one another do they form a unit.

Although there is more to the story than we have time to tell here, if you rely on the direct-comparison test to identify multiword verbs, you will most often be very close to the mark. In (71), *invite* is different from *invite up*, in (72) *run* and *run out* have quite distinct meanings, and in (73) and (74) *run* is quite different from *run over*.

Other multiword units All attributive processes (LV + Att and *be* + Att), all locative processes (*be* + Loc) and various idiomatic verbal expressions are also made up of two or more words. Note that attributes and locations are essential parts of their respective process units, but they are not usually considered elements in the verb group.

(75) In a telescope it [[**seems**] far profounder].
                   LV + Att
                   Pres MV   AdjG

(76) Then everything [[**was**] still].
                 be + Att
                 Past MV AdjG

(77) In three strides he [[**was**] at the door leading into the kitchen].
                          be + Loc
                   Past MV   PP

A note on particles, prepositions, and adverbs. You will probably have noticed that the same words appear capable of performing the jobs of (1) postposed particle in a multiword verb, (2) main preposition in a preposition group, and (3) main adverb in an adverb group. However, in the event that this feature of English hadn't already occurred to you, check out the sets in (78)–(80), (81)–(83), and (84)–(86).

(78) *Particle.* One can imagine them, covered with sand, excited and disordered, running up the little street in the bright sunlight just as the shop folks [were taking down] their shutters and people were opening their bedroom windows.

(79) *Preposition.* One of our chimneys cracked as if a shot had hit it, flew, and a piece of it came clattering [down the tiles] and made a heap of broken red fragments upon the flower bed by my study window.

(80) *Adverb.* For a minute he scarcely realized what this meant, and, although the heat was excessive, he clambered [down] into the pit close to the bulk to see the Thing more clearly.

(81) *Particle.* The uncovered part had the appearance of a huge cylinder, [caked over] and its outline softened by a thick scaly dun-coloured encrustation.

(82) *Preposition.* It had toppled [over the brim of the cylinder] and fallen into the pit, with a thud like the fall of a great mass of leather.

(83) *Adverb.* 'What ugly brutes!' he said. 'Good God! What ugly brutes!' He repeated this [over and over again].

(84) *Particle.* I (let ⌐myself⌐ in) with my latchkey, closed, locked, and bolted the door, staggered to the foot of the staircase, and sat down.

(85) *Preposition.* There were lights [in all the houses on the common side of the three villages], and the people there kept awake till dawn.

(86) *Adverb.* I saw my neighbour gardening, chatted with him for a time, and then strolled [in] to breakfast.

> As we noted earlier with *-ing*, it makes pretty good sense to recognize that some functional units have a very similar, perhaps even identical, appearance, even though they are doing different work in representing events. In this regard you might want to look ahead at what we will have to say about *that* in Chapter 9 (pp. 167–8).

On the other hand, idiomatic verbal expressions are generally thought of as unitary; for example, *be swept out of existence* in (87) is an idiomatic expression that means *eradicated*.

Trans

(87) The Tasmanians [were entirely swept out of existence].

        Past   Intens   MV   PP

        be + -ed/-en

        Idiomatic Expression

Practice with Terminology

What follows is a preview of the sentences that you will encounter in this chapter's Sentences for Analysis. Certain elements in each sentence have been underscored. Label each underscored element, using one or more of the terms shown below. Check the Glossary if you are not certain about the definition of any of the terms.

Aspect (specify perfective or progressive)	**Modality**	**Phrasal verb**
	Multiword verb	**Prepositional verb**
Core auxiliary	**Particle** (verb particle, postposed particle)	**Primary auxiliary**
Discontinuous constituent		**Progressive participle**
Intensifier	**Passive participle**	**Semiauxiliary**
Irregular verb	**Passive voice**	**Tense** (specify past or present)
Main verb	**Perfect participle**	

1 The grey clinker was <u>falling</u> off the circular edge of the end.

2 A large piece suddenly came <u>off</u> with a sharp noise.

3 The circular top of the cylinder <u>was</u> <u>rotating</u> on its body.

4 A black mark had <u>been</u> near him five minutes ago.

5 He <u>scarcely</u> understood the problem.

6 He <u>heard</u> a muffled grating sound.

7 Then the thing <u>came upon</u> him in a flash.

8 Something within the cylinder <u>was</u> <u>unscrewing</u> the top!

9 At once, with a quick mental leap, he <u>linked</u> the Thing with the flash upon Mars.

10 He <u>could</u> have burned his hands on the still-glowing metal.

11 Henderson stood <u>up</u>.

12 They <u>rapped</u> on the scaly burnt metal with a stick.

13 The shop folks were <u>taking</u> <u>down</u> their shutters.

14 A number of boys and unemployed men <u>had</u> already <u>started</u> for the common.

15 They <u>had</u> heard about the 'dead men from Mars'.

16 I have already <u>described</u> the appearance of that colossal bulk.

17 No doubt its impact had <u>caused</u> a flash of fire.

18 Nothing was to <u>be</u> <u>done</u> for the present.

19 There <u>had</u> been four or five boys at the edge of the Pit.

20 In the afternoon the appearance of the common <u>had</u> not <u>altered</u> very much.

21 A large number of gaily dressed ladies <u>must</u> have walked, in spite of the heat of the day, from Woking and Chertsey.

22 The burning heather had been <u>extinguished</u>.

23 An enterprising sweet-stuff dealer had sent his son <u>up</u> with a barrow-load of green apples and ginger beer.

24 Stent was <u>giving</u> directions in a clear, high-pitched voice.

25 The cylinder <u>was</u> now evidently much cooler.

26 Something <u>seemed to</u> have irritated him.

27 A large portion of the cylinder had been <u>uncovered</u>.

28 The crowd was <u>becoming</u> a serious impediment to their excavations.

29 A faint stirring <u>was</u> occasionally still audible within the case.

30 The case <u>appeared to</u> be enormously thick.

31 Everyone <u>seemed</u> greatly excited.

32 The crowd had <u>pushed</u> a young shop assistant from Woking into the hole again.

33 For a moment that circular cavity <u>seemed</u> perfectly black.

34 Everyone <u>expected</u> something a little unlike us terrestrial men.

35 The people on the other side of the pit were running <u>off</u>.

36 A big greyish rounded bulk, the size, perhaps, of a bear, was <u>rising</u> slowly and painfully out of the cylinder.

37 Two large dark-coloured eyes <u>were</u> regarding me steadfastly.

38 One <u>could</u> scarcely imagine the strange horror of its appearance.

39 Even at this first glimpse, I <u>was</u> overcome with disgust and dread.

40 There <u>was</u> something unspeakably nasty in the clumsy deliberation of the tedious movements.

41 Forthwith another of these creatures <u>appeared</u> darkly in the deep shadow of the aperture.

42 I could not <u>avert</u> my face from these things.

43 I had <u>had</u> a glimpse of the Martians.

44 Afterwards a thin rod <u>rose</u> up, joint by joint.

45 At its apex a circular disk <u>spun</u> with a wobbling motion.

46 Most of the spectators had <u>gathered</u> in one or two groups.

47 We <u>continued</u> watching for a time side by side.

48 I <u>heard</u> now a faint murmur from the crowd far away on the left, towards Woking.

49 There <u>was</u> scarcely an intimation of movement from the pit.

50 Some cabmen and others had <u>walked</u> boldly into the sand pits.

Analyzing and Reporting Verb Groups

Step 1: *Identifying processes* Bracket and label process type above the bracket.

Trans
(88) In Woking the shop folks [were taking down] their shutters

Step 2: *Identifying participants* By referring to your own personal experience, determine the number of participant roles that the process requires. In the clause find the role-players; bracket them and label participant functions above the bracket. Be aware that sometimes required participant roles are expressed by understood (missing) elements.

          Subj   Trans   **DirObj**

(89) **In Woking [the shop folks] [were taking down] [their shutters]**

In (89), the analysis proposes two participants: *the shop folks*, playing the role of tak*er*, and *their shutters* playing the role of tak*ee*.

Step 3: *Identifying circumstances* All of the remaining clause-level bracketable elements are circumstances. Bracket and label them by type.

   Place   Subj   Trans   DirObj

(90) **[In Woking] [the shop folks] [were taking down] [their shutters]**

In (90) one circumstance unit, a circumstance of place, is identified.

Step 4: *Labeling the main word for each bracketed word group* If clause-level bracketed units are phrases, sub-bracket all component word groups except one (we will assume that the remaining elements form a group). Label the main word for each sub-bracketed group.

   Place   Subj   Trans   DirObj

(91) [[In] Woking] [the shop folks] [were taking down] [their shutters]

     PG   NG   MN   MV   MN

Step 5: *Labeling adjective groups, adverb groups, and prepositional phrases*

   Place   Subj   Trans   DirObj

(92) [[In] Woking] [the shop folks] [were taking down] [their shutters]

     PG   NG   MN   MV   MN

Example (92) shows that the clause has no remaining adjective groups, adverb groups or prepositional phrases.

Step 6: *Labeling verb-group elements and taking stock* Remember that the left-hand edge of a verb group must have one of these three elements: tense, modal, or nonfinite clause marker. Be aware that *be*, *have*, and *do*, and all their various forms, can be main verbs as well as auxiliary verbs. Remember that the verb group can be discontinuous. Refer to Chart 5.1. Here's our final report.

   Place   Subj   Trans   DirObj

(93) [[In] Woking] [the shop folks] [were taking down] [their shutters]

     PG   NG   MN   Past MV   Particle   MN

                               be + -ing

Sentences for Analysis

The following sentences are adapted from *The War of the Worlds*. Analyze them and report your results as shown in the example below. Make certain that your analyses have the following features:

a Bracket processes, participants, and circumstances and label them by function at the top of the bracket.

b Sub-bracket as necessary, observing minimal bracketing conventions to isolate a preposition group (PG) from its complement or to isolate the verb group in *be*-plus- and linking-verb-plus- process types.

c Label the main word in each bracketed word group directly below its position in the group. Single-element groups are normally given the group label.

d Label adjective groups and adverb groups, sub-bracketing where necessary. Additionally, identify and label embedded prepositional phrases.

	Subj	Trans	DirObj	IndObj		Place	
(94)	[The Thing]	[had made]	[a pit]	[[for]	itself]	[[at] the edge	of the woods]
	MN	Past MV	MN	PG	ProG	PG	MN	PP
		have + *-ed/-en*					

* 1 The grey clinker was falling off the circular edge of the end.

2 A large piece suddenly came off with a sharp noise.

3 The circular top of the cylinder was rotating on its body.

* 4 A black mark had been near him five minutes ago.

5 He scarcely understood the problem.

6 He heard a muffled grating sound.

7 Then the thing came upon him in a flash.

8 Something within the cylinder was unscrewing the top!

9 At once, with a quick mental leap, he linked the Thing with the flash upon Mars.

10 He could have burned his hands on the still-glowing metal.

11 Henderson stood up.

* 12 They rapped on the scaly burnt metal with a stick.

13 The shop folks were taking down their shutters.

14 A number of boys and unemployed men had already started for the common.

15 They had heard about the 'dead men from Mars'.

16 I have already described the appearance of that colossal bulk.

17 No doubt its impact had caused a flash of fire.

18 Nothing was to be done for the present.

* 19 There had been four or five boys at the edge of the Pit.

20 In the afternoon the appearance of the common had not altered very much.

21 A large number of gaily dressed ladies must have walked, in spite of the heat of the day, from Woking and Chertsey.

22 The burning heather had been extinguished.

23 An enterprising sweet-stuff dealer had sent his son up with a barrow-load of green apples and ginger beer.

24 Stent was giving directions in a clear, high-pitched voice.

25 The cylinder was now evidently much cooler.

∗ 26 Something seemed to have irritated him.

27 A large portion of the cylinder had been uncovered.

28 The crowd was becoming a serious impediment to their excavations.

29 A faint stirring was occasionally still audible within the case.

30 The case appeared to be enormously thick.

31 Everyone seemed greatly excited.

32 The crowd had pushed a young shop assistant from Woking into the hole again.

∗ 33 For a moment that circular cavity seemed perfectly black.

34 Everyone expected something a little unlike us terrestrial men.

35 The people on the other side of the pit were running off.

36 A big greyish rounded bulk, the size, perhaps, of a bear, was rising slowly and painfully out of the cylinder.

37 Two large dark-coloured eyes were regarding me steadfastly.

38 One could scarcely imagine the strange horror of its appearance.

∗ 39 Even at this first glimpse, I was overcome with disgust and dread.

40 There was something unspeakably nasty in the clumsy deliberation of the tedious movements.

41 Forthwith another of these creatures appeared darkly in the deep shadow of the aperture.

∗ 42 I could not avert my face from these things.

43 I had had a glimpse of the Martians.

44 Afterwards a thin rod rose up, joint by joint.

45 At its apex a circular disk spun with a wobbling motion.

46 Most of the spectators had gathered in one or two groups.

∗ 47 We continued watching for a time side by side.

48 I heard now a faint murmur from the crowd far away on the left, towards Woking.

49 There was scarcely an intimation of movement from the pit.

∗ 50 Some cabmen and others had walked boldly into the sand pits.

Note: Suggested responses for the sentences marked by an asterisk (∗) are given at the back of the book. As a way of getting started on this activity, you might want to work first on those items. Where your responses and the suggested ones differ, you will want to get advice from your instructor. Very often, several interpretations might be appropriate.

Chapter 6

The Power of Beginnings

Preliminaries

Now that you are armed with some detail about the internal workings of verb groups, we can move on to considering how the leading edges of language units, verb groups included, have special significance.

The leading edge of any language unit usually has particular importance, if for no other reason than its ability to give a tip about the type of unit it belongs to. A determiner (see Chapter 7), for example, serves as a very clear delineator between what comes before, if anything, and the noun group that follows. A determiner generally appears only at the left-hand edge of a noun group, so it can faithfully forecast an upcoming main noun, which itself will make a significant contribution to the sense to be contained in the next larger unit. As we've shown in Chapter 5, the leading edge of a verb group must exhibit either tense, or a modal, or a nonfinite clause marker. These are the very reliable signals that an English language user automatically relies upon to keep the sense-making process rolling along smoothly.

With regard to the importance of its left-hand edge, a clause is no different from any other language unit. What happens at that beginning, or leading, edge of the clause makes a very significant contribution to the sense that the clause represents. The default expectation for English speakers is to hear (or read) the first-named participant (the *subject*) of a clause first, then the process, and then other participants and perhaps circumstances. In other words, the default setting for the order in which English-language clauses are expected to appear is **SVO**: subject, then verb, and then object. When given no other evidence, the English speaker's language processor hums along, doing its work using this default setting. It's not hard to imagine, then, that any changes in this expected order will affect our making sense of a clause. When our subject-then-verb-then-object expectation is violated, special attention is focused on the nature of the upcoming clause.

The Power of Beginnings

Let's consider some important cases of just how radically things change when the leading edge of the clause is manipulated: **yes/no questions**, requests and demands, and finally **content questions**.

Yes/no questions (interrogative clauses) and the discontinuous verb group A yes/no question is one that would require no more than a nod or a shake of the head in response.

> **(1) Are we such apostles of mercy as to complain if the Martians warred in the same spirit?**
>
> **(2) Did you see a man in the pit?**

To signal a yes/no question, English speakers wrap the verb group from the main clause process around the subject of the clause, thereby dislocating the left-hand edge of the verb group to the far left-hand edge of the clause. Doing so turns the verb group into a discontinuous constituent, and perhaps more significantly, it radically alters the beginning of the clause. Now, instead of first running into the subject of the clause (the default setting), you first encounter the left-hand edge of the verb group. Compare:

Default setting (default expectation)	**a** Subject **b** Verb **c** Object
Yes/no question (left-hand edge radically revised)	**a** Verb group starts **b** Subject **c** Verb group continues **d** Object

For example, the verb group in (3) is *could see*.

> **(3) You could see a man in the pit.**

If this were to be a question, the first element in the verb group, *could*, would be displaced to the left-hand edge of the clause, making the verb group *could see* become discontinuous, as shown in (4).

> **(4)** Discontinuous verb group
>
> 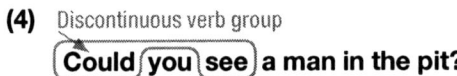 **a man in the pit?**

Here are some additional examples, adapted from *The War of the Worlds*.

(5) Discontinuous verb group

[**Was** *it* **seen**] **early in the morning?**

(6) Discontinuous verb group

[**Has** *the earth* **been**] **given over to them?**

(7) Discontinuous verb group

[**Had** *the Martian* **seen**] **me?**

The operator To make yes/no questions, English speakers don't select just any random element from the verb group. We select the element that is at the very leftmost edge. As we showed in Chapter 5, that element must be tense, or modal, or nonfinite clause marker.

However, yes/no questions are main (uppermost) clauses, so the nonfinite-clause-marker option is not available. Nonfinite clause markers occur only with embedded or subordinate clauses (much more on this in Chapters 9 and 10). With the nonfinite clause marker out of the picture, only tense and modal remain. If a modal is available, it appears to the left of the subject, and the yes/no question is formed, as in (4).

However, if no modal is available, then the element at the left-hand edge will be tense. But remember: tense has to be attached to a verb; it doesn't float around loose. This means that the *whole* verb-group element that bears tense is dislocated to the left of the subject, and then the yes/no question is formed, as in (5), (6), and (7).

The element that dislocates around the subject is called the **operator**. This is a simple signaling system, but it does run into one minor problem. Modern English speakers don't usually say things like (8).

(8) Took you pleasure from last night's supper?

A question like this was perfectly acceptable at one stage in the development of English, but not any longer; so present-day English adds one more provision to the system for signaling yes/no questions. In order to qualify as the cue for a yes/no question, the tense-bearing element from the left-hand edge of the verb group must be *something other than a main verb*, unless that verb happens to be *be*. This fact is in a way further evidence that the main verb *be* works mostly like a helper, even when it is the main verb. Chart 6.1 sums up the facts about the operator for your reference.

Chart 6.1 *The Operator*

Left-hand edge	Precentral space	Central Word	Right-hand edge
Tense (either present or past) or **Modal** or **Nonfinite clause marker**	**Semiauxiliaries** (with *be* or *have*) and **primary auxiliary verbs** or **the periphrastic auxiliary verb (dummy *do*)** If no other auxiliary is present and one is needed for Q or NEG	*Be* as main verb	Postposed particles Idiomatic elements

The **bold-print elements** function as the **operator** in questions (yes/no and *wh-*) and in clause-level (process) negation.

Questions: The operator appears at the left-hand edge of the verb group where we would expect tense, modal, or clause marker. Additionally, in all questions, the verb group is discontinuous (around the subject).

Negation: The negative word *not* (or the contraction *n't*) goes after the operator; the negative word *never* can go either before or after.

The periphrastic auxiliary, dummy *do* So what happens when the tensed element is a main verb other than *be*? Well, we use a stand-in operator, the word *do*. That's why (9) sounds much better to us than (8).

(9) *Did* you take pleasure from last night's supper?

This stand-in auxiliary is usually called ***dummy do***, but its formal name is ***periphrastic auxiliary***, which literally means *paraphrase for an auxiliary*. Some additional examples follow.

(10) *Did* English readers hear of it first in the issue of *Nature* dated August 2?

(11) *Did* the planet seem to grow larger and smaller?

(12) *Did* hundreds of observers see the flame that night?

Direct requests and demands (imperative clauses) and the zero modal (Ø).
To make direct requests and issue demands, we also radically alter the left-hand edge of the clause. For starters, we treat the subject as a missing element. A very unusual structure, indeed, and it provides a major cue to a listener's processing mechanism. That subject, for direct requests and demands, will always be *you* or *you all* (in the

United States, especially the southern states) or *you guys* (also in the United States, usually further north). The traditional way of referring to the missing-element subject of a direct request clause is to call it *You understood*.

That would pretty much be all of the story except that we haven't really accounted for what actually *is* at the left-hand edge of the direct request or demand clause, given that the subject isn't overtly expressed there. If we assume that the next unit in line is the verb group in a main-clause process, then the left-hand edge of the process becomes the left-hand edge of the whole clause. That means tense or modal or nonfinite clause marker must start the ball rolling because those are the only three elements that can be encountered at the left-hand edge of the verb group. But because direct requests and demands are main clauses, the nonfinite clause-marker option is not possible. That leaves only tense or modal. Which one is it?

If we try out any of the modals we know about to this point, they don't work very well either. For example, *Can be here tonight at midnight* isn't a direct request in English. We like *Be here tonight at midnight* much better. Even the modal *will*, which certainly has its own sense of obligation (for example, in the military-like *You WILL get your area squared away by 0600 hours!*) doesn't really work out very well. It requires a subject—no *You understood* allowed here—and you need to put some emphasis on *will*: *WILL get your area squared away by 0600 hours!* just doesn't express a demand any more than *CAN be here tonight at midnight*. That's why we should rule out the familiar modals, including *will*. (But don't lose that thought; we'll come back to it directly.)

We are apparently left with only tense, and if tense isn't the solution, then we might need to do a thorough re-evaluation of what can be at the left-hand edge of a verb group. So, let's tentatively settle on tense at the leading edge of a direct request. After all, the present-tense inflection for the *you* form, just like all the other forms except for the *he-she-it* third-person form, is zero, and zero is what we are looking for.

Unfortunately, this solution presents another problem. If we closely examine *Be here tonight at midnight*, or any other request using *be* as the main verb, we will be unhappy with tense as a solution. The direct request, *Be here tonight at midnight*, has no tense! It might appear to have zero as a tense marker because the normal second-person (*you*) form does use zero to mark present tense. However, remember that *be* has very unusual forms (see List 5.1): the tensed forms of *be* that go with *you* are either *are* (present) or *were* (past). So it must have no tense at all. If it did, we would have to say <u>*Are*</u> *here tonight at midnight* (present tense) or <u>*Were*</u> *here tonight at midnight* (past tense) instead of <u>*Be*</u> *here tonight at midnight*.

Time to do some backtracking through our reasoning. Demands and other direct requests are main clauses, not nonfinite clauses, so there is no need for a nonfinite clause marker at the left-hand edge of the verb group. And it cannot be tense—the example with *Be here tonight at midnight* shows that. And no modals we know about work either. What should we conclude?

We must either adjust our idea about nonfinite clause markers, expand our idea about tense, or fine-tune our inventory of modals. For reasons best left until Chapters 9 and 10, we probably do not want to permit main-clause nonfinite verb groups, especially given that direct requests and demands must have a timeframe (the present) and nonfinite verb groups cannot provide that. For a related reason, adding a third tense to accommodate direct requests and demands is not especially desirable; after all, we already have one fairly unitary present tense, and adding another tense would encroach on this one.

Therefore, I suggest expanding the list of modals to accommodate direct requests and demands. Requests and demands fit in with the kind of meanings that modals express, especially obligation, permission, probability, and possibility. For this reason we include ***zero modal (Ø)*** in the inventory of modals.

```
          Subj   Trans  DirObj Manner              Subj   Trans DirObj Manner
(13)   [(YOU)] [Ø Do] [it] [ [in] a rush], and [(YOU)] [Ø do] [it] [ [at] once].
          Zero MV ProG  PG     MN    Conj    Zero MV ProG  PG    AdvG
          Modal                             Modal
```

'Do it in a rush, and do it at once.'

Clause negation Although it might be a great way to do it, English doesn't alter the left-hand edge of the clause if the whole clause is to be negative: *NOT I enjoyed last night's meal* is not English.

It probably is a good idea not to do it that way anyway. We like to use negation for smaller units within the clause; by putting a negative at the beginning of the whole clause, we would run the risk of having just the first element negated rather than the whole clause.

Instead, to negate a clause, English speakers simply associate a negative word with the left-hand edge of the verb group, determining what qualifies as left-hand edge along the same lines that we use for yes/no questions and direct requests. And as with yes/no questions, when no other appropriate operator appears in the clause, we use dummy *do*. *Not I enjoyed last night's meal* turns out to be *I did not (or didn't) enjoy last night's meal*. Here are some examples from *The War of the Worlds*, in which the element at the left-hand edge of the verb group (or dummy *do*), as well as the negative word, is underscored.

(14) I <u>might not</u> have heard of the eruption at all had I not met Ogilvy.

(15) . . . it <u>had not</u> occurred to him that it might be hollow.

(16) He <u>did not</u> remember hearing any birds that morning.

(17) I <u>don't</u> like it.

(18) Those who <u>have never</u> seen a living Martian can scarcely imagine the strange horror of its appearance.

Main-clause *wh-* relationships: content questions We finish up this chapter with a topic that on first glance appears to be every bit as routine as the others we have touched upon. However, understanding the *wh-* **relationships** that occur in content questions provides a foundation for understanding one of the important ways that English speakers fit clauses together into larger units.

An adequate response to a content question, unlike one to a yes/no question, cannot be a nod or a shake of the head, unless by such a gesture you are not responding *to* the question but rather *about* the question.

Content questions generally require a more elaborate response. In addition, the exact nature of the expected response is controlled by the *wh-* word that appears at the left-hand edge of content questions. If you hear the word *why*, your sense-making mechanism goes into *reason* mode because *why* focuses attention on *reason*. With *where* you will begin thinking about *places*; *who* leads you to *people* (or personified entities, for example, we often refer to pets with *who*); *when* is a cue for *time*; *what* is a cue for *things*. It is handy to think of the *wh-* words in this way as information-focusing mechanisms. Here are some examples:

(19) '<u>What</u> does it mean?' he said. '<u>What</u> do these things mean?'

(20) '<u>Why</u> not shell the darned things strite off and finish 'em?' said the little dark man.

(21) '<u>Where's</u> your shells?' said the first speaker.

(22) '<u>How</u> are we to get to Leatherhead?' she said.

When *wh-* words work in this way, and they do so almost all the time, we will call them **markers**, because they are marking two things: (a) a significant focus of attention on the content specified by the *wh-* word, and (b) a shift in interpersonal relationship from *knower* to *questioner*.

To make a content question, we put a *wh-* **marker** in front of a regular yes/no question. That is, we first wrap the left-hand edge of the verb group around the subject, using the yes/no question signaling system. Then, in front of the clause, we add a *wh-* word: *what, when, where, which, who, whom, whose, why,* or *how.* (I know. *How* doesn't start with *wh-.*)

If you will look back at the examples, however, you will notice something very striking about them. Each has something missing from its event structure. For example, without its *wh-* marker, the questions in (19), partially repeated as (23), are ' __ does it mean?' and ' __ do these things mean?' They are each missing something: their direct objects. These missing elements are the **information gaps** that are the focus for the content questions. The elements are missing to allow the speaker to focus the listener's attention on the requested information.

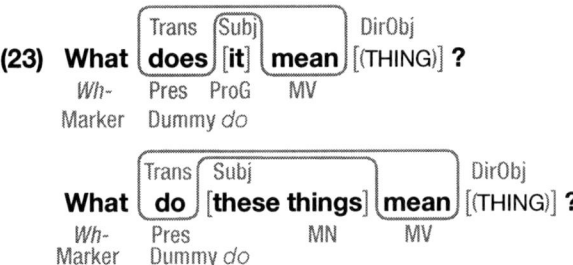

(23) What **does** [it] **mean** [(THING)] **?**

The *wh-* word *what* at the front of the clause is said to share a *wh-* relationship with this missing element, in this case the direct object (THING) in a transitive process. In principle, any part of the event structure (participants, attributes, locations, and circumstances) can be the information gap in a *wh-* relationship.

Something unusual occurs in *wh-* content questions in which the information gap is the subject of the clause and in which there is no verb-group element to act as **operator** and displace to the left of the (missing-element) subject. In such a case, we would expect to see the periphrastic auxiliary, dummy *do*, come into the picture. Example (24) is a normal *wh-* **question** in which the information gap is the subject of the clause—but notice that it sounds right without dummy *do*.

List 6.1 Wh- *Markers for Content Questions*

In a **content question**, if the *wh-* marker is:	The **information gap** will be a **missing element** related to:
Where (-ever)	→ a **Place**
Why (-ever)	→ a **Reason**
Who (-ever) or *Whom* (-ever)	→ a **Person**
When (-ever)	→ a **Time**
What (-ever)	→ a **Thing**
How (-ever)	→ a **Manner**, a **Means**, or a **Condition**; also a **Quantifying determiner** (see Chapter 7) or **Intensifier**
Whose (-ever)	→ a **Possessive determiner** (see Chapter 7)
Which	→ a **Determiner** (see Chapter 7)

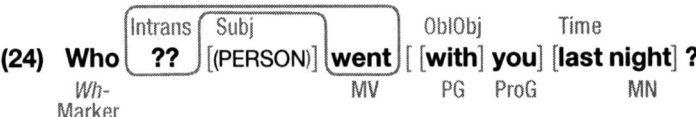

(24)   Who ?? [(PERSON)] went [[with] you] [last night] ?

If we were to use *do* as the operator in a case like this, it would clash with the use of *do* for emphasis. Example (25) is the same sentence, but with *do* at the displaced left-hand edge of the verb group. It sounds emphatic, doesn't it?

(25)   Who DID go with you last night?

Modern English saves this application for the emphatic *do* and does not require the dummy *do* operator in these *wh-* questions.

***Wh-* markers**   *Wh-* question words all start with *wh-* except *how*. A complete list of *wh-* words will be given after we have taken up the matter of embedded *wh-clauses* in Chapter 8. For content questions, the *wh-* markers and the information gaps correlate as shown in List 6.1. For embedded *wh-* relationships, the correlation will vary slightly in that the *wh-* word *which* will take on some additional work (see Chapter 8).

ACTIVITY **6.1**

Here are examples (21) and (22) again, abbreviated to include just their *wh-* questions. What are the missing elements that constitute the information gaps? Some suggested responses can be found at the back of the book.

(26) 'Where's your shells?'

(27) 'How are we to get to Leatherhead?'

Practice with Terminology

What follows is a preview of the sentences that you will encounter in this chapter's Sentences for Analysis. Certain elements in the sentences have been underscored. Label each underscored element using one or more of the following terms or an applicable term from a previous chapter. Check the Glossary if you are not certain about the definition of any of the terms.

Dummy *do* (periphrastic auxiliary)	Operator	Yes/no question
Imperative clause	*Wh-* marker	Zero modal
Negative clause	*Wh-* question	

1 The most extraordinary things <u>came to</u> my mind.

2 <u>Who was not affected by the newcomers</u>?

3 <u>Many people</u> had heard of the cylinders.

4 <u>Here, read Henderson's telegram.</u>

5 Why <u>did</u> his evening paper not print a special edition?

6 The great majority of people <u>were</u> inert.

7 <u>Were</u> people just <u>dining</u> all over the district?

8 Working men <u>were</u> <u>gardening</u> after the labours of the day.

9 Children were <u>being</u> put to bed.

10 Young people were wandering <u>through the lanes</u>.

11 <u>Was</u> there a murmur in the village streets?

12 Here and there a messenger caused <u>a whirl of excitement</u>.

13 How <u>could</u> the daily routine go on?

14 Even at Woking station and Horsell and Chobham all <u>was routine</u>.

15 A boy from the town was selling <u>papers with the afternoon's news</u>.

16 <u>Who</u> came into the station about nine o'clock?

17 When <u>did</u> half a dozen villas burn on the Woking border?

18   There were lights in all the houses on the common side of the three villages.

19   Keep awake!

20   What were you doing on Friday night?

21   A cylinder was sticking into the skin of our old planet Earth like a poisoned dart.

22   But the poison was not working yet.

23   Was the fever of war developing yet?

24   All night long the Martians were at work upon their machines.

25   Were the military authorities aware of the seriousness of the business?

26   A few seconds after midnight the second cylinder fell.

27   Saturday lives in my memory as a day of suspense.

28   I went into my garden before breakfast.

29   Had the Martians been surrounded by troops during the night?

30   Wouldn't the troops be able to destroy the Martians during the day?

31   The woods were still burning.

32   Walk down towards the common with me.

33   Where could I find a group of soldiers?

34   Would I be allowed over the canal?

35   I talked with some soldiers for a time.

36   I didn't tell them of my sight of the Martians on the previous evening.

37   Did any of them see the Martians?

38   Who had authorized the movements of the troops?

39   Would the reader like a description of that long morning?

40   I did not get a glimpse of the common.

41   Even the Chobham church tower was in the hands of the military authorities.

42   The people in the town were quite secure in the presence of the military.

43   Take a cold bath!

44   Could we go up to the railway station?

45   The Martians did not show an inch of themselves.

46   They seemed busy in their pit.

47   There was an almost continuous streamer of smoke.

48   Were they getting ready for a struggle?

49   The sight of all this armament and all this preparation greatly excited me.

50   It didn't seem a fair fight to me at that time.

> **Note:** You do not need to limit your choices to the new terms from this chapter. Where appropriate, use an applicable term from any previous chapter.

Analyzing and Reporting Yes/No Questions, Imperatives, Negatives, and Content Questions

Step 1: *Identifying processes* Bracket and label the process type above the bracket.

(28)   But where [**Intrans** are] we [to go] ?

Step 2: *Identifying participants* By referring to your own personal experience, determine the number of participant roles that the process requires. In the clause find the role-players; bracket them and label participant functions above the bracket. Be aware that sometimes required participant roles are expressed by understood (missing) elements.

(29)   But where [**Intrans** are] [**Subj** [we] to go] ?

In (29) the analysis proposes one participant: *we*, playing the role of go*er*.

Step 3: *Identifying circumstances* All of the remaining clause-level bracketable elements are circumstances. In this content question the *wh-* marker *where* must share a *wh-* relationship with a missing element in the clause. The missing element is a circumstance of place. Add the missing element; then bracket and label it by type.

(30)   But where [**Intrans** are] [**Subj** [we] to go] [**Place** [(PLACE)]] ?

Example (30) demonstrates that the clause has a missing element by putting it in parentheses and spelling it out in capital letters.

Step 4: *Labeling the main word for each bracketed word group (except missing elements)*

(31)   But where [**Intrans** are] [**Subj** [we] to go] [**Place** [(PLACE)]] ?
                                       ProG   MV

Example (31) demonstrates that *go* is the main verb of the discontinuous verb group *are to go*. *We* is a pronoun, and given that it is a single-word group, it gets the group label, ProG.

Step 5: *Labeling adjective groups, adverb groups and prepositional phrases*

(32)   But where [**Intrans** are] [**Subj** [we] to go] [**Place** [(PLACE)]] ?
                                       ProG   MV

There are no adjective groups, adverb groups, nor prepositional phrases in (32).

Step 6: *Labeling verb-group elements* Remember that the left-hand edge of a verb group must have one of these three elements (tense, modal, or nonfinite clause marker) and that one possibility for modal is the *zero modal*. Refer to Chart 5.1 (The Verb Group).

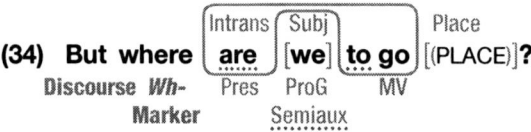

(33) **But where**   **are**   [**we**]   **to go**   [(PLACE)]?
            Intrans Subj Place
            Pres   ProG   MV
                 Semiaux

Step 7: *Looking for yes/no questions, imperatives, negatives, and content questions, and taking stock* Here is our final report:

(34) **But where**   **are**   [**we**]   **to go**   [(PLACE)]?
            Intrans Subj Place
Discourse Wh- Pres ProG MV
Marker   Semiaux

In (34) we've not bracketed *But* because it is not part of the event structure of the clause; however, we have labeled it as a *discourse* element because it serves to continue the narrative from the previous sentence. We've also labeled the *wh-* marker *where*, and we have left it unbracketed because it is not part of the event structure—it points to an information focus *(PLACE)* that is the related event-structure element.

Sentences for Analysis

The following sentences are adapted from *The War of the Worlds*. Analyze them and report your results as shown in the example. Make certain that your analyses have the following features:

a Bracket processes, participants, and circumstances and label them by function at the top of the bracket.
b Sub-bracket as necessary, observing minimal bracketing conventions.
c Label the main word in each bracketed word group directly below its position in the group. Single-element groups are normally given the group label.
d Label adjective groups and adverb groups, sub-bracketing where necessary. Additionally, identify and label embedded prepositional phrases.

       Subj   Trans   DirObj IndObj   Place
(35) [**The Thing**] [**had made**] [**a pit**] [[**for**] **itself**] [[**at**] **the edge of the woods**]
        MN   Past MV   MN   PG ProG   PG   MN   PP
               have + -ed/-en

1   The most extraordinary things came to my mind.

✽ 2   Who was not affected by the newcomers?

3   Many people had heard of the cylinders.

4   Here, read Henderson's telegram.

5   Why did his evening paper not print a special edition?

6   The great majority of people were inert.

✽ 7   Were people just dining all over the district?

8   Working men were gardening after the labours of the day.

9   Children were being put to bed.

10   Young people were wandering through the lanes.

11   Was there a murmur in the village streets?

12   Here and there a messenger caused a whirl of excitement.

13   How could the daily routine go on?

14   Even at Woking station and Horsell and Chobham all was routine.

15   A boy from the town was selling papers with the afternoon's news.

16   Who came into the station about nine o'clock?

✽ 17   When did half a dozen villas burn on the Woking border?

18   There were lights in all the houses on the common side of the three villages.

✽ 19   Keep awake!

20   What were you doing on Friday night?

21   A cylinder was sticking into the skin of our old planet Earth like a poisoned dart.

✽ 22   But the poison was not working yet.

23   Was the fever of war developing yet?

24   All night long the Martians were at work upon their machines.

25   Were the military authorities aware of the seriousness of the business?

26   A few seconds after midnight the second cylinder fell.

27   Saturday lives in my memory as a day of suspense.

28   I went into my garden before breakfast.

29   Had the Martians been surrounded by troops during the night?

✽ 30   Wouldn't the troops be able to destroy the Martians during the day?

31   The woods were still burning.

32   Walk down towards the common with me.

33   Where could I find a group of soldiers?

34   Would I be allowed over the canal?

35   I talked with some soldiers for a time.

✱ 36   I didn't tell them of my sight of the Martians on the previous evening.

37   Did any of them see the Martians?

✱ 38   Who had authorized the movements of the troops?

39   Would the reader like a description of that long morning?

40   I did not get a glimpse of the common.

41   Even the Chobham church tower was in the hands of the military authorities.

42   The people in the town were quite secure in the presence of the military.

✱ 43   Take a cold bath!

44   Could we go up to the railway station?

45   The Martians did not show an inch of themselves.

46   They seemed busy in their pit.

47   There was an almost continuous streamer of smoke.

✱ 48   Were they getting ready for a struggle?

49   The sight of all this armament and all this preparation greatly excited me.

50   It didn't seem a fair fight to me at that time.

Note: Suggested responses for the sentences marked by an asterisk (✱) are given at the back of the book. As a way of getting started on this activity, you might want to work first on those items. Where your responses and the suggested ones differ, you will want to get advice from your instructor. Very often, several interpretations might be appropriate.

Chapter 7

Noun Groups

Preliminaries

Here's what we have so far: language represents the events in ordinary everyday experience. At the level of the clause, the structure of language matches up nicely with the structure of events. In representing event structure, the process is the central element, the participants are the role-players and essential props, and the circumstances provide information about the when, where, why, and how of the event scenario.

In processes the verb group is often, though certainly not always, the main sense carrier—the main event representer, so to speak. In the verb group, the leading edge is central to a number of variations on clause beginnings: it can set up the clause as a statement, a question, a request, or a condition; or it can signal that the clause is nonfinite and subordinate (more on this in Chapter 9). In front of a yes/no question, a *wh-* marker can appear, converting the yes/no question into a *wh-* content question. *Wh-* words enter into a relationship with an information gap, which in the case of main-clause *wh-* questions represents the missing information that the response to the question is supposed to fill in.

Noun Groups

This chapter is about noun groups. We have already mentioned noun groups in connection with attributive and locative processes. In both *be*-plus-attribute and linking-verb-plus-attribute processes, the attribute can be either an adjective group or a noun group, as in (1), and in *be*-plus-location processes, the location can be a noun group, as in (2).

Attribute in an attributive process:

            LV + Att

(1) It [[seemed] such a little thing so bright and small and still].

         Past MV   NG

Location in a locative process:

> *be* + Loc
> **(2) In another minute it** [[**was**] **half a mile away**].
> Past MV   NG

We have also seen noun groups as the complement to a preposition group in prepositional phrases, as in (3), and we have seen noun groups representing circumstances, as in (4). Finally, of course, noun groups most frequently are to be found functioning as participants, as in (5).

Complement of preposition group:

> Time
> **(3) You know how that blackness looks** [[**on**] **a frosty starlight night**].
> PG   NG

Circumstance:

> Time
> **(4) This feeling was very strong upon me** [**that night**].
> NG

Participant:

> DirObj
> **(5) I could not avert** [**my face**] **from these things.**
> NG

Where noun groups fit in a clause In summary, we have found noun groups performing functions almost everywhere in a clause: as attributes in attributive processes, locations in locative processes, complements to preposition groups in prepositional phrases (*objects of the preposition*), circumstances, and, of course, participants.

Additionally in this chapter we shall note that noun groups can even be in the pre-central spot in adjective groups (for example, *British racing car* green or *lightning* fast), and noun groups can even be modifiers within other noun groups, either in front of or behind the main noun.

In (6) to (11) there are some further noun-group examples from *The War of the Worlds*. The obvious noun groups (and pronoun groups) are underscored, and toward the end of Chapter 8 we will come back and notice some less obvious ones in (6) and (7). You can go ahead and peek, if you want, at examples 40 and 41 in Chapter 8.

> **(6) However <u>it</u> is done, <u>a beam of heat</u> is <u>the essence of the matter</u>.**
>
> **(7) Whatever is combustible flashes into <u>flame</u> at <u>its touch</u>.**

The proform that is underscored in (6), *it*, would traditionally be called a **pronoun**, but a much more precise name might be **pronoun-group**. Pronouns, in other words, don't usually **corefer** with just a main noun but rather with an entire noun group. Notice that *its* (a proform functioning as a determiner) in example (7) corefers with *a beam of heat* in example (6), not just with the noun *beam*; *its* could therefore also be seen as a pro*noun-group*, not just a pro*noun*.

In these two examples noun groups can be seen in all three main-clause functional roles. In (6) *a beam of heat* is participant, and *the essence of the matter* is the attribute in a *be*-plus-attribute process. In (7), both *flame* and *its touch* are complements of preposition groups. Depending on your interpretation, *into flame* might be seen as a participant (playing the oblique role of **result**), or perhaps it is part of the idiomatic expression *flash into flame*. Likewise, *at its touch* might be treated as either a circumstance of manner (telling how the matter flashes into flame) or a participant (playing the agent role), depending on the sense that you derive from the context.

ACTIVITY **7.1**

Take a minute to figure out the noun-group functions in examples (8) to (11). Some responses are available at the back of the book.

(8) That night nearly forty people lay under the starlight about the pit, charred and distorted beyond recognition, and all night long the common from Horsell to Maybury was deserted and brightly ablaze.

(9) The news of the massacre probably reached Chobham, Woking, and Ottershaw about the same time.

(10) As yet, of course, few people in Woking even knew that the cylinder had opened, though poor Henderson had sent a messenger on a bicycle to the post office with a special wire to an evening paper.

(11) Stent and Ogilvy, anticipating some possibilities of a collision, had telegraphed from Horsell to the barracks as soon as the Martians emerged, for the help of a company of soldiers to protect these strange creatures from violence.

Noun-group elements You have probably noticed that, within the boundaries of the underscored noun groups in examples (6) to (11), many different specifiers, modifiers, and complements are represented. Here are some examples (all of these potentialities, and then some, are summarized in Chart 7.1).

Chart 7.1 *The Noun Group*

Left-hand edge	Precentral space	Central Word	Right-hand edge
Determiners (Det)	Adjective group Noun group Prepositional phrase Clause Adverb group	Main noun	Prepositional phrase Clause Adjective group Noun group Adverb group

Note: Entire noun groups can be within the scope of an intensifier.

Three types of determiners (These are listed in the order in which they generally appear with respect to each other. These are not intended to be exhaustive lists.)

Predeterminers:	all (of), half (of), most (of), both (of), some (of), a cup of, double, such, one-third, three times, what, . . .
Primary determiners:	the, a(n), this, that, these, those, each (of), no, enough (of), every, either (of), neither (of), my, our, his, her, its, their, Possessive NGs, whose, which, . . .
Postdeterminers:	cardinal and ordinal numbers, additional, further, last, next, older, younger, . . .

(12) [a beam of heat]
   Det MN   PP

(13) [flame]
     NG

(14) [nearly forty people]
       Det   MN

(15) [the rooms below]
   Det   MN   AdvG

(16) [about [the same time]]
   Intens Det Det MN
   (AdvG)

(17) [poor Henderson]
    AdjG   MN

(18) [some possibilities of a collision
   Det   MN   PP

Tests for identifying nouns Traditionally it has been said that nouns name persons, places, or things. That's a start, of course, but the whole unit *people in these latter times* in example (19) below refers to persons, so perhaps the right thing to say is that entire units headed by nouns name persons, places, or things. However, *up to the station*, a prepositional phrase, is a place in (20), and *the telescope vibrating* *with the activity of the clockwork*, an entire nonfinite clause, is a thing in (21). It should be clear that nouns and groups headed by nouns are not the only constituents that designate persons, places, and things.

(19) People in these latter times scarcely realize the abundance and enterprise of our nineteenth-century papers.

(20) I went home, had some tea, and walked up to the station to waylay him.

(21) It was as if it quivered, but really this was the telescope vibrating with the activity of the clockwork.

However, nouns do have one unique structural property: they very frequently can be made plural. If you can pluralize a word, either you have a noun on your hands, or by making it plural, you have changed a word from some other word category into a noun.

(22) Scattered <u>groups</u> were hurrying from the direction of Woking, and one or two <u>persons</u> were returning.

(23) There were raised <u>voices</u>, and some sort of struggle appeared to be going on about the pit.

(24) Strange <u>imaginings</u> passed through my mind.

You might also be able to recognize a noun by the form it takes. Nouns can end in *-(i)an, -age, -al, -ant, -ation, -dom, -ee, -er, -ery, -ess, -ette, -ful, -hood, -ing, -ism, -ist, -ite, -ity, -ment ,-ness, -or, -ship,* and *-ster*. In (25) are some examples of nouns that exhibit these endings. But you need to take care; some of these endings are also characteristic of other **lexical** categories.

(25) Mart<u>ian</u>, carri<u>age</u>, sign<u>al</u>, assist<u>ant</u>, veget<u>ation</u>, king<u>dom</u>, employ<u>ee</u>, wagon<u>er</u>, machin<u>ery</u>, silhou<u>ette</u>, ship<u>ful</u>, neighbor<u>hood</u>, even<u>ing</u>, hero<u>ism</u>, balloon<u>ist</u>, meteor<u>ite</u>, profund<u>ity</u>, move<u>ment</u>, dark<u>ness</u>, vend<u>or</u>, profess<u>orship</u>, pun<u>ster</u>

Here's a summary of tests for identifying nouns.

Inflections	Nouns can often be made plural. Noun groups can be made possessive.
Derivational endings	-(i)an, -age, -al, -ant, -ation, -dom, -ee, -er, -ery, -ese, -ess, -ette, -ful, -hood, -ing, -ism, -ist, -ite, -ity, -ment, -ness, -or, -ship, -ster
Syntax	Nouns fit into the main noun position in a noun group; therefore they can be preceded by a determiner.

Main noun Every word group has a head word. In a noun group the ***main noun*** (MN) is the head of the group.

Noun groups are unique among word groups in a couple of ways. First, only noun groups can normally be initiated by a determiner. By the way, that's another fairly surefire way to identify a noun: a noun is the kind of word that heads a group that is initiated by a determiner. This test might be even more reliable than trying the pluralization test because not all nouns can be pluralized.

However, a bit more interesting and stable is the second unique feature of noun groups: exactly the same set of structures can occur in the precentral space directly in front of the main noun as can occur at the right-hand edge, following the main noun. Adjective groups, noun groups, prepositional phrases, clauses, and the occasional adverb group (for example, *three years ago*, *five miles away*) can all appear either before or after the main noun in a noun group. But as you can see in Chart 7.1, the set of constituents that can appear before the main noun is in a different order from the set that can occur after it. This is because the probability of any member of the set happening before the main noun is different than the probability of that member occurring after it (except the adverb group, which is rare in either place). Adjective groups and noun groups are the items with the highest probability of occurring between determiners and main nouns. Similarly, prepositional phrases and clauses have the highest probability for following main nouns. Here are some examples taken from *The War of the Worlds*.

Adjective group preceding main noun:

    (26) every <u>available</u> pocket

Noun group preceding main noun:

    (27) a nocturnal <u>newspaper</u> reporter

Prepositional phrase preceding main noun (not common—none to be found in The War of the Worlds*):*

    (28) an <u>over-the-top</u> performance

Clause preceding main noun:

    (29) its <u>guarding</u> giants

Adverb group preceding main noun (not common—none to be found in The War of the Worlds*):*

    (30) far-away places with strange-sounding names (some might prefer to call *far-away* an adjective group)

Prepositional phrase following main noun:

    (31) the strength <u>of the Martians</u>

Clause following main noun:

    (32) things <u>that people had dropped</u>

Adjective group following main noun:

    (33) something <u>very strange</u>

Noun group following main noun (compare with 'Apposition' later in this chapter):

    (34) The <u>dinner</u>, <u>a cold one</u>

Adverb group following main noun:

    (35) The crowd <u>far away on the left</u>

Here is a short passage from *The War of the Worlds*. See how well you do at identifying the elements of the underscored noun groups by comparing them with the chart and with the examples above (we're going to work further on them just below). Two of the underscored groups contain embedded *wh-* clauses. We take up this topic in some detail in the next chapter, so you might simply suspend your consideration of embedded *wh-* clauses until then.

    (36) There, among <u>some young pine trees</u> and furze bushes, I stopped, panting, and waited <u>further developments</u>. <u>The common round the sand pits</u> was dotted with people, standing like myself in <u>a half-fascinated terror</u>, staring at these creatures, or rather at the heaped <u>gravel at the edge of the pit in which they lay</u>. And then, with a renewed horror, I saw <u>a round, black object</u> bobbing up and down on the edge of the pit. It was <u>the head of the shopman who had fallen in</u>, but showing as a little black object against <u>the hot western sun</u>. Now he got his shoulder and knee up, and again he seemed to slip back until <u>only his head</u> was visible. Suddenly he vanished, and I could have fancied <u>a faint shriek</u> had reached me. I had a momentary impulse to go back and help him that my fears overruled.

Determiners In (36), you might have noticed that with the exception of just one group, *only his head*, all of the underscored noun groups are initiated by determiners. This is not an unusual arrangement. Noun groups, especially those with a singular main noun, usually do contain a determiner or two. And in (36), even in the one apparent exceptional case, *only his head*, the noun group itself is *his head*, which is initiated by a determiner. The word *only* fits into the class of items that we are calling *intensifiers*. In this case the job that the intensifier does is to focus attention on the noun group itself, and therefore it has the entire group rather than just the main noun in its scope.

Here all of the selected noun groups in example (36) are isolated and the determiners underscored:

(37) <u>some</u> young pine trees

<u>further</u> developments

<u>The</u> common round the sand pits

<u>a</u> half-fascinated terror

<u>the</u> heaped gravel at the edge of the pit in which they lay

<u>a</u> round, black object

<u>the</u> head of the shopman who had fallen in

<u>the</u> hot western sun

only <u>his</u> head

<u>a</u> faint shriek

The function of determiners is to point out, or determine, the head noun with which they group. Determiners accomplish this goal by counting, designating, indicating, isolating, quantifying, sequencing, specifying, and so forth. Subgroups of determiners are often identified: *the*, *a*, and *an* are often called **articles**. *This*, *that*, *these*, and *those* are the **demonstratives** or *demonstrative pronouns*. The determiners *my*, *our*, *your*, *his*, *her*, *its*, *their*, and *whose* are referred to as **possessives** or *possessive pronouns*.

In doing their jobs, determiners contrast significantly with adjectives, whose main work is to attribute qualities to the main noun, or to describe, characterize, assign distinguishing features, traits, properties or peculiarities to the main noun.

Here once again are the noun groups from example (36), this time with their adjective groups underscored.

(38) some <u>young</u> pine trees (*pine* is a noun, not an adjective)

a <u>half-fascinated</u> terror

the <u>heaped</u> gravel at the edge of the pit in which they lay

a <u>round</u>, <u>black</u> object

the <u>hot</u> <u>western</u> sun

a <u>faint</u> shriek

Compare the following:

Determiners	Adjectives
some	young
further	half-fascinated
the	heaped
a	round
his	black
	hot
	western
	faint

The determiners *all*, *both*, and *any* can be displaced to a spot following the main noun (as in 39). They can also displace even further, to a spot just after the operator (as in 40):

(39) **Meeting with no response, [they both] concluded the man or men inside must be insensible or dead.** (compare with *both of them . . .*)

(40) **She turned without a word—they [were both panting]—and they went back to the lady.** (compare with *both of them . . .*)

Adjective groups and prepositional phrases You will find adjective groups performing two primary functions: (a) modifying or complementing the main noun within a noun group as shown in (38), and (b) as the attribute in *be*-plus-attribute or linking-verb-plus-attribute processes. For detail about the structure of adjective groups, look back to the appropriate sections of Chapter 4.

Prepositional phrases were also dealt with in some detail in Chapter 4. However, here is a quick synopsis of some of the particulars. First, the prepositional phrase is made up of two units—a preposition group and a complementary unit, often called the *object of the preposition*, either a noun group, a pronoun group, a clause, or an adverb group.

(41) **My wife was curiously silent [[throughout] the drive],** ↻
                             Preposition   Complement
                             Group

→ **and seemed oppressed [[with] forebodings of evil].**
                    Preposition   Complement
                    Group

Second, prepositional phrases have two main event-structure (clause-level) functions: Preposition groups mark the participant role in oblique objects (42), and preposition groups introduce circumstances (43).

(42) **The description of their death, as it was seen by the crowd, tallies very closely <u>with my own impressions</u>.**

(43) **In the sudden thud, hiss, and glare of the igniting trees, the panic-stricken crowd seems to have swayed hesitatingly <u>for some moments</u>.**

Third, prepositional phrases can also perform other functions at levels below the event structure within clauses: they can be attributes in attributive processes (44), they can be locations in locative processes (45), and they can be satellites modifying or complementing main nouns within noun groups, adjectives within adjective groups, and adverbs within adverb groups (46).

(44) **No doubt, ran the report, the situation was <u>of the strangest and gravest description</u>, but the public was exhorted to avoid and discourage panic.**

(45) **'We are <u>in the midst of it</u>,' I said, 'quiet as it is.'**

(46) **Far away <u>to the southeast</u>, marking the quiet, we heard the Martians hooting to one another, and then the air quivered again with the distant thud of their guns.**

Finally, prepositional phrases can also work outside clauses as carriers of discourse functions (47).

(47) **And, <u>in the second place</u>, we all overlooked the fact that such mechanical intelligence as the Martian possessed was quite able to dispense with muscular exertion at a pinch.**

Putting Units Together

Up to this point we have shown that clauses work by bringing together word groups and phrases to represent the event structures (processes, participants, and circumstances) of ordinary experience.

And we have shown that word groups work by bringing together units of various sizes such as words, word groups, phrases, and clauses into units that are headed by a main word. The main word is like a magnet to which the various other units are drawn as satellites. We have not yet provided much detail about the way clauses fit into word groups, but in a way, that is what the rest of this book is all about.

In the next chapter we will take an extended look at the way that noun groups act as docking mechanisms for clauses, creating the nested-boxes effect that we have called *embedding*. As with noun groups, but to a less significant extent, adjective groups and adverb groups also function as host sites for embedded clauses; we will consider adjective groups with embedded clauses in Chapter 10.

Conjoining But first we will consider the ways that words, word groups, phrases, or clauses can be strung together in parallel, creating lists of items in an equivalence relationship. The word *paratactic* will be used here to describe the *strung-together* relationship (*para-* means *at the same level* and **tactic** means *arranged*). Other terms that might be used are **conjoining** and **compounding**. The words that signal this sort of relationship (words like *and*, *or*, and *but*) are **conjunctions** (or *conjuncts*). In general, units may be conjoined that are (a) clause-level components of equivalent functional status or (b) units of equivalent status within word groups and phrases. A number of the possibilities are shown in examples (48) to (59).

Main adverbs:

(48) . . . was being watched <u>keenly</u> *and* <u>closely</u> . . .

(49) . . . was rising <u>slowly</u> *and* <u>painfully</u> out of the cylinder.

Main verbs:

(50) . . . they were <u>scrutinized</u> *and* <u>studied</u>, . . .

(51) Air was *either* <u>entering</u> *or* <u>escaping</u> at the rim with a thin, sizzling sound.

Main adjectives:

(52) Ogilvy moved about, <u>invisible</u> *but* <u>audible</u>.

(53) . . . they both concluded the man or men inside must be <u>insensible</u> *or* <u>dead</u>.

Main nouns:

(54) . . . the <u>light</u> *and* <u>heat</u> it receives from the sun is barely half of that received by this world . . .

(55) Dense clouds of <u>smoke</u> *or* <u>dust</u>, . . .

Main determiners:

(56) There were <u>four</u> *or* <u>five</u> boys sitting on the edge of the Pit.

(57) . . . transferring everything from the <u>second</u> *and* <u>third</u> cylinders.

Noun groups:

(58) I think everyone expected to see a man emerge—possibly <u>something a little unlike us terrestrial men</u>, *but* <u>in all essentials a man</u>.

Prepositional phrases:

(59) A great bank of dust was perpetually renewed <u>by the hurrying feet of horses</u> *and* <u>by men and women on foot</u>, *and* <u>by the wheels of vehicles of every description</u>.

Clauses:

> **(60)** **There was a lot of shouting, *and* one man was even jesting.**

Apposition A second way of putting units together in a parallel manner is apposition. Apposition works very much like conjoining in that two equivalent units together perform the function that might otherwise be performed by a single unit. However, in a strict sense, apposition differs from conjoining and embedding in several ways. First, it is not usually signaled by a conjunction or other marker. Second, either one of the members of the appositive set can usually substitute for the other; whereas *all* of the elements that share a conjoined relationship are needed to convey sense, in an appositive relationship, *either* of the elements could do the job. So, third, the elements in an appositive relationship refer to exactly the same elements of the event structure; that is, they are said to be strictly ***coreferential***. Fourth, and finally, an appositive relationship functions as one constituent of the event structure; therefore, each of the appositive elements realizes exactly the same function in the clause. In sentences (61), (62), and (63) that function is direct object; in (64) the function is subject.

> **(61)** **I might not have heard of the eruption at all had I not met Ogilvy, the well-known astronomer, at Ottershaw.**
>
> DirObj   Appositive
> [[Ogilvy] [the well-known astronomer]]

> **(62)** **. . . and pointed out Mars, a bright dot of light creeping zenithward, towards which so many telescopes were pointed.**
>
> DirObj   Appositive
> [[Mars] [a bright dot of light creeping zenithward]]

> **(63)** **That sobered him a little; and when he saw Henderson, the London journalist, in his garden, he called over the palings and made himself understood.**
>
> DirObj   Appositive
> [[Henderson] [the London journalist]]

> **(64)** **Among these were a couple of cyclists, a jobbing gardener I employed sometimes, a girl carrying a baby, Gregg the butcher and his little boy, and two or three loafers and golf caddies who were accustomed to hang about the railway station.**
>
> Subj   Appositive
> [[Gregg] [the butcher]]

Embedding, subordinating In contrast to both conjoining and apposition, subordination and embedding are ways of tucking one structure into another, as opposed to stringing them together. The word *hypotactic* will be applied here to describe the subordinate and embedded relationships (*hypo-* means *at a lower level* and *tactic* means *arranged*). The term *embedded* generally applies to word groups, prepositional phrases, and clauses that are positioned INSIDE of word groups; the term *subordinate* is generally applied only to clauses that are positioned OUTSIDE of word groups and that are functioning as constituents of the event structure (process, participant, circumstance) in a *host clause*. In the next three chapters we will consider these ideas in some detail.

Practice with Terminology

What follows is a preview of the sentences that you will encounter in this chapter's Sentences for Analysis. Certain elements in the sentences have been underscored. Label each underscored element using one or more of the following terms or an applicable term from a previous chapter. Check the Glossary if you are not certain about the definition of any of the terms.

Apposition	Conjoining	Determiner	Missing element
Article	Demonstrative	Embedding	Possessive

1   My younger brother was in London.

2   He was a medical student.

3   He heard nothing of the arrival until Saturday morning.

4   The morning papers contained lengthy special articles on the planet Mars.

5   The papers on Saturday contained a brief and vague telegram.

6   The telegram concluded with hopeful words.

7   The Martians have not moved from their pit.

8   Probably this is due to the relative strength of the earth's gravitational energy.

9   All the students in my brother's biology class were intensely interested in the Martians.

10   There were no signs of any unusual excitement in the streets.

11   The afternoon papers puffed scraps of news under big headlines.

12   They told nothing beyond the movements of troops about the common.

13   Nothing more of the fighting was known that night, the night of my drive to Leatherhead and back.

14   My brother felt no anxiety about us.

15   The cylinder was a good two miles from my house.

16   In London on Saturday night <u>there</u> was a thunderstorm.

17   Trains <u>could</u> not reach Woking because of an accident that night.

18   <u>The</u> nature of the accident my brother could not ascertain.

19   <u>Even</u> the railway authorities did not clearly know at that time.

20   A <u>nocturnal</u> newspaper reporter mistook my brother for the traffic manager.

21   My brother resembles <u>that</u> railway official.

22   Few people, <u>except</u> the railway officials, connected the accident with the Martians.

23   <u>Plenty of</u> Londoners did not hear of the Martians until the panic of Monday morning.

24   The majority of people in London <u>do</u> not read Sunday papers.

25   The habit of personal security is deeply fixed in <u>the Londoner's</u> mind.

26   The newspapers made startling reports but Londoners ignored <u>them</u>.

27   About seven o'clock last night the Martians <u>came out</u> of the cylinder.

28   They moved about under <u>an</u> armour of metallic shields.

29   They <u>have</u> completely wrecked Woking station and the adjacent houses.

30   <u>No</u> details could be reported by the papers.

31   The field guns have been <u>absolutely</u> useless against their armour.

32   The Martians <u>appear to</u> be moving slowly towards Chertsey or Windsor.

33   No one in London knew positively of the nature of the <u>armoured</u> Martians.

34   None of the telegrams could have been written by an eyewitness <u>of their advance</u>.

35   My brother <u>went to church</u> at the Foundling Hospital in the morning.

36   There he heard allusions to the invasion, and <u>a special prayer for peace</u>.

37   The train service was now <u>very much</u> disorganized.

38   <u>Quite a number of</u> people were standing about the station.

39   They had <u>been expecting</u> friends from places on the South-Western network.

40   A man in a blue <u>and</u> white blazer addressed my brother.

41   The <u>vague</u> feeling of alarm had spread to the clients of the underground railway.

42   The crowd in the station was immensely excited by the passage of trucks <u>full of soldiers</u>.

43   A little while after <u>that</u> a squad of police came into the station.

44   They cleared the public <u>off the platforms</u>.

45   My brother went out into the street <u>again</u>.

46   Five of the machines <u>had been</u> moving towards the Thames.

47   One, by a happy chance, had <u>been</u> destroyed.

48   In the <u>other</u> cases the shells had missed.

49   The batteries had been <u>at once</u> annihilated by the Heat-Rays.

50   The Martians had <u>retreated</u> to their triangle of cylinders again.

Note: You do not need to limit your choices to the new terms from this chapter. Where appropriate, use an applicable term from any previous chapter.

Analyzing and Reporting Noun Groups

Step 1: *Identifying processes* Bracket and label with the process type above the bracket.

                          Trans
(65)   **The Martians [had killed] a number of people with a quick-firing gun**

Step 2: *Identifying participants* By referring to your own personal experience, determine the number of participant roles that the process requires. In the clause find the role-players; bracket them and label participant functions above the bracket. Be aware that sometimes required participant roles are expressed by understood (missing) elements and that sometimes more than just the required participant roles are expressed.

        Subj   Trans   DirObj   OblObj
(66)   **[The Martians] [had killed] [a number of people] [[with] a quick-firing gun]**

In (66), the analysis proposes three participants: *The Martians*, playing the role of kill*er*, *a number of people* playing the role of kill*ee*, and *with a quick-firing gun* as an essential prop, the instrument.

Step 3: *Identifying circumstances* All of the remaining clause-level bracketable elements are circumstances. Bracket and label them by type.

        Subj   Trans   DirObj   OblObj
(67)   **[The Martians] [had killed] [a number of people] [[with] a quick-firing gun]**

Example (67) demonstrates that this clause has no circumstance units.

Step 4: *Labeling the main words* Label the main word for each bracketed word group. If clause-level bracketed units are phrases, sub-bracket all component word groups except one (we will assume that the remaining elements form a group). Label the main word for each sub-bracketed group; single-element groups normally take the group label.

<pre>
        Subj   Trans   DirObj   OblObj
(68) [The Martians] [had killed] [a number of people] [[with] a quick-firing gun]
         MN   MV   MN   PG   MN
</pre>

Step 5: *Labeling adjective groups, adverb groups, and prepositional phrases*

<pre>
        Subj   Trans   DirObj   OblObj
(69) [The Martians] [had killed] [a number of people] [[with] a quick-firing gun]
         MN   MV   MN   PG   AdjG   MN
</pre>

Step 6: *Labeling verb-group elements* Refer to Chart 5.1 (The Verb Group).

<pre>
        Subj   Trans   DirObj   OblObj
(70) [The Martians] [had killed] [a number of people] [[with] a quick-firing gun]
         MN   Past MV   MN   PG   AdjG   MN
                    have + -ed/-en
</pre>

Step 7: *Labeling noun-group elements and taking stock* Refer to Chart 7.1 (The Noun Group). Here is our final report:

<pre>
        Subj   Trans   DirObj   OblObj
(71) [The Martians] [had killed] [a number of people] [[with] a quick-firing gun]
       Det   MN   Past MV   Det   MN   PG   Det AdjG   MN
                    have + -ed/-en
</pre>

Sentences for Analysis

The following sentences are adapted from *The War of the Worlds*. Analyze them and report your results as shown in the example below. Make certain that your analyses have the following features:

a Bracket processes, participants, and circumstances and label them by function above the bracket.

b Sub-bracket as necessary, observing minimal bracketing conventions.

c Label elements in all word groups. Single-element groups are normally given the group label.

<pre>
        Subj   Trans   DirObj   IndObj Place
(72) [The Thing] [had made] [a pit] [[for] itself] [[at] the edge of the woods]
       Det   MN   Past MV   Det MN   PG   ProG   PG Det   MN   PP
                  have + -ed/-en
</pre>

✱ 1 My younger brother was in London.

2 He was a medical student.

3 He heard nothing of the arrival until Saturday morning.

4 The morning papers contained lengthy special articles on the planet Mars.

 * 5   The papers on Saturday contained a brief and vague telegram.

 6   The telegram concluded with hopeful words.

 7   The Martians have not moved from their pit.

 8   Probably this is due to the relative strength of the earth's gravitational energy.

 9   All the students in my brother's biology class were intensely interested in the Martians.

 10   There were no signs of any unusual excitement in the streets.

 11   The afternoon papers puffed scraps of news under big headlines.

 * 12   They told nothing beyond the movements of troops about the common.

 13   Nothing more of the fighting was known that night, the night of my drive to Leatherhead and back.

 14   My brother felt no anxiety about us.

 15   The cylinder was a good two miles from my house.

 16   In London on Saturday night there was a thunderstorm.

 17   Trains could not reach Woking because of an accident that night.

 * 18   The nature of the accident my brother could not ascertain.

 19   Even the railway authorities did not clearly know at that time.

 * 20   A nocturnal newspaper reporter mistook my brother for the traffic manager.

 21   My brother resembles that railway official.

 22   Few people, except the railway officials, connected the accident with the Martians.

 23   Plenty of Londoners did not hear of the Martians until the panic of Monday morning.

 24   The majority of people in London do not read Sunday papers.

 25   The habit of personal security is deeply fixed in the Londoner's mind.

 * 26   The newspapers made startling reports but Londoners ignored them.

 27   About seven o'clock last night the Martians came out of the cylinder.

 28   They moved about under an armour of metallic shields.

 29   They have completely wrecked Woking station and the adjacent houses.

 30   No details could be reported by the papers.

 * 31   The field guns have been absolutely useless against their armour.

 32   The Martians appear to be moving slowly towards Chertsey or Windsor.

 33   No one in London knew positively of the nature of the armoured Martians.

 34   None of the telegrams could have been written by an eyewitness of their advance.

 35   My brother went to church at the Foundling Hospital in the morning.

 36   There he heard allusions to the invasion, and a special prayer for peace.

✳ 37   The train service was now very much disorganized.

38   Quite a number of people were standing about the station.

39   They had been expecting friends from places on the South-Western network.

✳ 40   A man in a blue and white blazer addressed my brother.

41   The vague feeling of alarm had spread to the clients of the underground railway.

42   The crowd in the station was immensely excited by the passage of trucks full of soldiers.

43   A little while after that a squad of police came into the station.

44   They cleared the public off the platforms.

45   My brother went out into the street again.

✳ 46   Five of the machines had been moving towards the Thames.

47   One, by a happy chance, had been destroyed.

48   In the other cases the shells had missed.

49   The batteries had been at once annihilated by the Heat-Rays.

50   The Martians had retreated to their triangle of cylinders again.

> **Note:** Suggested responses for the sentences marked by an asterisk (✳) are given at the back of the book. As a way of getting started on this activity, you might want to work first on those items. Where your responses and the suggested ones differ, you will want to get advice from your instructor. Very often, several interpretations might be appropriate.

Chapter 8

Embedded
Wh- Clauses

Preliminaries

At the end of the last chapter, we had begun to consider how language units fit together. You have had plenty of practice identifying noun groups, some of which have other word groups and phrases embedded within them—for example, adjective groups or prepositional phrases. In this chapter and the next two we are going to expand on this idea that one language unit can be tucked into another.

In this chapter we are going to observe that *wh-* clauses, which we first discussed as content questions in Chapter 6, can also embed in noun groups. Then in Chapters 9 and 10 we will find out how other clause types, the non*wh-* clauses, not only embed in host word groups but can also serve as event-structure constituents (as participants, circumstances, and attributes in attributive processes).

This chapter builds on what we have said already about noun groups by combining three familiar ideas:

a Word groups have edges and main words.

b Words, word groups, and phrases can sometimes act like nested dolls. You can often take the lid off one, only to encounter another waiting for you right inside the first.

c *Wh-* markers enter into a coreference relationship with an information gap.

Even though these ingredients, taken individually, might not impress you as being particularly potent, taken together they account for one of the most frequently used structures in English: the embedded *wh-* clause.

Here comes that part of the story.

Embedded *Wh-* Clauses

To understand embedded *wh-* clauses, it is best to start with the topic of *wh-* questions. You will recall from Chapter 6 that *wh-* questions have three essential components:

a a *wh- marker* to the left of the left-hand edge of the clause,

b a *discontinuous verb group* that signals question structure, and

c an *information gap* (a missing element).

Moreover, *wh-* questions stand alone as main clauses:

(1) **Who would Ogilvy invite up?**

(2) **Why should the Martians come to Earth?**

(3) **When did the first cylinder open?**

(4) **Where could the people be safe?**

The structure of main-clause *wh-* questions is this: (a) *wh-* marker, (b) left-hand edge of the verb group, (c) subject, (d) remainder of the event structure. For example, here are these four structural elements in (1):

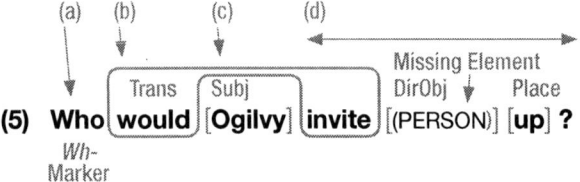

Now here's the main point: in addition to serving as content questions, *wh-* structures can also function as elements in a noun group. However, once they are embedded in a noun group, they lose their independent function as questions, and they therefore have no need for the question-cueing discontinuity of the verb group. With their verb groups reunited and their missing elements indicated in parentheses, *wh-* clauses (1) to (4) would look like this:

(6) *who* **Ogilvy would invite** (PERSON) **up**

(7) *why* **the Martians should come to Earth** (REASON)

(8) *when* **the first cylinder opened** (TIME)

(9) *where* **the people could be safe** (PLACE)

No longer main-clause questions, whose verb groups must be discontinuous, these *wh-* clauses have only two of the three features that characterize *wh-* questions:

a the *wh- marker* at the left-hand edge of the clause, and

b the missing-element coreferential *information gap.*

Clauses such as these are always embedded in a noun group, usually behind the main noun, and the information gap in the embedded clause is no longer the focused content of a question. Instead, the *wh-* marker and the gap match up with elements of the host noun group, usually the main noun, to provide continuity between the host noun group and the embedded clause.

In examples (10) to (13) the main noun/information-gap sets are underscored in each complex. The first member of each set is the head word of the bracketed noun group in the host clause, and the second is a missing element, essential to the event structure, in the embedded clause.

> (10) **The narrator was** [**the person who Ogilvy would invite** (PERSON) **up**].
>
> Embedded Clause

Two combined clauses are distinguishable here; one ( ) is an embedded element in the other ( ).

  The narrator was the person.

  Ogilvy would invite (PERSON) **up.**

Here are some more examples (their combining clauses are specified below each one).

> (11) [**The reason why the Martians should come to Earth** (REASON)] ↻
>
> Embedded Clause
>
> ⇀ **was not at first clear.**

  The reason was not at first clear.

  The Martians should come to Earth (REASON).

> (12) **Ogilvy was not there at** [**the time when the first cylinder opened** (TIME)].
>
> Embedded Clause

  Ogilvy was not there at the time.

  The first cylinder opened (TIME).

> (13) **There was** [**no place where the people could be safe** (PLACE)].
>
> Embedded Clause

  There was no place.

  The people could be safe (PLACE).

Examples (10) to (13) are clause complexes formed from two event structures. These complexes can be represented by substituting a numbered triangle for the embedded clause () at the appropriate spot in the host noun group.

> **A note about conventions for reporting embedded clauses.** The reporting convention used in (14) has been called the *triangle convention* because of the numbered triangle (▲) that replaces the embedded clause.

(14) **The narrator was the person who Ogilvy would invite up** .

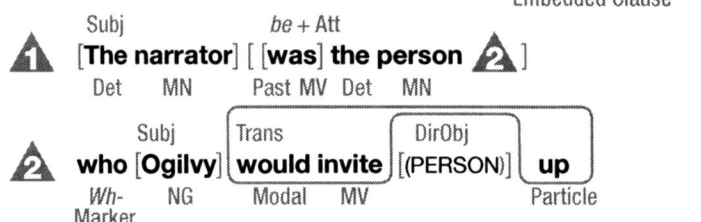

We will continue to use minimal bracketing for the clause elements. Across the top of each clause, we label the bracketed constituents with functional designations for processes, participants, and circumstances; below the clause we label the elements of the word groups. In a moment you should try out your hand on examples (11) to (13). Before you do, however, now might be a good time to return to example (36) in the previous chapter, repeated below at (15), where we had postponed consideration of a couple of the word groups: (a) *the heaped gravel at the edge of the pit in which they lay*, and (b) *the head of the shopman who had fallen in*.

(15) **There, among some young pine trees and furze bushes, I stopped, panting, and waited further developments. The common round the sand pits was dotted with people, standing like myself in a half-fascinated terror, staring at these creatures, or rather at the heaped gravel at the edge of the pit in which they lay. And then, with a renewed horror, I saw a round, black object bobbing up and down on the edge of the pit. It was the head of the shopman who had fallen in, but showing as a little black object against the hot western sun. Now he got his shoulder and knee up, and again he seemed to slip back until only his head was visible. Suddenly he vanished, and I could have fancied a faint shriek had reached me. I had a momentary impulse to go back and help him that my fears overruled.**

Reports for the two underscored units in (15) are given at (16) and (17).

(16)

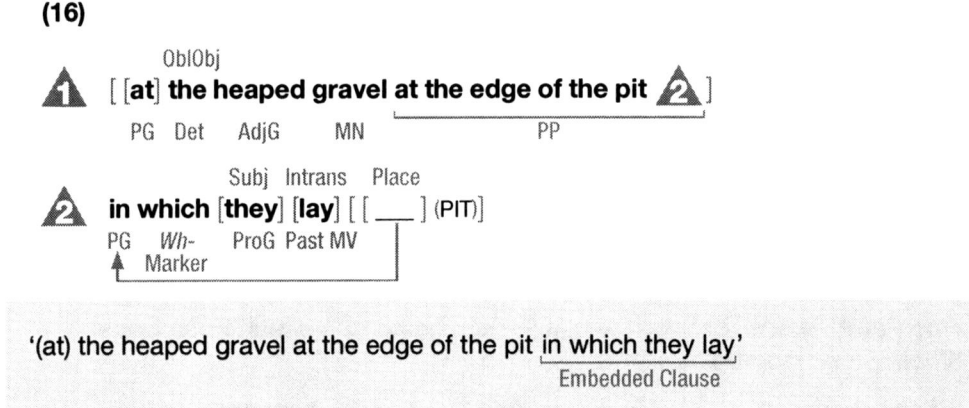

'(at) the heaped gravel at the edge of the pit in which they lay'

Embedded Clause

Note the formal style of *in which they lay* in (16)—as opposed to, say, *that they lay in*. The preposition group *in* is represented as having been displaced from its more conversational spot for this formal style (known as ***formal preposing***).

(17)

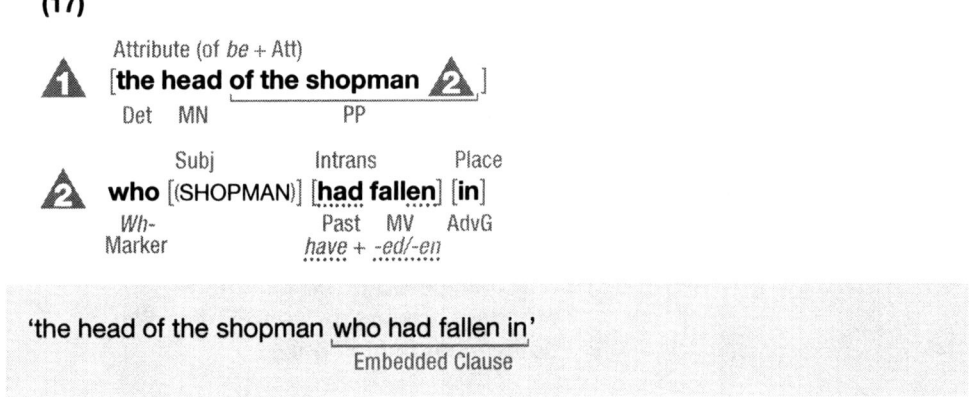

'the head of the shopman who had fallen in'

Embedded Clause

ACTIVITY 8.1

Now it's your turn. Make triangle-convention reports for examples (11) to (13). Remember:

a The gap in the embedded clause is always represented in upper-case letters and parentheses; its content matches up with the head of the host noun group.

b The triangle symbol for the embedded clause is placed right at the spot where the embedded clause is located in the host noun group.

Some suggested responses for (11) to (13) are given at the back of the book.

List 8.1 Wh- *Markers for Embedded Clauses*

In an embedded clause, if the *wh-* marker is:	The *wh-* gap will be a missing element coreferent with:
Where (*-ever, -soever*)	➡ a Place heading the host noun group
Why (*-ever*)	➡ a Reason heading the host noun group
Who (*-ever, -soever*) or **Whom** (*-ever, -soever*)	➡ a Person heading the host noun group
When (*-ever*)	➡ a Time heading the host noun group
What (*-ever, -soever*)	➡ a Thing heading the host noun group
How (*-ever, -soever*)	➡ a Manner, a Means, or a Condition heading the host noun group; also a Quantifier
Whose (*-ver, -soever*)	➡ a Possessive determiner related to the head of the noun group
Which (*-ever*) and **That**	➡ a range of items that could be heads in the host noun group, including places, reasons, persons, times, things, manners, means, or conditions; also a determiner (**which** only)

Wh- question markers and *wh-* embedded clause markers are almost, but not quite, the same set (see List 8.1). First, the word *which*, when it is used to mark a *wh-* embedded clause, usually signals a gap containing a thing; however, its use is often extended to take in people, places, reasons, times, and perhaps other categories. Moreover, an additional marker, *that*, joins the set, which like *how* does not begin with *wh-* and like *which* has a very wide range of applications. Moreover, the *wh-* markers *what* and *how* are normally restricted to noun groups in which the main noun (the head of the group) is a missing element (see 'The headless version' under 'Types of embedded *wh-* clauses').

Types of embedded *wh-* clauses All embedded *wh-* clauses have three coreferential elements:

   a the **main noun** or **pronoun** in the host noun group

b a ***wh-* marker** that is coreferent with one or more of the elements in the host noun group, almost always the main noun, and

c a ***wh-* gap** with which the marker and the host group main noun must corefer

Given that missing elements figure so prominently in *wh-* relationships, let's first pause to notice that of the three coreferential elements—main noun, marker, and gap—listed in (a), (b), and (c), the information gap is *always* a missing element. That leaves only the other two to vary between being overt and being missing. There is almost never any variation from these contents. However, once the familiar principle of *missing elements*, which applies across all of English, is expanded to include not only the information gap in the embedded clause but also, potentially, the main noun, several types of *wh-* embedded clause can be identified.

In the balance of this chapter we provide some detail about the four major varieties of *wh-* embedded clauses: the ***normal version***, the ***missing-marker version***, the *whiz* ***version***, and the ***headless version***.

The normal version Only the *wh-* gap is a missing element. For example,

(18) . . . a man with a microscope might scrutinize the transient creatures that swarm and multiply in a drop of water.

Embedded Clause

 A man with a microscope might scrutinize the transient creatures.

 (CREATURES) swarm and multiply in a drop of water.

(19) . . . the earth must have accelerated its cooling to the temperature at which life could begin.

Embedded Clause

 The earth must have accelerated its cooling to some temperature.

 Life could begin at (TEMPERATURE).

The missing-marker version The *wh-* gap and the marker are both missing elements. For example,

(20) He stood at the edge of the pit the Thing had made for itself.

Embedded Clause

 He stood at the edge of the pit.

 The Thing had made (PIT) for itself.

(21) Here and there were things people had dropped.

Embedded Clause

 Here and there were things.

 People had dropped (THINGS).

The *whiz* version The *whiz* variety also exploits the missing-element principle. However, in this version THREE elements are missing: (1) any form of *be*, except the one in a *there*-plus-*be* process (see Chart 8.1), (2) the content of the *wh-* gap, and (3) the *wh-* marker itself. (The form of *be* in the embedded clause is reflected in the *-iz* of the name *whiz*, because of the pronunciation of *is*, a form of *be*.)

(22) **This blaze was the casting of the huge gun, in the vast pit** ↻
→ **sunk into their planet.**
Embedded Clause

 This blaze was the casting of the huge gun, in the vast pit.

 → (PIT) (WAS) **sunk into their planet.**

(23) **He compared it to a colossal puff of flame** ↻
→ **suddenly and violently squirted out of the planet.**
Embedded Clause

 He compared it to a colossal puff of flame.

 (FLAME) (WAS) **suddenly and violently squirted out of the planet.**

> **A note about prepositional phrases embedded in noun groups** When an embedded *whiz* clause is used that is missing the *be* of a *be*-plus-location process, where the location is a prepositional phrase, the only part that is overt and apparent is the prepositional phrase, as shown in (24), (25), and (26) below. This analysis can't be offered as an explanation for all prepositional phrases that are **postmodifiers** (complements) in noun groups, but it might explain the locative ones. For simplicity's sake, we will normally treat embedded prepositional phrases as such and not as embedded *whiz* clauses.

(24) **I was very glad to do as he asked, and so became one of the privileged** ↻
→ **spectators** (WHO WERE) **within the contemplated enclosure.**
Embedded Clause

 I was very glad to do as he asked, and so became one of the privileged ↻
→ **spectators.**

 (SPECTATORS) (WERE) **within the contemplated enclosure.**

(25) **Then suddenly the trees** (THAT WERE) **in the pine wood ahead of me** ↻
Embedded Clause

→ **were parted.**

 Then suddenly the trees were parted.

 (TREES) (WERE) **in the pine woods ahead of me.**

Chart 8.1 *The Forms of Be That Participate in Whiz Clauses*

The **bold-print elements** participate in *whiz* clauses

Left-hand edge	Precentral space	Central Word		Right-hand edge
Tense (either present or past) or Modal or Nonfinite clause marker	Combinations of **semiauxiliary verbs** and **primary auxiliary verbs** or **the periphrastic auxiliary verb** (dummy *do*) If no other auxiliary is present and one is needed for Q or NEG	**Main verb** (except in *there* + *be*)		Postposed particles Idiomatic elements

Note: Intensifiers can fit in almost anywhere.

Semiauxiliary verbs with *be*:   be able to, be about to, be bound to, be fixin' to, be going to, be inclined to, be liable to, be supposed to, be to, be willing to . . .

Primary auxiliaries with *be*:   *be* + *-ing*   (progressive aspect)
                                        be + *-ed/-en*   (passive voice)

Process types with main verb *be*:   *be* + attribute (*be* + Att)
                                            be + location (*be* + Loc)

(26)   'Shut up, you fool!' said a man (WHO WAS) **near me** to a yelping dog.
                                    ‾‾‾‾‾‾‾‾‾‾‾‾‾‾‾‾‾‾‾‾‾‾‾‾
                                         Embedded Clause

   'Shut up, you fool!' said a <u>man</u> to a yelping dog.

   (MAN) (WAS) **near me.**

The headless version The *wh-* gap in the embedded clause and the main noun in the host noun group are both missing elements. The host noun group for headless *wh-* clauses functions as attribute, or complement of preposition group, or participant (as in 27), or as circumstance as in (28).

(27)   No one on earth has explained <u>why the shots ceased after the tenth.</u>
                                         Embedded Clause

   No one on earth has explained (REASON).

   The shots ceased after the tenth (REASON).

(28)   Something fell with a crash <u>where the road opens out on the common.</u>
                                         Embedded Clause

   Something fell with a crash (PLACE).

   The road opens out on the common (PLACE).

Let's look now at each of these four types to see how the noun groups in the examples look in the form of triangle-convention reports. The next few pages have several models for you to examine. Chart 8.1 outlines the forms of *be* that participate in *whiz* clauses.

Triangle-convention reports for the normal version Here is a generic picture of the normal *wh-* embedded clause in its host noun group. The examples given earlier are reported below it in triangle-convention form.

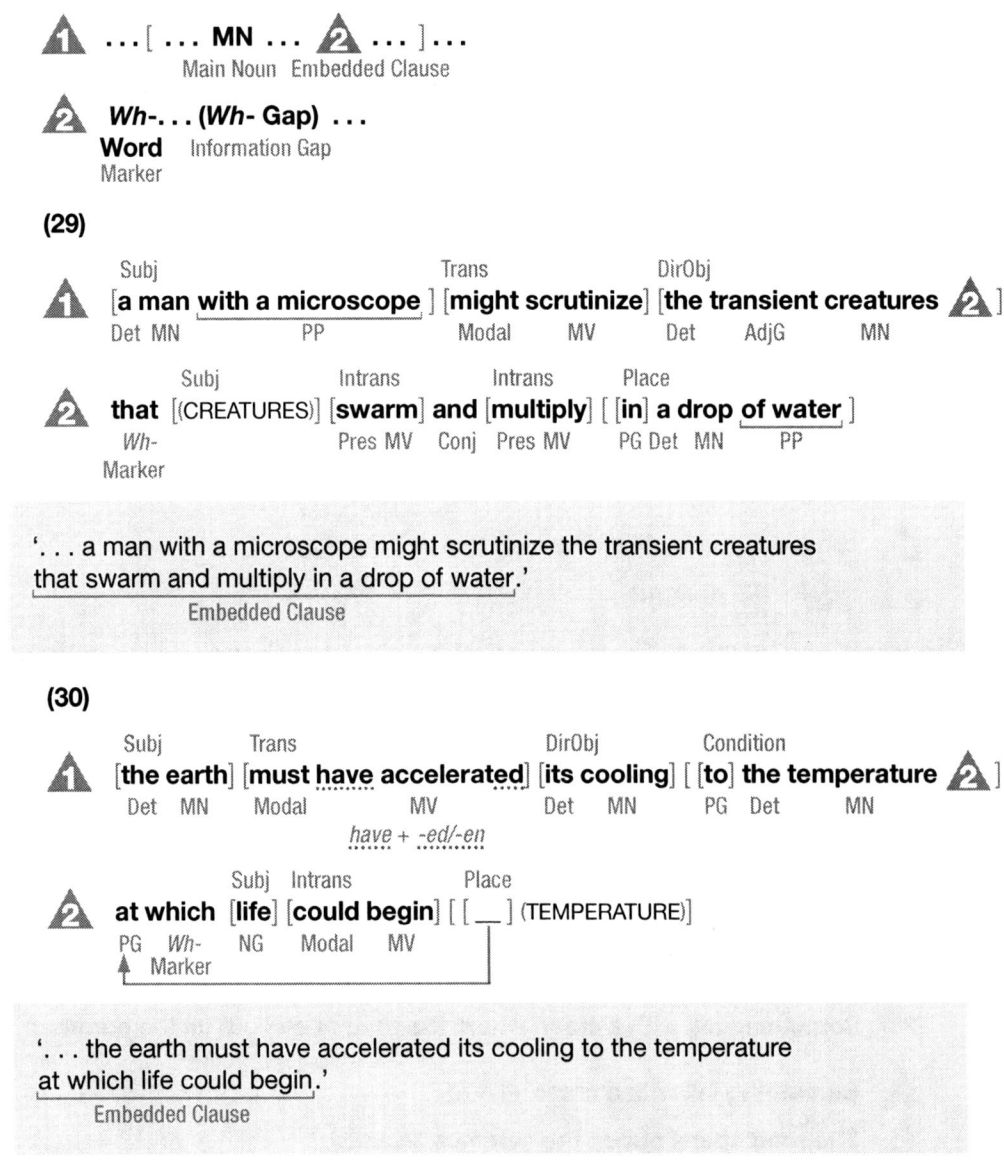

(29)

'. . . a man with a microscope might scrutinize the transient creatures that swarm and multiply in a drop of water.'
                Embedded Clause

(30)

'. . . the earth must have accelerated its cooling to the temperature at which life could begin.'
                Embedded Clause

Triangle-convention reports for the missing-marker version Here is a generic picture of the missing-marker *wh-* embedded clause in its host noun group. The examples given earlier are reported below it in triangle-convention form.

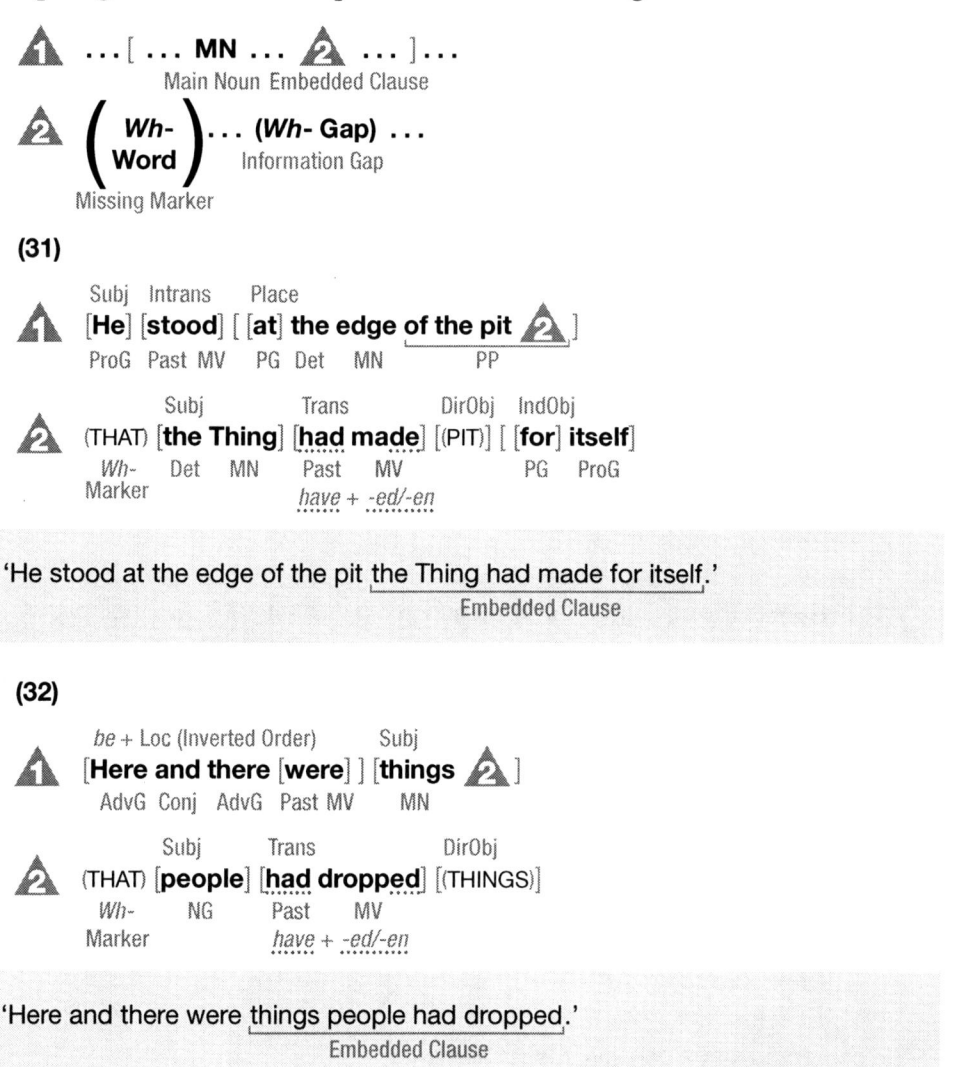

(31)

'He stood at the edge of the pit the Thing had made for itself.'
Embedded Clause

(32)

'Here and there were things people had dropped.'
Embedded Clause

Triangle-convention reports for the *whiz* version Here is a generic picture of the *(wh-) (wh- gap) (BE)* embedded clause, the *whiz* clause, in its host noun group. The examples given earlier are reported below it in triangle-convention form. See Chart 8.1 for the forms of *be* that participate in *whiz* embedded clauses.

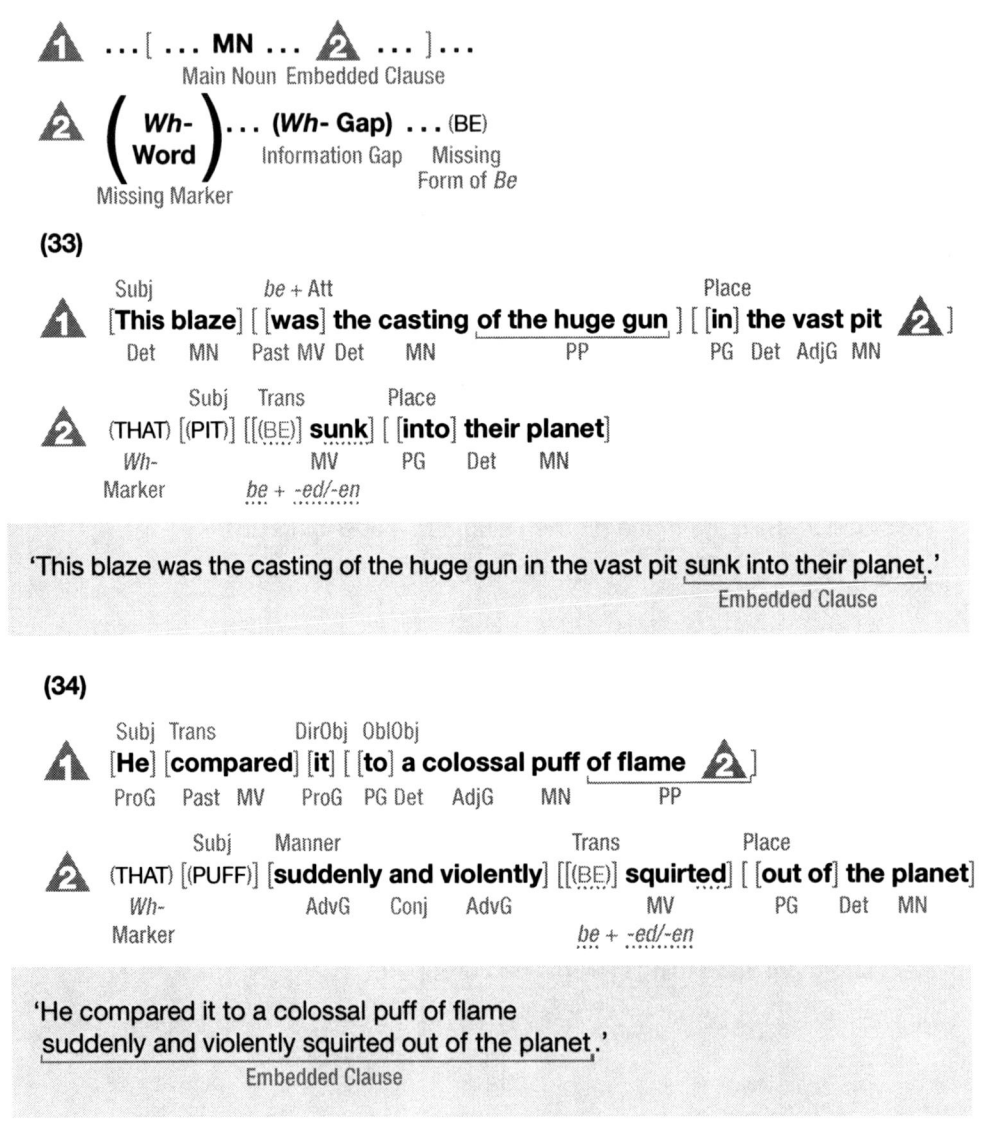

(33)

'This blaze was the casting of the huge gun in the vast pit sunk into their planet.'
                                                                    Embedded Clause

(34)

'He compared it to a colossal puff of flame
suddenly and violently squirted out of the planet.'
                      Embedded Clause

Triangle-convention reports for the headless version Here is a generic picture of the headless *wh-* embedded clause in its host noun group. The examples given earlier are reported below it in triangle-convention form.

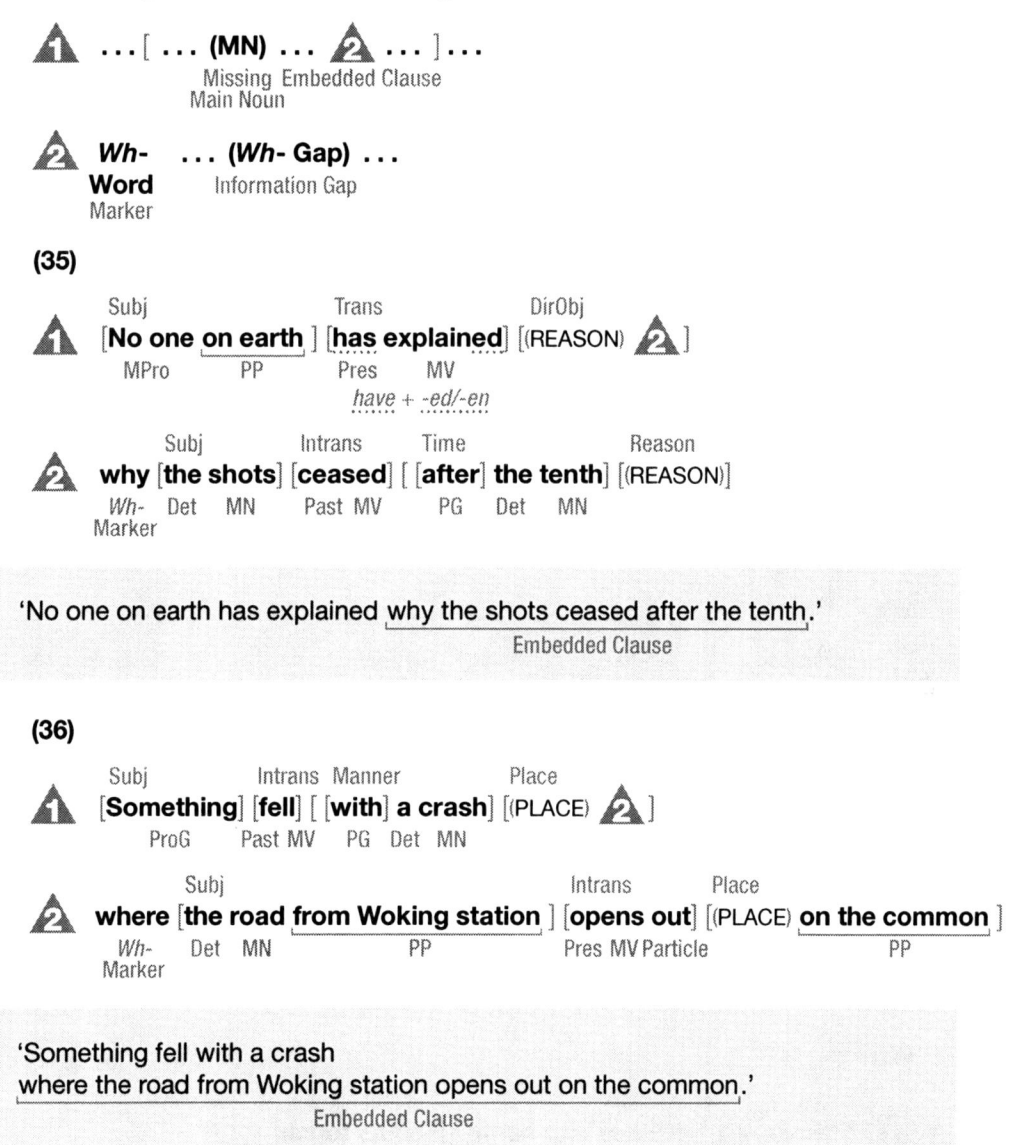

‹1 ... [... **(MN)** ... ‹2 ...] ...
          Missing Embedded Clause
          Main Noun

‹2 **Wh-**   ... **(Wh- Gap)** ...
  Word   Information Gap
  Marker

(35)

     Subj   Trans   DirObj
‹1 [**No one on earth**] [**has explained**] [(REASON) ‹2]
   MPro   PP   Pres   MV
                       have + -ed/-en

       Subj   Intrans   Time   Reason
‹2 **why** [**the shots**] [**ceased**] [[**after**] **the tenth**] [(REASON)]
  Wh- Det   MN   Past MV   PG   Det   MN
  Marker

‘No one on earth has explained why the shots ceased after the tenth.’
                                 Embedded Clause

(36)

    Subj   Intrans Manner   Place
‹1 [**Something**] [**fell**] [[**with**] **a crash**] [(PLACE) ‹2]
   ProG   Past MV   PG   Det MN

      Subj   Intrans   Place
‹2 **where** [**the road from Woking station**] [**opens out**] [(PLACE) **on the common**]
  Wh-   Det   MN   PP   Pres MV Particle   PP
  Marker

‘Something fell with a crash
where the road from Woking station opens out on the common.’
                        Embedded Clause

Discontinuity: extraposition *Wh-* embedded clauses can be extraposed to the right toward the end of a clause. Discontinuity is a **syntactic** resource that English exploits, as was noted, for example, in Chapter 6 with respect to the role of the left-hand edge of the verb group in the specification of questions. Moreover, Chapter 10 describes in some detail the role of **extraposition** in expressions with non*wh-*clauses. Here we demonstrate extraposed *wh-* embedded clauses, which result in discontinuous noun groups.

(37) The star left a greenish streak behind it that glowed for some seconds.

(38) We saw a rush of smoke, far away up the river, that jerked up into the air.

(39) Then came a violent crash, quite close to us, that shook the ground.

Finally, in Chapter 7 we said that with regard to examples (5) through (10) in that chapter we might want to come back and take notice of some noun groups that were less than completely obvious. Check out examples (6) and (7) from Chapter 7 again, repeated below as (40) and (41). *However it is done* and *Whatever is combustible* are both noun groups, each with a headless *wh-* embedded clause.

(40)

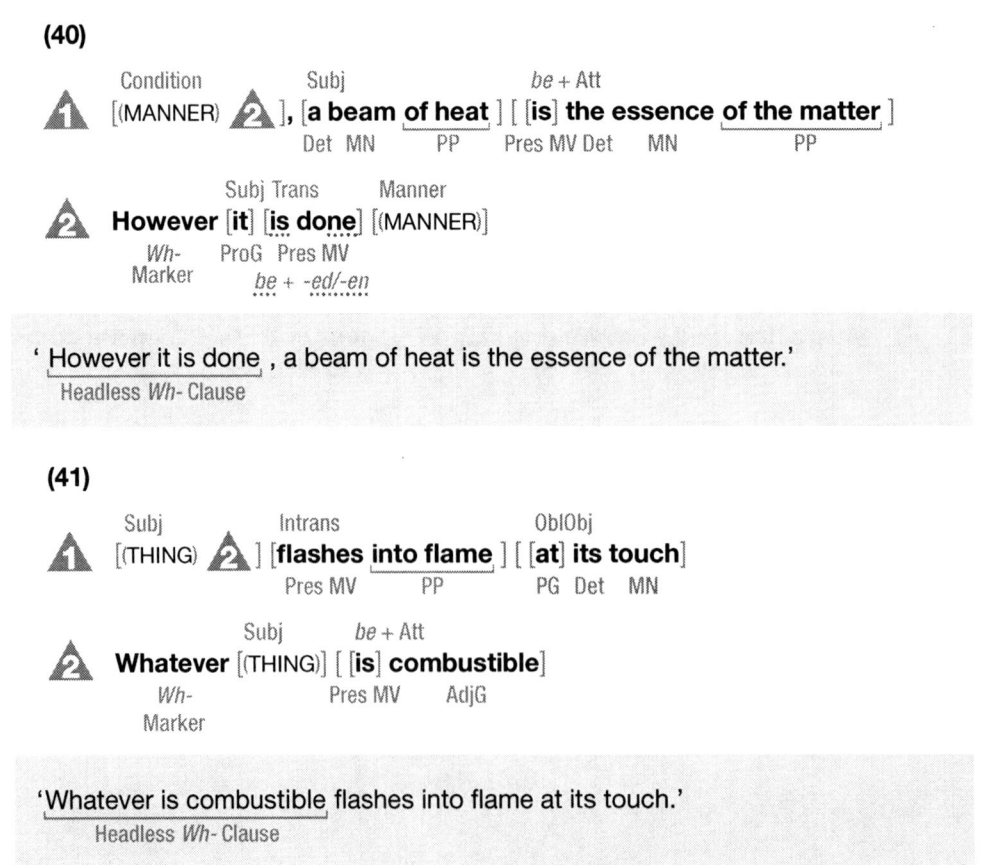

	Condition		Subj		*be* + Att
1	[(MANNER)	**2**],	[a beam of heat]	[[is]	the essence of the matter]
			Det MN	PP	Pres MV Det MN PP

		Subj	Trans	Manner
2	However	[it]	[is done]	[(MANNER)]
	Wh- Marker		ProG Pres MV	
			be + *-ed/-en*	

' However it is done , a beam of heat is the essence of the matter.'
Headless *Wh-* Clause

(41)

	Subj		Intrans	OblObj
1	[(THING)	**2**]	[flashes into flame]	[[at] its touch]
			Pres MV PP	PG Det MN

		Subj	*be* + Att
2	Whatever	[(THING)]	[[is] combustible]
	Wh- Marker		Pres MV AdjG

'Whatever is combustible flashes into flame at its touch.'
Headless *Wh-* Clause

Restrictive and nonrestrictive relationships between clauses Sometimes an embedded clause is absolutely necessary to the identification of the head of the host noun group. On the other hand, sometimes the embedded clause simply adds information, but not information that is vital to knowing the unique identity of the host main noun. When embedded information is vital, it is called ***restrictive***. When it is not absolutely necessary to the identification of the host main noun, it is called ***nonrestrictive***. Generally, these terms are applied just to embedded *wh-* clauses, but you will occasionally see them used in reference to any satellite of the main noun within a noun group and sometimes to other forms of modification, too. Here are some examples of restrictive and nonrestrictive *wh-* clauses from *The War of the Worlds*. Notice that one convention of written English punctuation is that the nonrestrictive clauses are all set off by commas.

Restrictive

(42)   And this was the little world in which I had been living securely for years ,
                                      Embedded Clause
        this fiery chaos!

(43)   The officers who were not actively engaged stood and stared over the
                        Embedded Clause
        treetops southwestward, and the men digging would stop every now
                                               Embedded Clause
        and again to stare in the same direction.

(44)   The people who landed there from the boats went tramping off
                    Embedded Clause
        down the lane.

Nonrestrictive

(45)   Except the lodge at the Orphanage, which was still on fire , none of the
                                        Embedded Clause
        houses had suffered very greatly here.

(46)   The idea people seemed to have here was that the Martians were simply
        formidable human beings, who might attack and sack the town , to be
                                    Embedded Clause
        certainly destroyed in the end.

(47)   London, which had gone to bed on Sunday night oblivious and inert ,
                    Embedded Clause
        was awakened, in the small hours of Monday morning, to a vivid sense
        of danger.

Apposition and embedding It has frequently been noted that some *whiz*-type nonrestrictive embedded clauses look (and sometimes sound) a whole lot like appositives. In some instances it may be difficult to distinguish one from the other, even with ample surrounding context. That is, it is often possible for a structure to be *interpreted* as either an appositive or as a nonrestrictive *wh-* embedded clause. However, appositives and *wh-* clauses are structurally distinct, as we mentioned in the last chapter. Appositives are functional coequals, *wh-* clauses are embeddings. Here's an example of what I mean.

> (48) As my brother began to realize the import of all these things, he turned hastily to his own room, put all his available money—*some ten pounds altogether*—into his pockets, and went out again into the streets.

The coequal elements in an appositive relationship refer to exactly the same elements of the event structure; that is, they are said to be strictly coreferential. And in (48), the *whiz*-type embedded clause (*some ten pounds altogether*) might appear superficially to have the same event-structure reference as *all his available money*.

However, on closer inspection, it is clear that the sense of *all his available money* gets lost when you substitute *some ten pounds altogether* for it. *Put all his available money into his pockets* and *put ten pounds altogether into his pockets* are equivalent only if their equivalence can somehow be recovered from the rest of the context. The purpose of *some ten pounds altogether* is to specify the extent of *his available money*, so the two elements are not coequal; the one specifies rather than renames the other.

Likewise, an appositive relationship functions as one constituent of the event structure, and each of the appositive elements can realize exactly the same function in the clause. However, given that in (48) *some ten pounds altogether* specifies *available money*, it cannot function as the direct object of *put*, as it would if it were appositive.

Now, compare (49), in which the appositive *the Astronomer Royal* is completely interchangeable with *Stent*. In (50), *Lord Hilton* and *the lord of the manor* are also appositive alternates for one another.

> (49) Going to the edge of the pit, I found it occupied by a group of about half a dozen men—Henderson, Ogilvy, and a tall, fair-haired man that I afterwards learned was <u>Stent, the Astronomer Royal</u>, with several workmen wielding spades and pickaxes. Stent was giving directions in a clear, high-pitched voice.

> (50) As soon as Ogilvy saw me among the staring crowd on the edge of the pit he called to me to come down, and asked me if I would mind going over to see <u>Lord Hilton, the lord of the manor</u>.

Practice with Terminology

What follows is a preview of the sentences that you will encounter in this chapter's Sentences for Analysis. Certain elements in the sentences have been underscored. Label each underscored element using one or more of the following terms or an applicable term from a previous chapter. Check the Glossary if you are not certain about the definition of any of the terms.

Adjective clause	Hypotactic relationship	Relative clause
Adverb clause	Missing element	*Wh-* clause (specify 'normal,'
Embedding	Nominal (noun) clause	'missing-marker,' '*whiz*,' or
Extraposition	Paratactic relationship	'headless')
Formal preposing	Participial phrase	*Wh-* gap
		Wh- marker

> **Note:** You do not need to limit your choices to the new terms from this chapter. Where appropriate, use an applicable term from any previous chapter.

1   That last stage of exhaustion, <u>to us still incredibly remote</u>, has become a present-day problem for the inhabitants of Mars.

2   This blaze <u>may have been</u> the casting of the huge gun from which their shots were fired at us.

3   I felt my way <u>in the darkness</u> to the little table where the siphon stood.

4   <u>Whatever</u> is combustible flashes into flame at its touch.

5   A little crowd surrounded <u>the</u> huge hole in which the cylinder lay.

6   I do not know when they learned of the things <u>happening beyond the hill</u>.

7   When he saw Henderson, <u>the London journalist</u>, in his garden, he called over the palings.

8   The little group of black specks carrying the flag of white <u>had been</u> swept out of existence.

9   Among the group of bystanders were a girl carrying a baby and a gardener <u>I sometimes employed</u>.

10   I met <u>two or three</u> loafers and golf caddies who usually hung about the railway station.

11   He was standing on the cylinder, which [. . .] was now evidently much cooler.

12   <u>How</u> he came to be standing on the cylinder nobody could guess.

13   We don't know what's in the <u>confounded</u> mechanism.

14   There was a mouth under the eyes, <u>the lipless brim of which</u> quivered and panted.

15   <u>A number of</u> shop people, attracted by the stories they had heard, were walking over the Horsell Bridge.

16   What could <u>be going</u> on there?

17 I noted a little black knot of men, the foremost of whom was waving a white flag.

18 A quantity of luminous greenish smoke came out of the pit in three distinct puffs, which drove up straight into the still air.

19 I heard the sudden squeal of a horse that was suddenly stilled.

20 The common seemed now dark, except where its roadways lay grey and pale.

21 Overhead the stars were mustering in a sky that was still a pale, bright, almost greenish blue.

22 The Martians and their appliances were altogether invisible, save for that thin mast upon which their restless mirror wobbled.

23 They are the most sluggish things I ever saw.

24 How could Mars have inhabitants who were signalling us?

25 In Woking the shops had closed when the tragedy happened.

26 Nobody knows how the Martians are able to slay men so swiftly and so silently.

27 Those who have never seen a living Martian can scarcely imagine the strange horror of its appearance.

28 There may have been a crowd of three hundred people at this place, besides those leaving the road.

29 There were three policemen too, one of whom was mounted.

30 There was some booing from those thoughtless and excitable souls to whom a crowd is always an occasion for noise and horse-play.

31 Where the road grows narrow and black between the high banks the crowd jammed, and a desperate struggle occurred.

32 I could not tell them what I had seen.

33 But I told my wife the things I had seen.

34 The dinner, which was a cold one, had already been served.

35 I pointed out the bright dot of light that so many telescopes were pointed toward.

36 They may keep the pit and kill people who [. . .] come near them, but they cannot get out of it.

37 People rattling Londonwards peered into the darkness and saw a thin veil of smoke driving across the stars.

38 You could not have found one human being whose emotions were not affected by the newcomers.

39 I have already described the behaviour of the men and women to whom I spoke.

40 When I saw her deadly white face, I ceased abruptly.

41 They did not know who had authorized the movements of the troops.

42 You can't tell what they might do.

43 I was not satisfied by what I already knew.

44 When the <u>next</u> flash came, I saw a sturdy man, cheaply but not shabbily dressed.

45 I <u>narrowly</u> escaped an accident at the corner of the road to Pyrford, where a knot of people stood with their backs to me.

46 For a minute he scarcely realiz<u>ed</u> what this meant.

47 Machine it was, with long tentacles, <u>one of which</u> gripped a young pine tree.

48 I saw along the western horizon a <u>blood-red</u> glow that crept slowly up the sky.

49 It <u>was the landlord of the Spotted Dog, whose conveyance I had taken</u>.

50 I overcame the repugnance natural to one <u>who had never before touched a dead body</u>.

A note on terminology In many traditional grammars, normal embedded *wh-* clauses are referred to as **relative clauses** or **adjective clauses**, and their *wh-* marker is called a **relative pronoun**. Missing-marker embedded *wh-* clauses are said to have a zero relative pronoun. Moreover, headless embedded *wh-* clauses are called either **nominal relatives, nominal clauses** or **noun clauses** if they function as subject, object, or attribute, and **adverb clauses** if they function as circumstance. Finally, embedded *wh-* clauses in which both the *wh-* marker and a form of the primary auxiliary *be* are missing (*whiz* version) are traditionally not called clauses but rather **participial phrases**—and more recently **reduced relatives**.

However, we have settled here on the uniform term, *wh-* clause, to unite these divergent terms into one. Using the term *wh-* clause recognizes that all process-based units are clauses. It also avoids the problem of applying to entire clauses the part-of-speech labels **adjective**, **adverb**, and **noun**. We trade a couple of terms (*wh-* **clause** and *wh-* **marker**) for many (**relative clause, adjective clause, relative pronoun, zero relative pronoun, nominal relative, nominal clause, noun clause, adverb clause, participial phrase, and reduced relative**).

Analyzing and Reporting Multiclausal Sentences

In much the same way that we have followed a step-by-step process in analyzing and reporting the structure of individual clauses, we should also adopt a procedure by which the details of clause complexes containing two or more clauses can be observed and reported. One idea is to follow a charting procedure, keeping track of the steps you have taken to analyze the complex. Each step should be something that you are confident about doing. Here is an example:

> **(51) The sailors and lightermen had to fight savagely against the people who swarmed upon them from the riverfront.**

Step 1: *Identifying processes* Start a chart by identifying processes and opening up the minimal number of functional spots for the requisite participant roles for each one. Label the process and participant functions. In example (51) there are two processes:

> The sailors and lightermen <u>had to fight</u> savagely against the people
> who <u>swarmed</u> upon them from the riverfront.

The chart:

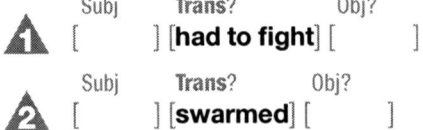

Both *fight* and *swarm* could entail either one or two directly expressible participant roles, so let's tentatively call them transitive and open places for two participants for each, just to be safe. While you are identifying processes and opening up participant slots on the chart, take note of passive-voice verb groups (*be + -ed/-en*). The passive voice is accompanied by a participant-function reversal in which an active-voice object appears as the passive-voice subject, and the active-voice subject appears as an oblique object, usually introduced with *by*. In the example we are developing here, there are no passive-voice clauses.

Step 2: *Studying the complex and filling in the requisite participant slots on the chart* Using the logic of the event structure to do this step, seek out the role-players that are required for each process; they will usually be right in the neighborhood of the process. The only directly expressed role-players for either process in this example are the subjects (the second of which is a missing element), so let's change the label for both from 'Trans' to 'Intrans'. After you do this step, the only clause content left unaccounted for in the complex will be circumstances, clause markers, or relationship and discourse elements. Below the participants are underscored:

> The sailors and lightermen had to fight savagely against the people
> who swarmed upon them from the riverfront.

The chart continues:

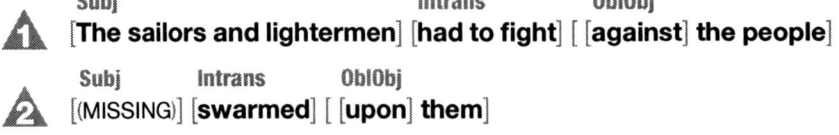

Step 3: *Doing the math* Every complex has hypotactic and paratactic relationships among clauses, and all of these relationships are marked as either (a) conjoined, or (b) *wh-*, or (c) non*wh-*. However, one of the clauses is the host clause and does not have a marker. Therefore, after you count the processes, you subtract one (for the host clause), and the remainder will be the number of marked clauses, and therefore

the number of markers, you will find. *Take care:* some *wh-* clauses could be double-marked (see Chapter 10), and it's always possible that a marker could be understood (a missing element). Take your time over this step; it'll be worth it.

Here's the math for our example:

	Two processes identified:	2
minus	One (for the host clause):	−1
yields	<u>One</u> marker needed:	1

Step 4: *Finding markers and adding them to your chart* Remember that all markers (except the nonfinite clause markers, free *-ing* and *to*, which are at the far left-hand edge of the verb group—see Chapter 9) occur out in front of the clause. All markers (including free *-ing* and *to*) are charted and reported to the left of their clauses. Allow for the formal style in which preposition groups and determiners that might otherwise be inside the boundaries of a clause get pulled out to form a unit with the marker—see, for example, (42) above. Our example here has an overt *wh-* marker:

**The sailors and lightermen had to fight savagely against the people
who swarmed upon them from the riverfront.**

Subj   Intrans   OblObj
Host ① [**The sailors and lightermen**] [**had to fight**] [[**against**] **the people**]

Subj   Intrans   OblObj
② **who** [(MISSING)] [**swarmed**] [[**upon**] **them**]

After this step, the only items left to account for in the clause complex must be either (a) circumstances or (b) relationship and discourse elements.

Step 5: *Taking stock* Locate circumstance, relationship, and discourse units. The remaining units in the clause complex are underscored.

**The sailors and lightermen had to fight <u>savagely</u> against the people
who swarmed upon them <u>from the riverfront</u>.**

What do you make of what's left? Here are a couple of possibilities:

savagely sounds like the way in which the sailors and lightermen had to fight, so it probably belongs in the circumstance category

from the riverfront sounds like a place from which something originates—also a circumstance

Step 6: *Adding circumstance, relationship, and discourse units to your chart* Amend participants as required. Fill in missing elements as required. You might have to refer to the context of the passage.

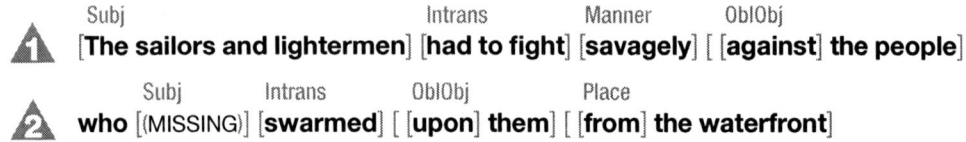

All that remains is to make sure that each embedded and subordinate clause has a place to dock in its host clause. In this example we still have not resolved the problem of the missing-element subject in the *wh-* clause—and because the nature of the event structure would lead us to conclude that it was the *people* that did the swarming, we have the ideal spot at which to plug in the *wh-* clause: just to the right of *people* in the oblique object in the upper clause.

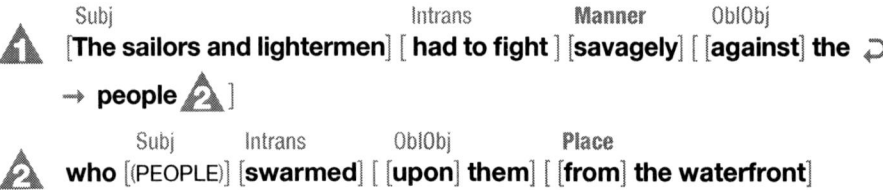

Step 7: *Finishing the triangle-convention report* The 'chart' has evolved into a triangle-convention report. All that remains is to observe minimal bracketing and labeling protocol.

'The sailors and lightermen had to fight savagely against the people who swarmed upon them from the riverfront.'

Sentences for Analysis

The following sentences are adapted from *The War of the Worlds*. Analyze them and report your results as shown in the example below. Make certain that your analyses have the following features:

a Bracket processes, participants, and circumstances and label them by function at the top of the bracket.

b Sub-bracket as necessary, observing minimal bracketing conventions.

c Label elements in all word groups. Single-element groups are normally given the group label.

d Follow the triangle convention in reporting embedded clauses.

(52)

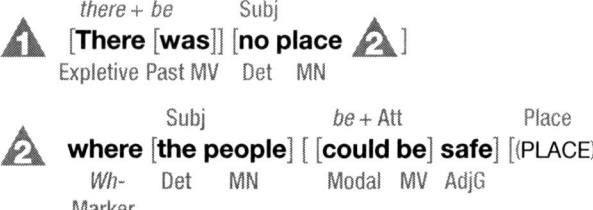

1 That last stage of exhaustion, to us still incredibly remote, has become a present-day problem for the inhabitants of Mars. (***Whiz***)

✱ 2 This blaze may have been the casting of the huge gun from which their shots were fired at us. (**Formal preposing**)

3 I felt my way in the darkness to the little table where the siphon stood.

4 Whatever is combustible flashes into flame at its touch.

5 A little crowd surrounded the huge hole in which the cylinder lay. (**Formal preposing**)

6 I do not know when they learned of the things happening beyond the hill.

7 When he saw Henderson, the London journalist, in his garden, he called over the palings.

8 The little group of black specks carrying the flag of white had been swept out of existence. (***Whiz***)

✱ 9 Among the group of bystanders were a girl carrying a baby and a gardener I sometimes employed.

10 I met two or three loafers and golf caddies who usually hung about the railway station.

11 He was standing on the cylinder, which was now evidently much cooler. (**Normal**)

12 How he came to be standing on the cylinder nobody could guess.

13 We don't know what's in the confounded mechanism.

* 14 There was a mouth under the eyes, the lipless brim of which quivered and panted. (**Formal preposing**)

15 A number of shop people, attracted by the stories they had heard, were walking over the Horsell Bridge.

16 What could be going on there?

17 I noted a little black knot of men, the foremost of whom was waving a white flag.

18 A quantity of luminous greenish smoke came out of the pit in three distinct puffs, which drove up straight into the still air. (**Normal**)

19 I heard the sudden squeal of a horse that was suddenly stilled.

20 The common seemed now dark, except where its roadways lay grey and pale.

* 21 Overhead the stars were mustering in a sky that was still a pale, bright, almost greenish blue. (**Normal**)

22 The Martians and their appliances were altogether invisible, save for that thin mast upon which their restless mirror wobbled.

23 They are the most sluggish things I ever saw. (**Missing-marker**)

24 How could Mars have inhabitants who were signalling us? (**Normal**)

25 In Woking the shops had closed when the tragedy happened.

26 Nobody knows how the Martians are able to slay men so swiftly and so silently. (**Headless**)

27 Those who have never seen a living Martian can scarcely imagine the strange horror of its appearance.

28 There may have been a crowd of three hundred people at this place, besides those leaving the road.

* 29 There were three policemen too, one of whom was mounted. (**Formal preposing**)

30 There was some booing from those thoughtless and excitable souls to whom a crowd is always an occasion for noise and horse-play.

31 Where the road grows narrow and black between the high banks the crowd jammed, and a desperate struggle occurred.

32 I could not tell them what I had seen. (**Headless**)

33 But I told my wife the things I had seen. (**Missing-marker**)

34 The dinner, which was a cold one, had already been served. (**Normal**)

35 I pointed out the bright dot of light that so many telescopes were pointed toward. (**Normal**)

36 They may keep the pit and kill people who come near them, but they cannot get out of it.

37 People rattling Londonwards peered into the darkness and saw a thin veil of smoke driving across the stars.

✳ 38   You could not have found one human being whose emotions were not affected by the newcomers. (**Normal**)

39   I have already described the behaviour of the men and women <u>to whom I spoke.</u> (**Formal preposing**)

40   When I saw her deadly white face, I ceased abruptly.

41   They did not know <u>who had authorized the movements of the troops.</u>

42   You can't tell <u>what they might do.</u> (**Headless**)

43   I was not satisfied by what I already knew.

✳ 44   When the next flash came, I saw a sturdy man, <u>cheaply but not shabbily dressed.</u> (**Headless; *Whiz***)

45   I narrowly escaped an accident at the corner of the road to Pyrford, <u>where a knot of people stood with their backs to me.</u>

46   For a minute he scarcely realized <u>what this meant.</u> (**Headless**)

47   Machine it was, with long tentacles, one of which gripped a young pine tree. (**Formal preposing**)

48   I saw along the western horizon a blood-red glow that crept slowly up the sky.

✳ 49   It was the landlord of the Spotted Dog, <u>whose conveyance I had taken.</u>

50   I overcame the repugnance natural to one who had never before touched a dead body. (***Whiz*; Normal**)

Note: Suggested responses for the sentences marked by an asterisk (✳) are given at the back of the book. As a way of getting started on this activity, you might want to work first on those items. Some of the other items have a hint. The *wh-* clause is underscored in some, and the *wh-* clause type is provided for some others. Where your responses and the suggested ones differ, you will want to get advice from your instructor. Very often, several interpretations might be appropriate.

Chapter 9

Non*wh-* Subordinate Clauses

Preliminaries

The primary function of language is to represent the events that occur in our ordinary everyday experience.

At the level of the clause, the structure of language is in very nice balance with the structure of events. The main constituents of clauses and those of events are very much the same. Processes represent the core nature of events. Participants play the roles and act as essential props. Circumstances set the scene by providing details about the when, where, why, and how of an event.

In representing event structure, the process is the central element, and the verb group is most often the main bearer of the core sense of the event. Verb groups also figure centrally in specifying whether a clause is to be taken as a statement, a question, a request, or a condition. The verb group can also signal that the clause is nonfinite and therefore not the main (uppermost) clause. Clauses with nonfinite verb groups can be either subordinate or embedded; we turn to these matters in this chapter and the next.

Clauses can be put together by either (a) conjoining one with another in a series or sequence, or (b) sliding one into another, much as one might stack one mixing bowl or one measuring spoon inside another. Chapter 8 gave some consideration to one form of clause combining: *wh-* embedding. In this chapter we consider an additional type, **non*wh-* subordination**.

Then Chapter 10 will take up two additional forms of combining, **non*wh-* embedding** and **non*wh-* apposition**, and it will, additionally, consider some English-language structures, *wh-* **hybrids** and *wh-* **double-markeds**, which appear to combine the features of *wh-* relationships on the one hand and non*wh-* clause marking on the other.

Non*wh*- Subordinate Clauses

Here again is the passage from *The War of the Worlds* that we first used back in Chapter 1. This time I have put four clause markers in boxes. The clauses that follow these markers are not embedded in noun groups nor are their markers *wh*- words. These are non*wh*- clauses.

(1) No one would have believed in the last years of the nineteenth century (that) this world was being watched keenly and closely by intelligences greater than man's and yet as mortal as his own; (that) as men busied themselves about their various concerns they were scrutinized and studied, perhaps almost as narrowly as a man with a microscope might scrutinize the transient creatures that swarm and multiply in a drop of water. With infinite complacency men went to and fro over this globe about their little affairs, serene in their assurance of their empire over matter. It is possible (that) the infusoria under the microscope do the same. No one gave a thought to the older worlds of space as sources of human danger, or thought of them only to dismiss the idea of life upon them as impossible or improbable. It is curious to recall some of the mental habits of those departed days. At most terrestrial men fancied ((THAT)) there might be other men upon Mars, perhaps inferior to themselves and ready to welcome a missionary enterprise. Yet across the gulf of space, minds that are to our minds as ours are to those of the beasts that perish, intellects vast and cool and unsympathetic, regarded this earth with envious eyes, and slowly and surely drew their plans against us. And early in the twentieth century came the great disillusionment.

The word *that* Seven occurrences of *that* have been marked in the passage above. You will recognize three of them (the third, sixth, and seventh, underscored) as markers of *wh*- relationships (isolated as examples (2), (3), and (4) below).

(2) . . . the transient creatures that swarm and multiply in a drop of water.

(3) . . . minds that are to our minds as ours are to those of the beasts that perish, . . .

(4) . . . the beasts that perish, . . .

The other four occurrences mark clauses that are not *wh*- embedded clauses. These four (the first, second, fourth, and fifth, in text boxes) mark the non*wh*- subordinate clauses that are isolated below at (5), (6), (7), and (8).

(5) . . . that this world was being watched keenly and closely by intelligences greater than man's and yet as mortal as his own . . .

(6) ... that ... they were scrutinized and studied, perhaps almost as narrowly as a man with a microscope might scrutinize the transient creatures that swarm and multiply in a drop of water.

(7) ... that the infusoria under the microscope do the same.

(8) ... (THAT) there might be other men upon Mars, perhaps inferior to themselves and ready to welcome a missionary enterprise.

The word *that* has more than one job. It might in fact be best considered as more than one word. Examples (2) through (8) show that *that* can be used as both a *wh*- marker and as a **non*wh*- marker**.

Here are some examples of other uses for *that*. In (9), *that* is a pronoun, in (10) it is a determiner, and in (11) it is part of the **comparative** marker set, *so ... that*. *That* can even be used as an intensifier: I'll bet you didn't know it had *that* many uses! *That* is in a league with *be* when it comes to its pervasiveness and versatility.

(9) ... the midday temperature barely approaches *that* of our coldest winter.

(10) *That* last stage of exhaustion ... has become a present-day problem for the inhabitants of Mars.

(11) The thought of the confined creature was *so* dreadful to him *that* he forgot the heat and went forward to the cylinder to help turn.

Other non*wh*- markers Non*wh*- clauses are introduced by a very large set of markers that does not overlap the set of *wh*- markers, except, as we just saw, the word *that* (and, very rarely, *when*). By comparison with the non*wh*- markers, the *wh*- set is tiny, indeed. Here's a sampling of non*wh*- markers (see List 9.1):

after, although, as, as far as, as if, as long as, as soon as, as though, assuming (that), because, before, but that, considering (that), even if, excepting (that), for ... to, free -ing, given (that), granted (that), granting (that), if, in that, in order that, in the event that, like, now (that), once, provided (that), providing (that), seeing (that), since, so (that), such that, supposing (that), that, though, till, to, (to), unless, until, whereas, whereupon, whether, while, ...

A non*wh*- clause introduced by all but four of these has either tense or modal at the left-hand edge of its verb group. However, when either the free -*ing* or the *to* marker occurs (underscored above), the marker itself is at the left-hand edge of the verb group, displacing both tense and modal. These two are the **nonfinite clause markers**, so called because they cannot contribute to the timeframe of an event in the way that both tense and modal can (see Chapter 5).

List 9.1 *Some Common (and Not-So-Common) Clause Markers*

For *wh-* clauses (Chapter 8)	how, however, howsoever, that, what, whatever, whatsoever, when, whenever, where, wherever, wheresoever, which, whichever, who, whoever, whosoever, whom, whomever, whomsoever, whose, whosesoever, why, whyever
For non*wh-* clauses (this chapter)	after, although, as, as far as, as if, as long as, as soon as, as though, assuming (that), because, before, but that, considering (that), even if, excepting (that), for, for . . . to, free *-ing*, given (that), granted (that), granting (that), if, in that, in order that, in order to, in the event that, like, now (that), once, poss . . . free *-ing*, provided (that), providing (that), seeing (that), since, so (that), such that, supposing (that), that, (that), though, till, to, (to), unless, until, when, whereas, whereupon, whether (to), while, . . .

Free *-ing* is called 'free' because it does not occur in combination with a form of *be*, as it would if it were part of the auxiliary in a verb group. This is demonstrated in (12). Free *-ing* sometimes appears as *poss(essive)* . . . *-ing* in its more formal applications. In these places, the free *-ing* form of the verb will be accompanied by the possessive (*poss*) form of the subject of the clause, as in (13). You will rarely encounter this structure in contemporary English; it might in fact sound very formal, perhaps even peculiar, to you.

Free -ing:

  (12) **Looking through the telescope, one saw a circle of deep blue and the little round planet swimming in the field.**

Poss . . . -ing (*a variant of Free* -ing)

  (13) **He was full of speculation that night about the condition of Mars, and scoffed at the vulgar idea of its having inhabitants who were signalling us.**

Traditionally, non*wh-* subordinate clauses introduced by free *-ing* (or poss . . . *-ing*) have been called **gerunds** or **gerund phrases** and sometimes **participles** or **participial phrases**. However, to keep things simple, we will just use the name of the marker and call them *free -ing clauses* or use the generic term *nonfinite clause*, which can also be used in referring to any non*wh-* subordinate clause marked with *to*.

The marker *to*, which introduces **infinitives** (or infinitive clauses), sometimes appears as part of the discontinuous set *for . . . to*, as shown in (14).

> **(14) It was too far for me to recognize anyone there, but afterwards I learned that Ogilvy, Stent, and Henderson were with others in this attempt at communication.**

An infinitive clause can also appear to be missing a marker altogether, in which case it is said to be the **zero infinitive** or the **bare infinitive**. When the *to* is missing, the left-hand edge of the verb group appears to be empty.

> **(15) He grew calmer telling me and trying to make me <u>see</u> the things he had seen.**

To detect that the verb group in (15) has a nonfinite missing marker, try substituting the word *cause* for *make*. Do you hear *to* pop up in front of *see*? With some verbs, like *cause*, we expect to hear *to*, with others, like *make*, we don't.

The particle *to* that appears at the end of several semiauxiliary verbs (such as *appear to*, *be able to*, *be about to*, and so forth) is historically related to the nonfinite non*wh*- marker *to*. In fact, the entire category of semiauxiliary verb is very fluid, reflecting the process by which some main verbs have come to be used as auxiliaries as the language changed over time.

You will notice that many of the non*wh*- markers in List 9.1 are just like *that* in that they do double and triple and quadruple duty—sometimes as particles in multiword verbs, sometimes as main prepositions in preposition groups, sometimes as main adverbs in adverb groups, and so forth.

You might also have noticed that some non*wh*- markers begin with the letters *w* and *h*. Their spelling does not automatically qualify them as *wh*- markers, of course. In order to be a *wh*- marker, a word must be able to signal an information gap. The words in this list that begin with *wh*- (*whereas, whereupon, whether, while*) cannot do that. Try it out. Can you begin a normal content question with *while*?

Non*wh*- subordination The term *subordination* is applied to non*wh*- clauses that appear anywhere you might otherwise find a noun group. Well, *nearly* anywhere (see below). In a sense, then, whereas embedded *wh*- clauses (Chapter 8) serve to expand noun groups, non*wh*- subordinate clauses appear to function as noun-group substitutes—when you consider the wide range of uses to which noun groups can be put.

Where noun groups fit in a clause (reprise) As we established back in Chapter 7, you will find noun groups performing functions almost everywhere in a clause:

a Noun groups can be attributes in attributive processes.

b Noun groups can be locations in locative processes.

c Noun groups can be complements to preposition groups.

d Noun groups can represent circumstances.

e Noun groups can represent participants.

f Noun groups can be in the pre-central spot in adjective groups.

g Noun groups can be modifiers within other noun groups.

Non*wh*- subordinate clauses can be found performing most of these noun-group functions. Non*wh*- subordinate clauses will be found *nearly* anywhere you might otherwise find a noun group. Non*wh*- subordinate clauses occupy a bracketed unit all by themselves *almost* any place that a noun group otherwise could be. I say *nearly* and *almost* because it is unlikely that you would find a non*wh*- clause naming a location in a locative process (b). Similarly, non*wh*- clauses don't usually appear in adjective groups or noun groups in front of the main word (f and g), although they can be embedded in adjective groups and noun groups after the main word (more on this in Chapter 10).

In (h), (i), and (j), we provide a summary of the places where you are likely to encounter non*wh*- subordinate and embedded clauses:

h Non*wh*- subordinate clauses appear as constituents of the event structure itself as noun groups otherwise would do: as participants, or circumstances, or as attributes in processes.

i Non*wh*- subordinate clauses can serve as complements to preposition groups to form prepositional phrases, another high-frequency function for noun groups.

j Finally, as we will see in Chapter 10, in contrast to non*wh*- subordinate clauses, non*wh*- embedded clauses can be found as complements in noun groups and adjective groups following the main word.

ACTIVITY **9.1**

Several examples of non*wh*- subordinate clauses occur in the following passages from *The War of the Worlds*. The non*wh*- clauses and their markers are underscored. Decide whether the non*wh*- clauses function as either process, participant, circumstance, or complement to preposition groups. Some suggested responses are given at the back of the book.

Don't be concerned that this might seem a bit overwhelming here. We will unravel some of the complexities as the chapter moves along.

(16) The secular cooling that must someday overtake our planet has already gone far indeed with our neighbour. Its physical condition is still largely a mystery, but we know now that even in its equatorial region the midday temperature barely approaches that of our coldest winter. Its air is much more attenuated than ours, its oceans have shrunk until they cover but a third of its surface, and as its slow seasons change huge snowcaps gather and melt about either pole and periodically inundate its temperate zones. That last stage of exhaustion, which to us is still incredibly remote, has become a present-day problem for the inhabitants of Mars. The immediate pressure of necessity has brightened their intellects, enlarged their powers, and hardened their hearts. And looking across space with instruments, and intelligences such as we have scarcely dreamed of, they see, at its nearest distance only 35,000,000 of miles sunward of them, a morning star of hope, our own warmer planet, green with vegetation and grey with water, with a cloudy atmosphere eloquent of fertility, with glimpses through its drifting cloud wisps of broad stretches of populous country and narrow, navy-crowded seas.

(17) I remember how I sat on the table there in the blackness, with patches of green and crimson swimming before my eyes.

(18) He was full of speculation that night about the condition of Mars, and scoffed at the vulgar idea of its having inhabitants who were signalling us.

Non*wh*- clauses are accounted for in triangle-convention reports just as *wh*- clauses are. The major difference between the two is that subordinate non*wh*- clauses can occupy a functional bracketed (often labeled) space of their own. That is, they are most often constituents of clauses or complements of preposition groups. On the other hand, *wh*- clauses are *always* embedded in a noun group. Chart 9.1 shows the distinction between reporting conventions for *wh*- and non*wh*- clauses.

Chart 9.1 *A Comparison of Wh- Clause Embedding with Nonwh- Clause Subordination*

Embedded *wh*- clause	
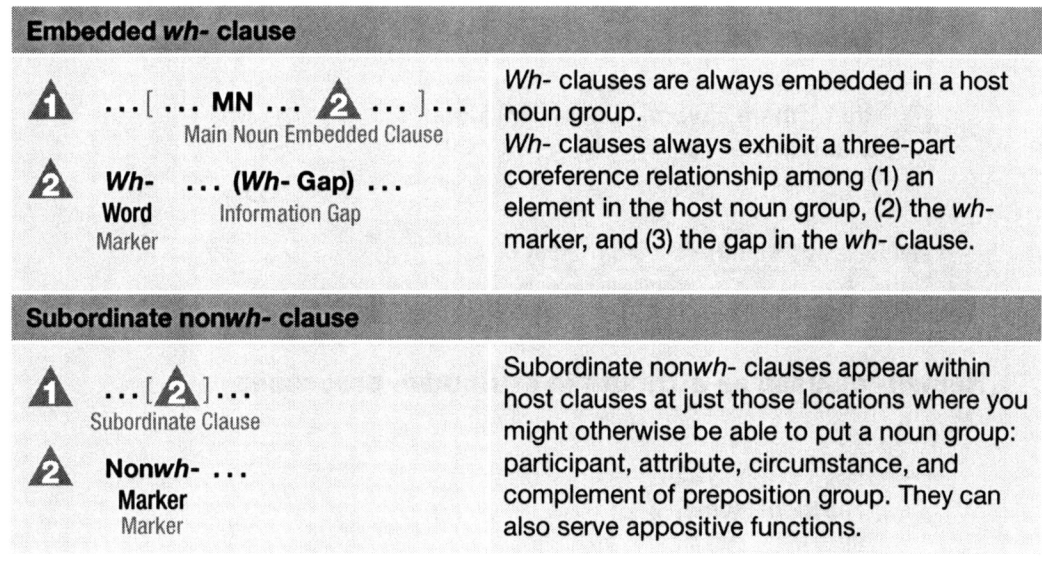	*Wh*- clauses are always embedded in a host noun group. *Wh*- clauses always exhibit a three-part coreference relationship among (1) an element in the host noun group, (2) the *wh*- marker, and (3) the gap in the *wh*- clause.

Subordinate non*wh*- clause	
	Subordinate non*wh*- clauses appear within host clauses at just those locations where you might otherwise be able to put a noun group: participant, attribute, circumstance, and complement of preposition group. They can also serve appositive functions.

In addition to their subordinate function, non*wh*- clauses can be embedded (see Chapter 10) as complements in host noun groups. However, in contrast to the *wh*- information gaps in embedded *wh*- clauses, missing participants in non*wh*- clauses cannot exhibit coreference relationships with the main noun in the host noun group. Non*wh*- clauses can also be embedded as complements in adjective groups (*wh*- clauses cannot).

Here are several examples of the various functions that can be performed by non*wh*-subordinate clauses.

Nonwh- clauses as participant

(19)

'Denning, our greatest authority on meteorites, stated that the height of its first appearance was about ninety or one hundred miles.'

(20)

△1   Subj Time Trans   DirObj
    [**I**] [**still**] [**believed**] [△2]
    ProG AdvG Past MV

△2   *there + be*   Subj   Place
    that [**there** [**were**]] [**men**] [[**in**] **Mars**]
    Non*wh-* Expletive Past MV NG   PG   NG
    Marker

'I still believed <u>that there were men in Mars</u>.'
Subordinate Clause

Non*wh-* clauses as attribute in attributive processes

(21)

△1   Subj   *be + Att*
    [**His idea**] [[**was**] △2]
    Det MN   Past MV

△2   Subj   Intrans   Manner   Place
    that [**meteorites**] [**might be falling**] [[**in**] **a heavy shower**] [[**upon**] **the planet**]
    Non*wh-*   NG   Modal   MV   PG Det AdjG   MN   PG   Det   MN
    Marker   *be + -ing*

'His idea was <u>that meteorites might be falling in a heavy shower upon the planet</u>.'
Subordinate Clause

(22)

△1   Subj   *be + Att*
    [**All** △2][[**was**] △3]
    MPro   Past MV

△2   Subj Trans DirObj
    (THAT) [**I**] [**felt**] [(ALL)]
    Wh- ProG Past MV
    Marker

△3   Subj *be + Att*
    that [**it**] [[**was**] **something very strange**]
    Non*wh-* ProG Past MV MPro   AdjG
    Marker

'All I felt was <u>that it was something very strange</u>.'
Subordinate Clause

Non*wh*- clauses as circumstance

(23)

        Means   Subj   Trans   DirObj
        [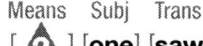] [one] [saw] [a circle of deep blue]
        ProG Past MV Det MN   PP

                Subj   Intrans   OblObj
    free *-ing* [(ONE)] [look] [[through] the telescope]
  Non*wh*- Marker   MV   PG   Det   MN

'Looking through the telescope , one saw a circle of deep blue.'
       Subordinate Clause

(24)

     Subj Time   Intrans   OblObj Time   Condition
     [I] [never] [dreamed] [[of] it] [then] [ ]
     ProG AdvG   Past MV   PG ProG AdvG

         Subj Intrans
    as   [I] [watched]
  Non*wh*- ProG   Past MV
  Marker

'I never dreamed of it then as I watched.'
       Subordinate Clause

Non*wh*- clauses as complement of a preposition group

(25)

     Subj Trans   DirObj Means
    [he] [discovered] [it] [only [[through]]]
    ProG   Past   MV   ProG Intens   PG
                  (AdvG)

          Subj   Trans   DirObj
    free *-ing* [(HE)] [notice] [▲3]
  Non*wh*- Marker   MV

        Subj   *be* + loc Time
    that [a black mark 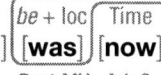] [was] [now] at the other side of the circumference
  Non*wh*- Det AdjG   MN   Past MV AdvG   PP
  Marker

        Subj   *be* + loc   Time
    that [(MARK)] [[had been] near him] [five minutes ago]
  Wh- Marker   Past MV   PP   Det   MN   AdvG
               have + *-ed/-en*

'. . . he discovered it only through noticing that a black mark that had been near ⊃
    Subordinate Clause ⌋

→ him five minutes ago was now at the other side of the circumference.'
    → Subordinate Clause continues

(26)

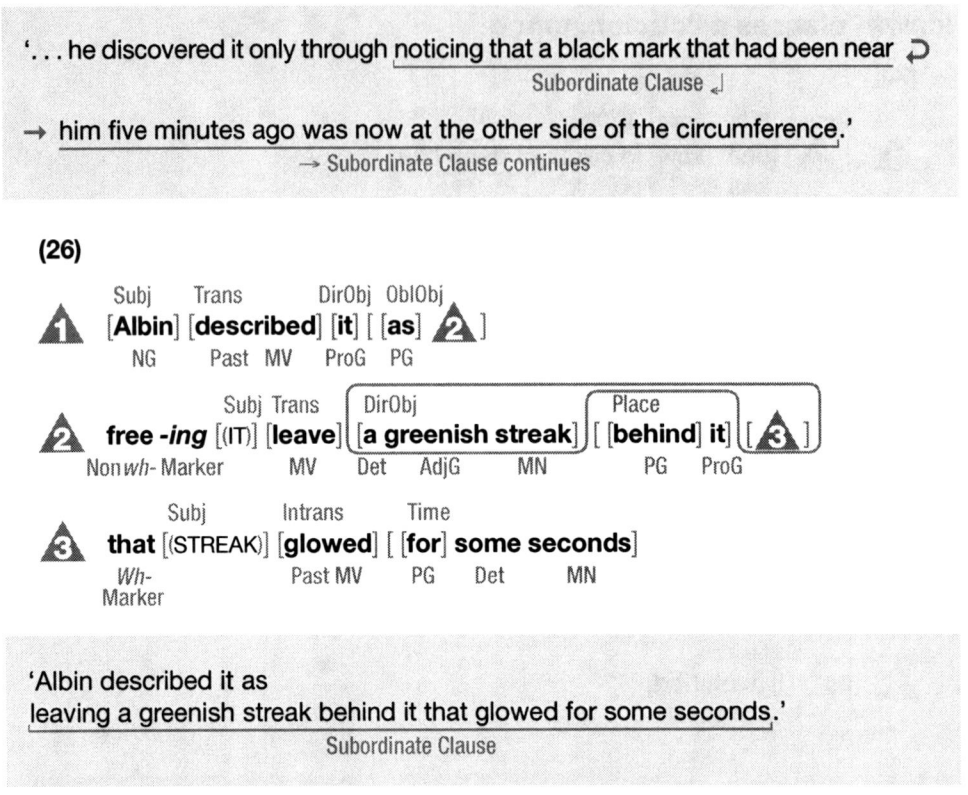

'Albin described it as
leaving a greenish streak behind it that glowed for some seconds.'
    Subordinate Clause

The rationale for treating the non*wh- leave* clause in (26) as the complement of a preposition group (an oblique object) in the host *describe* clause is given in the discussion of the object complement that follows.

The matter of object complements Traditionally, certain non*wh-* subordinate clauses functioning as either direct or oblique objects have been treated not as clause-size structures but as word-group elements in the higher clause. Here are some examples:

(27) **We elected her captain of the team.**

(28) **Buzz painted the old barn gray.**

(29) **The people found him a boring talk-show host.**

The underscored portions of examples (27) to (29) all appear to be attributes in an attributive relationship in much the same way that the attribute in a *be*-plus-attribute or linking-verb-plus-attribute process is in an attributive relationship with the subject of the clause. (*She was*) *captain of the team*, (*The old barn*) *became gray*, and (*He was*) *a boring talk-show host* seem like fair paraphrases for the underscored parts of examples

(27) to (29). Because of this relationship between the underscored portions and another word group apparently functioning as an object in the clause, these clause constituents have traditionally been called **object complements**. So, for example, in (27) *her* would be analyzed as the direct object and *captain of the team* would be an object complement. Likewise, in (28) *the old barn* would be the direct object and *gray* would be an object complement. And in (29) *him* would be the direct object and *a boring talk-show host* would be an object complement. An object complement can be either a noun group or an adjective group.

However, this sort of analysis is not consistent with the assumption that clauses represent event structures. Here's what I mean. If you carefully examine the event structure in (27), you will probably agree that *we elected her* and *she will be captain of the team* are the reasonable ways to express the two events that are being represented by the entire sentence *We elected her captain of the team*. Likewise, in (28), *Buzz painted the old barn* and *The old barn became gray* are the components of *Buzz painted the old barn gray*. We usually get the clearest picture of the way that language works if we start with the event structure this way. (We'll get back to (29) in a minute.)

Notice, additionally, that an accurate paraphrase for (27) might be *We elected her <u>to be</u> captain of the team*. This being the case, we might consider an alternative to the object complement analysis: a *two-clause* analysis may come closer to representing the events in question. In effect, we will say that two things were *elected* or *chosen*. The first is *her*. The second is *her being captain of the team*. Examples (30) and (31) represent (27) and (28) after they are analyzed as host clauses with subordinate non*wh*- clauses instead of simple clauses with object complements. If for (31) *Buzz painted the old barn <u>to be</u> gray* doesn't sound very good, try to extract the *cause* idea: might *Buzz caused the old barn <u>to be</u> gray* be better?

(30)

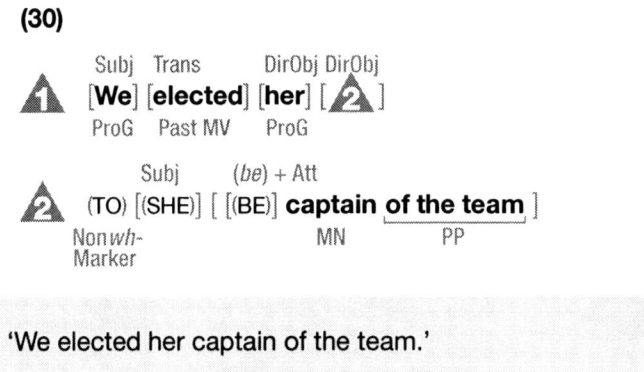

'We elected her captain of the team.'

(31)

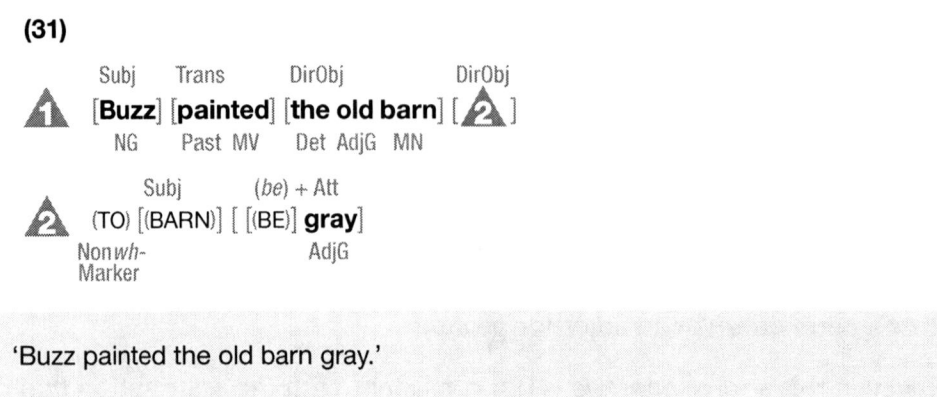

'Buzz painted the old barn gray.'

Raising However, the case of (29) is certainly far less clear. Is *The people found him* a good representation of the event structure? I'd say not. *The people found him* is not a part of the meaning of *The people found him a boring talk-show host*. So it is worthwhile noting that (27) and (28) share a feature that (29) does not have. In (27) and (28) there is actually a noun-group object in the event structure of the host clause, a direct object. We did elect *her*. Buzz did paint *the old barn*. But in the event represented in (29) the people did not *find him*. Technically, there is no direct object for an object complement to complement.

This being the case, the problem is to account for why the first-named participant in the subordinate clause (the *be a boring talk-show host* clause) appears in the form that an object ought to take (*him* rather than *he*). One suggestion has been that because the subordinate clause is initiated following the process, its subject shows up in the part of the sentence where an English speaker expects to hear an object (sometimes called *object territory*). *Him* functions as the subject of the subordinate clause, but it has the *form* of an object. This particular type of disharmony between form and function is often referred to as **raising**. The subject of the subordinate clause, which ought to be *he* (*He is a boring talk-show host*) is raised to the object territory of the host clause (*The people find him*). A particular set of processes, of which *find* is a member, appear to work this way when they are host-clause processes. They include *assume, believe, consider, expect, imagine,* and *hate,* among others.

We will have cause to refer to the *raising* concept again in Chapter 10, so tuck it away for future reference. Meanwhile, here at (32) is a triangle-convention report that treats the subordinate non*wh*- clause in (29) as direct object:

(32)

'The people found him a boring talk-show host.'

ACTIVITY 9.2

Here are a couple of examples from *The War of the Worlds*. Try your hand at an analysis and triangle-convention report for each one. Suggested responses are given at the back of the book.

> (33) **Can you imagine a milking stool tilted and bowled violently along the ground?**

> (34) **But instead of a milking stool imagine it a great body of machinery on a tripod stand.**

Absolute clauses Sometimes a non*wh*- clause of circumstance, marked with a nonfinite free -*ing* at the left-hand edge of the verb group, will have an overt (not a missing element) subject that is not coreferent with the subject of the host clause. This is an English-language structure known as an ***absolute clause***, and you will almost always find it in written, rather than spoken, English.

One type of absolute clause Compare (35) and (36) below. In example (35), the free -*ing* manner-circumstance clause (emphasized with underscoring) exhibits an expected coreference relationship between its missing subject and the subject of the host clause. That is, the *he* who hid under a dead horse is the same *he* who was doing the peeping out. However, notice that in (36) the subject of the condition-circumstance clause (*headlike hood . . .*) is not missing and it is not strictly coreferent with the subject in the host clause. This -*ing* clause in (36) is an absolute, so named, more or less, because of this lack of strict coreference.

> (35) **He had hid under the dead horse for a long time, <u>peeping out furtively across the common.</u>**

(36) **Then the monster had risen to its feet and had begun to walk leisurely to and fro across the common among the few fugitives, <u>headlike hood turning about exactly like the head of a cowled human being.</u>**

Here are a couple more sentences, adapted from *The War of the Worlds*, in which free *-ing* absolute clauses serve as circumstances in the host clause.

(37) **He had been consumed with thirst until he found one of the water mains near the railway arch smashed, <u>the water bubbling out like a spring upon the road.</u>**

In (37) *the water*, which is the subject in the free *-ing bubbling* clause is not coreferent with *one of the water mains*, the subject of the host clause.

(38) **In the midst of it all the worthy vicar was very pluckily holding an early celebration, <u>bell jangling out above the excitement.</u>**

As was the case in (37), in (38) the lack of strict coreference between the subject of the free *-ing* condition-circumstance, *bell jangling out above the excitement*, and the subject of the host clause signals the presence of an absolute clause.

A second type of absolute clause Another type of absolute clause is a clause of circumstance for which the non*wh-* marker is missing and in which a form of *be* from *be* + Att or *be* + Loc is also missing. As with the other absolutes that we have considered, the subject of the subordinate clause is overt (not missing) and it is not coreferent with the subject in the host clause.

(39) **Then, realizing that he was deserted, he dodged round and made off down the lane after the chaise, <u>the sturdy man close behind him, and the fugitive, who had turned now, following remotely.</u>**

Example (39) has two free *-ing* absolute clauses of circumstance; one is a *be*-plus-location process (*(BEING) close behind him*) and the other an intransitive process (*following remotely*). These two clauses have different subjects (*the sturdy man* and *the fugitive*), neither of which is coreferent with the subject (*he*) of the host clause. The first (*close behind him*) is missing a form of *be* and its clause marker, free *-ing*. The *following remotely* clause is free *-ing* absolute.

(40) **A brewer's dray rumbled by, <u>two near wheels splashed with fresh blood.</u>**

Example (40) has a condition circumstance that is expressed in an absolute clause, *two near wheels splashed with fresh blood*. As with the first absolute in (39), (40) is missing a form of *be* and its clause marker, free *-ing*.

Absolute clauses can sometimes be paraphrased as complements of the preposition group *with*. For example, the sentence in (36) might be paraphrased as in (41). Likewise, (37) might be paraphrased as in (42), (38) as in (43), and so forth.

(41) **Then the monster had risen to its feet and had begun to walk leisurely to and fro across the common among the few fugitives, <u>with</u> headlike hood turning about exactly like the head of a cowled human being.**

(42) **He had been consumed with thirst until he found one of the water mains near the railway arch smashed, <u>with</u> the water bubbling out like a spring upon the road.**

(43) **In the midst of it all the worthy vicar was very pluckily holding an early celebration, <u>with</u> bell jangling out above the excitement.**

(44) **Then, realizing that he was deserted, he dodged round and made off down the lane after the chaise, <u>with</u> the sturdy man close behind him, and the fugitive, who had turned now, following remotely.**

(45) **A brewer's dray rumbled by, <u>with</u> two near wheels splashed with fresh blood.**

Here is a report of sentence (40), repeated as (46), and its paraphrase using *with* at (47):

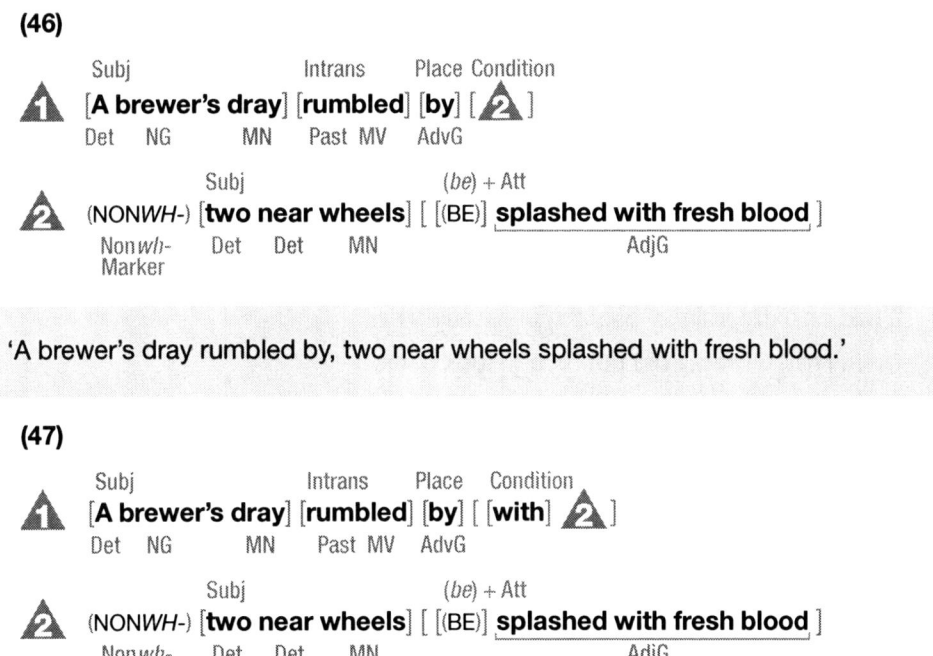

(46)

```
        Subj                    Intrans    Place  Condition
   1   [A brewer's dray] [rumbled] [by] [ 2 ]
        Det   NG          MN      Past MV  AdvG

              Subj                  (be) + Att
   2   (NONWH-) [two near wheels] [ [(BE)] splashed with fresh blood ]
        Nonwh-   Det   Det   MN                     AdjG
        Marker
```

'A brewer's dray rumbled by, two near wheels splashed with fresh blood.'

(47)

```
        Subj                    Intrans    Place  Condition
   1   [A brewer's dray] [rumbled] [by] [ [with] 2 ]
        Det   NG          MN      Past MV  AdvG

              Subj                  (be) + Att
   2   (NONWH-) [two near wheels] [ [(BE)] splashed with fresh blood ]
        Nonwh-   Det   Det   MN                     AdjG
        Marker
```

'A brewer's dray rumbled by, with two near wheels splashed with fresh blood.'

See what you make of the underscored clause back at (17). An absolute, right?

Practice with Terminology

What follows is a preview of the sentences that you will encounter in this chapter's Sentences for Analysis. Certain elements in the sentences have been underscored. Label each underscored element using one or more of the following terms or an applicable term from a previous chapter. Check the Glossary if you are not certain about the definition of any of the terms.

Absolute clause	Non*wh-* marker	Subordinate clause
Hypotactic relationship	Object complement	
Nonfinite clause	Raising	

1 Afterwards I learned that Ogilvy, Stent, and Henderson were with others in an attempt at communication.

2 The deep blue sky overhead seemed to darken abruptly as the puffs of luminous greenish smoke arose.

3 Then, by the light of their own destruction, I saw the group staggering and falling.

4 As the unseen shaft of heat passed over them, pine trees burst into fire, and every dry furze bush became with one dull thud a mass of flames.

5 I perceived it coming towards me by the flashing bushes in its path.

6 If that death had swept through a full circle, it must inevitably have slain me in my surprise.

7 As it passed, it spared me, and left the night about me suddenly dark and unfamiliar.

8 The undulating common seemed now dark almost to blackness, its roadways lying grey and pale under the deep blue sky of the early night.

9 Suddenly, like a thing falling upon me from without, came—fear.

10 It had an extraordinary effect in unmanning me.

11 Once I had turned, I did not dare to look back.

12 I remember feeling that this mysterious death would leap after me from the pit about the cylinder and strike me down.

13 Many think that in some way the Martians are able to generate an intense heat in a chamber of practically absolute non-conductivity.

14 They project this intense heat by means of a polished parabolic mirror, much as the mirror of a lighthouse projects a beam of light.

15 I thought the news of the massacre probably reached Chobham, Woking, and Ottershaw about the same time.

16 You may imagine the young people making this novelty the excuse for walking together and enjoying a trivial flirtation.

17 As yet, of course, few people in Woking even knew that the cylinder had opened.

18 As these folks came out by twos and threes upon the open, they found little knots of people talking excitedly.

19   To protect the strange creatures from violence, Stent and Ogilvy <u>had</u> telegraph<u>ed</u> from Horsell to the barracks for the help of a company of soldiers.

20   After <u>telegraphing for help</u>, they returned to lead that ill-fated advance.

21   If the elevation of the mirror <u>had been a few yards higher</u>, none could have lived to tell the tale.

22   An invisible hand lit the bushes as it hurried towards them <u>through the twilight</u>.

23   Then the beam swung close over their heads, bring<u>ing</u> down in crumbling ruin a portion of the gable of the house nearest the corner.

24   Suddenly a mounted policeman <u>came</u> galloping through the confusion with his hands clasped over his head, screaming.

25   Three persons were <u>crushed</u> and <u>trampled</u> there, and left to die amid the terror and the darkness.

> **Note:** You do not need to limit your choices to the new terms from this chapter. Where appropriate, use an applicable term from any previous chapter.

Analyzing and Reporting Multiclausal Sentences

As was noted at the end of Chapter 8, when clause complexes contain two or three clauses or even more, it can sometimes become a chore to keep up with the analysis—not because it is so tough, but because it is so long. This is when following a charting procedure can really help you keep track of the steps you have taken to analyze the complex.

Here are two examples: one has three clauses (a host clause, a *wh-* clause, and a non*wh-* clause) and the other is a six-clause monster. The three-clause example is far more typical of the size of English-language clause complexes. Only rarely would you be asked to analyze anything so complicated as a monstrous clause complex comprising six clauses. But perhaps an example from way out there in the Twilight Zone will help you see that you are developing what it takes to do even the most complicated analyses. First the three-clause complex:

> (48)   **Then the small handbag disgorged a mass of sovereigns that**
> **seemed to break up into separate coins as it struck the ground.**

Step 1: *Identifying processes* Start a chart by identifying processes and opening up the minimal number of functional spots for the requisite participant roles for each one. Label the process and participant functions. In the example there are three processes:

> **Then the small handbag <u>disgorged</u> a mass of sovereigns**
> **that <u>seemed to break up</u> into separate coins as it <u>struck</u> the ground.**

The chart:

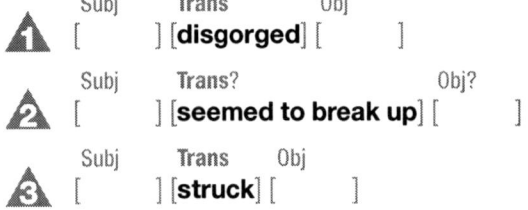

	Subj	Trans	Obj
1	[ ]	[disgorged]	[ ]

	Subj	Trans?	Obj?
2	[ ]	[seemed to break up]	[ ]

	Subj	Trans	Obj
3	[ ]	[struck]	[ ]

Disgorged requires two participant roles, *break up* can require either one or two, but we open places for two just to be safe, and *struck* requires two. While you are identifying processes and opening up participant slots on the chart, take note of any passive-voice verb groups (*be* + *-ed/-en*). Each is accompanied by a participant-function reversal: an active-voice object appears as the passive-voice subject, and the active-voice subject appears as an oblique object, usually introduced with *by*. In the example being developed, there are no passive-voice clauses.

Step 2: *Studying the complex and filling in the requisite participant slots on your chart* Using the logic of the event structure to do this step, seek out the role-players that are required for each process; they will usually be right in the neighborhood of the process. Remember that some participants might be missing elements. After this step, the only clause content left unaccounted for in the complex is either circumstances, clause markers, or relationship and discourse elements. Here, the participants are underscored:

> **Then <u>the small handbag</u> disgorged <u>a mass of sovereigns</u>**
> **that <u>seemed to break up</u> <u>into separate coins</u> as <u>it</u> struck <u>the ground</u>.**

	Subj	Trans	DirObj
1	[the small handbag]	[disgorged]	[a mass of sovereigns]

	Subj	Trans?	Obj?
2	[ ]	[seemed to break up]	[[into] separate coins]

	Subj	Trans	DirObj
3	[it]	[struck]	[the ground]

Step 3: *Doing the math* Every complex has hypotactic and paratactic relationships among clauses, and all of these relationships are marked as either (1) conjoined, (2) *wh-*, or (3) non*wh-*. However, one of the clauses is the host clause and will not have a marker. Therefore, after you count the processes, you can subtract one (for the host clause), and the remainder will be the number of marked clauses, and therefore

the number of markers, you will find. *Take care*: some *wh-* clauses could be double-marked (see Chapter 10). And it's always possible that a marker could be a missing element. Take your time at this step; it'll pay off.

Here's the math for our example:

Three processes identified: 3

minus One (for the host clause): −1

yields <u>Two</u> markers needed: 2

Step 4: *Finding markers and adding them to your chart* Remember that all markers (except the nonfinite clause markers, free *-ing* and *to*, which are at the far left-hand edge of the verb group—see Chapter 9) occur out in front of the clause. All markers (including free *-ing* and *to*) are charted and reported to the left of their clauses. Allow for the formal style in which preposition groups and determiners that might otherwise be inside the boundaries of a clause get pulled out to form a group with the marker. Our example has two overt markers, one *wh-* and one non*wh-*:

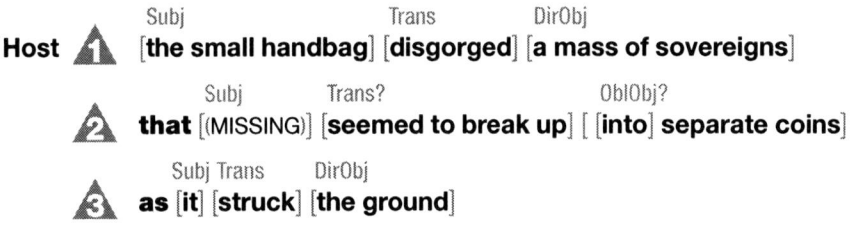

**Then the small handbag disgorged a mass of sovereigns
that seemed to break up into separate coins as it struck the ground.**

		Subj	Trans	DirObj
Host	⚠1	[the small handbag]	[disgorged]	[a mass of sovereigns]

	Subj	Trans?	OblObj?
⚠2 **that**	[(MISSING)]	[seemed to break up]	[[into] separate coins]

	Subj	Trans	DirObj
⚠3 **as**	[it]	[struck]	[the ground]

After this step, the only items left to account for in the clause complex will have to be either (a) circumstances or (b) relationship and discourse elements.

Step 5: *Taking stock* Locate circumstance, relationship, and discourse units. Here's the clause complex as it stands after processes, participants, and markers have been transferred to your chart; the remaining units are underscored.

**Then the small handbag disgorged a mass of sovereigns
that seemed to break up into separate coins as it struck the ground.**

What do you make of what is left? *Then* sounds like one of two things. Either it is a time reference, telling something about the timeframe of the event of disgorging, or it is a discourse unit that helps get the sequence of events lined up in order. I vote for it being a discourse item.

How should we resolve the questions of *seemed to break up* and *into separate coins*? We have tentatively identified *seemed to break up* as transitive and *into separate coins* as an oblique object. However, *seemed to break up* here appears to mean *seemed to dissolve*, and that sounds like a one-participant process. Could *into separate coins* be a resultant condition—a condition-circumstance? Time to decide. Let's treat *seemed to break up* as an intransitive process with a condition-circumstance.

Step 6: *Adding circumstance, relationship, and discourse units to your chart* Amend participants as required. Fill in missing elements as required. You might have to refer to the context of the passage.

> **Then the small handbag disgorged a mass of sovereigns**
> **that seemed to break up into separate coins as it struck the ground.**

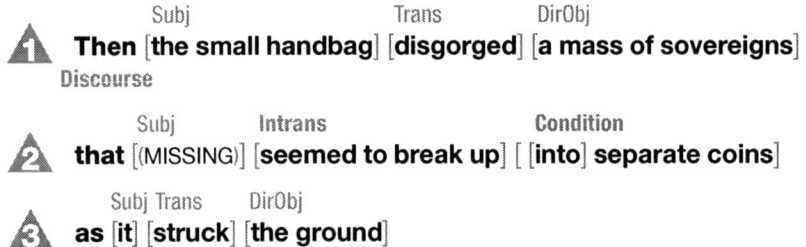

All that remains is to make sure that each embedded and subordinate clause has a place to dock in its host clause. In this example, we still have not resolved the problem of the missing-element subject in the *wh-* clause (introduced by *that*), and since the logic of the event structure would lead us to conclude that it was the *mass of sovereigns* that broke up, we have the ideal spot at which to plug in the *wh-* clause: just to the right of *sovereigns* in the direct object in the upper clause. The non*wh-* clause introduced by *as* seems to be telling about the circumstances surrounding the breaking up of the coins. Let's treat it as a circumstance of time at the end of the second clause.

Subj Trans   DirObj

△3   as [it] [struck] [the ground]

Step 7: *Finishing the triangle-convention report* The 'chart' has evolved into a triangle-convention report. All that remains is to observe minimal bracketing and labeling protocol.

           Subj   Trans   DirObj

△1   Then [the small handbag] [disgorged] [a mass of sovereigns △2]

Discourse Det AdjG   MN   Past MV   Det MN   PP

           Subj   Intrans   Condition   Time

△2   that [(MASS)] [seemed to break up] [[into] separate coins] [△3]

Non*wh*-   Past   MV Particle PG   AdjG   MN
Marker   Semiaux

     Subj Trans   DirObj

△3   as [it] [struck] [the ground]

Non*wh*- ProG Past MV Det   MN
Marker

> 'Then the small handbag disgorged a mass of sovereigns that seemed to break up into separate coins as it struck the ground.'

And now for the six-clause monster:

(49) **There had been a hasty consultation, and since the Martians were evidently, in spite of their repulsive forms, intelligent creatures, it had been resolved to show them, by approaching them with signals, that we too were intelligent.**

Step 1: *Identifying processes* Start a chart by opening up the minimal number of functional spots for the requisite participant roles. Label the process and participant functions. The example appears to have six processes.

(49) **There had been a hasty consultation, and since the Martians were evidently, in spite of their repulsive forms, intelligent creatures, it had been resolved to show them, by approaching them with signals, that we too were intelligent.**

The chart

     there + *be*   Subj

△1 [There [had been]] [   ]

     Subj   *be* + Att

△2 [   ] [[were] intelligent creatures]

     Subj   **Trans**   Obj

△3 [   ] [had been resolved] [   ]

      Subj   **Trans** Obj   Obj
4 [   ] [**show**] [   ] [   ]

      Subj   **Trans**   Obj
5 [   ] [**approach**] [   ]

      Subj   **be** + Att
6 [   ] [[**were**] **intelligent**]

While you are identifying processes and opening up participant slots on the chart, take note of passive-voice verb groups (*be* + *-ed/-en*). Passive voice is accompanied by a participant-function reversal in which an active-voice object appears as the passive-voice subject, and the active-voice subject appears as an oblique object, usually introduced by *by*. In the example developing here, the process in clause **3**, *had been resolved*, has both perfective aspect (*have* + *-ed/-en*) and passive voice (*be* + *-ed/-en*). Revise your chart to accommodate participant-function reversals:

      Subj   Trans   **OblObj**
3 [   ] [**had been resolved**] [   ]

Step 2: *Studying the complex and filling in the requisite participant slots on your chart* The logic of the event structure will help you complete this step; just look for the required role-players, usually somewhere right near the process. Remember that some participants might be missing elements. After this step, all that is left unaccounted for in the complex will have to be (a) circumstances, (b) markers, or (c) relationship and discourse elements. Here the overt participants are underscored:

> **There had been a hasty consultation**, and since **the Martians were**
> evidently, in spite of their repulsive forms, intelligent creatures,
> **it** had been resolved to show **them**, by approaching **them** with signals,
> that **we** too were intelligent.

            there + *be*   Subj
1 [**There** [**had been**]] [**a hasty consultation**]

  Subj   *be* + Att
2 [**the Martians**] [[**were**] **intelligent creatures**]

  Subj Trans   **OblObj**
3 [**4**] [**had been resolved**] [(MISSING)]

  Subj   Trans   Obj   Obj
4 [(MISSING)] [**show**] [**them**] [**6**]

  Subj   Trans   Obj
5 [(MISSING)] [**approach**] [**them**]

  Subj   *be* + Att
6 [**we too**] [[**were**] **intelligent**]

Step 3: *Doing the math* Every complex has hypotactic and paratactic relationships among clauses, and all of these relationships are marked as (1) conjoined, (2) *wh-*, or (3) non*wh-*. However, one of the clauses is the host clause and does not have a marker. Therefore, after you count the processes, you can subtract one (for the host clause); the remainder will be the number of marked clauses, and therefore markers, you find. Take care: some *wh-* clauses could be double-marked (see Chapter 10). And it is always possible that a marker could be a missing element (understood). Take your time at this step; it'll pay off.

Here's the math for our example:

	Six processes identified:	6
minus	One (for the host clause):	−1
yields	<u>Five</u> markers needed:	5

Step 4: *Finding markers and adding them to your chart* Remember that all markers (except the nonfinite clause markers, free *-ing* and *to*, which are at the far left-hand edge of the verb group; see above) occur out in front of the clause. All markers (including free *-ing* and *to*) are charted and reported to the left of their clauses. Allow for the formal style in which preposition groups and determiners that might otherwise be inside the boundaries of a clause get pulled out to form a group with the marker. Here the five markers are underscored:

> **There had been a hasty consultation, <u>and</u> <u>since</u> the Martians were evidently, in spite of their repulsive forms, intelligent creatures, it had been resolved <u>to</u> show them, by approach<u>ing</u> them with signals, <u>that</u> we too were intelligent.**

Host **1**   *there + be*   Subj
     [**There** [**had been**]] [**a hasty consultation**]

2   Subj   *be + Att*
    since [**the Martians**] [[**were**] **intelligent creatures**]

3   Subj   Trans   OblObj
    and [**4**] [**had been resolved**] [(MISSING)]

4   Subj   Trans   Obj   Obj
    to [(MISSING)] [**show**] [**them**] [**6**]

5   Subj   Trans   Obj
    free -ing [(MISSING)] [**approach**] [**them**]

6   Subj   *be + Att*
    that [**we too**] [[**were**] **intelligent**]

After this step, all that is left to account for in the clause complex is either (a) circumstances or (b) relationship and discourse elements.

Step 5: *Taking stock* Locate circumstance, relationship, and discourse units. Here is the clause complex as it now stands after you have transferred processes, participants, and markers to your chart. The remaining units are underscored:

> **There had been a hasty consultation, and since the Martians were
> evidently, in spite of their repulsive forms, intelligent creatures,
> it had been resolved to show them, by approaching them with signals,
> that we too were intelligent.**

What do you make of what is left? Here are some ideas.

Evidently sounds like a speaker's judgment, so I would put it in the relationship category.

In spite of their repulsive forms sounds like a condition under which the Martians are operating, and that makes it circumstance.

It is the expletive of non*wh-* extraposition; this accounts for why the subject (the *show* clause) comes after the verb group *had been resolved*.

Here *by* has to introduce an oblique object or circumstance, and because we have already accounted for all participant roles, it must introduce circumstance of means.

And *with signals* must be either a circumstance or a required prop (a participant); it is your call, but it seems essential to me. I'd go back and add it as a participant.

Step 6: *Adding circumstance, relationship, and discourse units to your chart* Amend participants as required. Fill in missing elements as required. You might have to refer to the context of the passage.

> **There had been a hasty consultation, and since the Martians were
> evidently, in spite of their repulsive forms, intelligent creatures,
> it had been resolved to show them, by approaching them with signals,
> that we too were intelligent.**

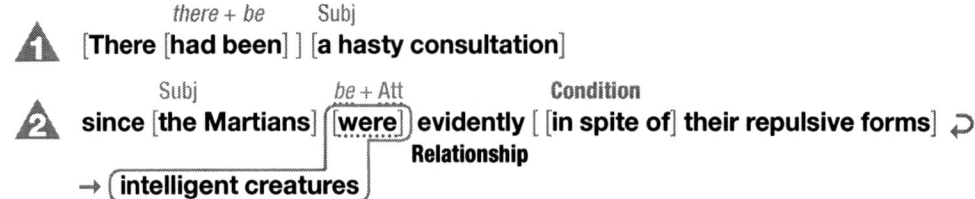

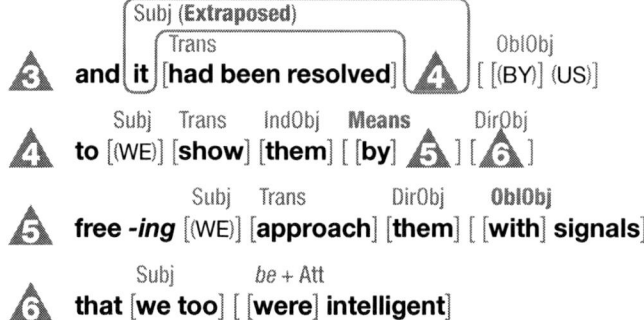

3 — Subj (Extraposed) / Trans / ObiObj
and it [had been resolved] 4 [[(BY)] (US)]

4 — Subj Trans IndObj **Means** DirObj
to [(WE)] [show] [them] [[by] 5] [6]

5 — Subj Trans DirObj **OblObj**
free -*ing* [(WE)] [approach] [them] [[with] signals]

6 — Subj be + Att
that [we too] [[were] intelligent]

All that remains is to make sure that each embedded and subordinate clause has a place to dock in its host clause. We have now placed three (the ▲ symbols show where they go), and we are left only to account for the non*wh*- clause introduced by *since*, clause [⒉]. It sounds like circumstance to me, telling the condition under which the deputation resolved to approach the Martians.

> **There had been a hasty consultation, and since the Martians were evidently, in spite of their repulsive forms, intelligent creatures, it had been resolved to show them, by approaching them with signals, that we too were intelligent.**

Let's get clauses ⒉ and ⒊ renumbered and put in the correct order:

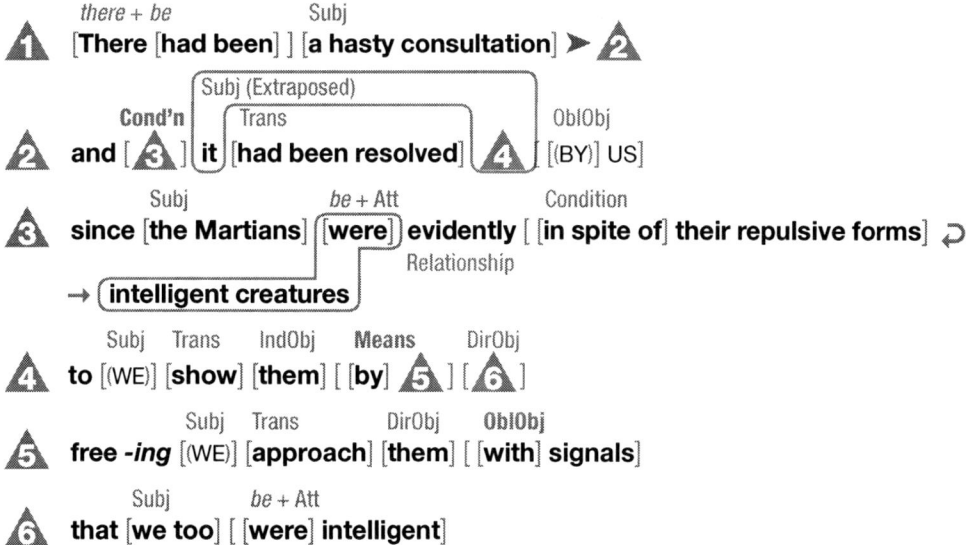

1 — there + be / Subj
[There [had been]] [a hasty consultation] ➤ ⒉

2 — **Cond'n** / Subj (Extraposed) / Trans / ObiObj
and [⒊] it [had been resolved] 4 [(BY)] US]

3 — Subj be + Att Condition
since [the Martians] [were] evidently [[in spite of] their repulsive forms] ↻
Relationship
→ (intelligent creatures)

4 — Subj Trans IndObj **Means** DirObj
to [(WE)] [show] [them] [[by] 5] [6]

5 — Subj Trans DirObj **OblObj**
free -*ing* [(WE)] [approach] [them] [[with] signals]

6 — Subj be + Att
that [we too] [[were] intelligent]

Step 7: *Making a triangle-convention report* Take care to observe minimal bracketing and labeling protocol. Here is the report for this six-clause example:

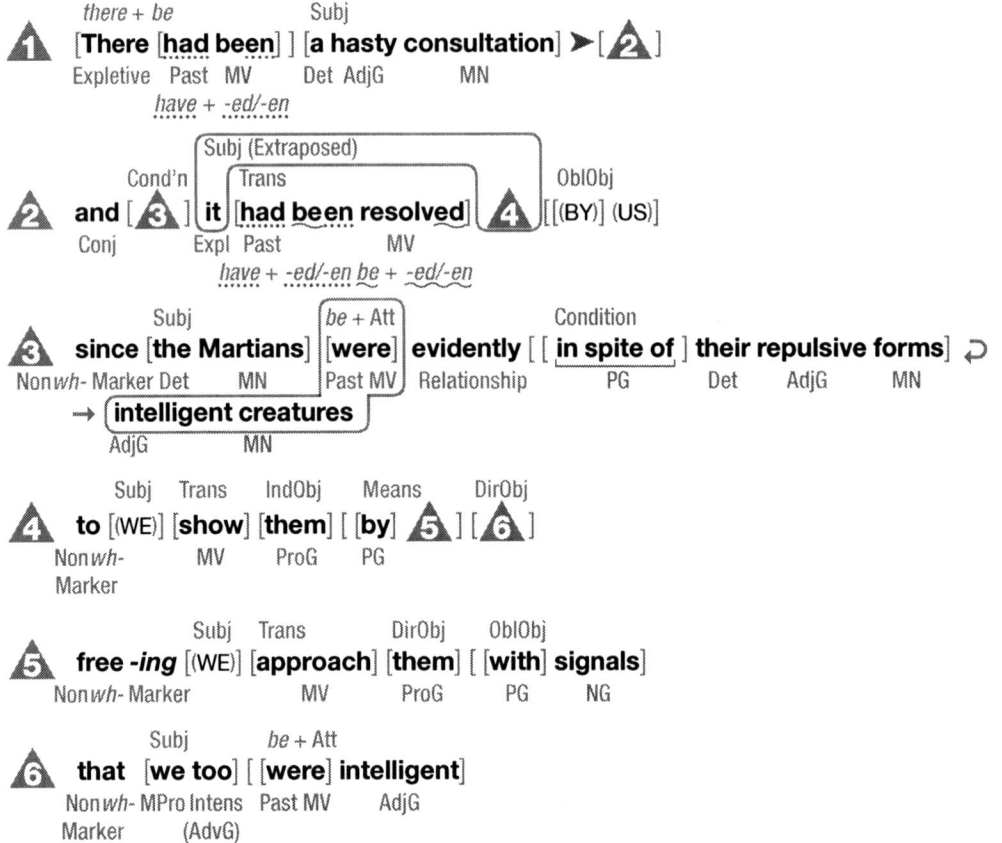

Sentences for Analysis

The following sentences are adapted from *The War of the Worlds*. Analyze them and report your results as shown in the two preceding examples. Make certain that your analyses have the following features:

a Bracket processes, participants, and circumstances and label them by function at the top of the bracket.

b Sub-bracket as necessary, observing minimal bracketing conventions.

c Label elements in all word groups. One-element groups should be given a group label.

d Follow the triangle convention in reporting embedded and subordinate clauses.

(50)

Subj   Trans   DirObj

1   **Then** [**the small handbag**] [**disgorged**] [**a mass of sovereigns** **2**]

Discourse Det   AdjG   MN   Past MV   Det   MN   PP

Subj   Intrans   Condition   Time

2   **that** [(MASS)] [**seemed to break up**] [[into] separate coins] [**3**]

Non*wh*-   Past Semiaux   MV Particle   PG   AdjG   MN
Marker

Subj   Trans   DirObj

3   **as**   [**it**] [**struck**] [**the ground**]

Non*wh*- ProG   Past MV   Det   MN
Marker

'Then the small handbag disgorged a mass of sovereigns
that seemed to break up into separate coins as it struck the ground.'

1   Afterwards I learned that Ogilvy, Stent, and Henderson were with others in an attempt at communication. (**Direct Object**)

2   The deep blue sky overhead seemed to darken abruptly as the puffs of luminous greenish smoke arose.

3   Then, by the light of their own destruction, I saw the group staggering and falling.

✱ 4   As the unseen shaft of heat passed over them, pine trees burst into fire, and every dry furze bush became with one dull thud a mass of flames. (**Condition**)

5   I perceived it coming towards me by the flashing bushes in its path. (**Direct Object**)

6   If that death had swept through a full circle, it must inevitably have slain me in my surprise. (**Condition**)

7   As it passed, it spared me, and left the night about me suddenly dark and unfamiliar.

8   The undulating common seemed now dark almost to blackness, its roadways lying grey and pale under the deep blue sky of the early night. (**Condition**)

9   Suddenly, like a thing falling upon me from without, came—fear.

✱ 10   It had an extraordinary effect in unmanning me. (**Complement of PG**)

11   Once I had turned, I did not dare to look back.

12   I remember feeling that this mysterious death would leap after me from the pit about the cylinder and strike me down. (**Direct Objects**)

13   Many think that in some way the Martians are able to generate an intense heat in a chamber of practically absolute non-conductivity.

14   They project this intense heat by means of a polished parabolic mirror, much as the mirror of a lighthouse projects a beam of light. (**Manner**)

✳ 15 I thought the news of the massacre probably reached Chobham, Woking, and Ottershaw about the same time.

16 You may imagine the young people making this novelty the excuse for walking together and enjoying a trivial flirtation.

17 As yet, of course, few people in Woking even knew that the cylinder had opened. (**Direct Object**)

18 As these folks came out by twos and threes upon the open, they found little knots of people talking excitedly.

✳ 19 To protect the strange creatures from violence, Stent and Ogilvy had telegraphed from Horsell to the barracks for the help of a company of soldiers.

20 After telegraphing for help, they returned to lead that ill-fated advance. (**Complement of PG; Condition**)

21 If the elevation of the mirror had been a few yards higher, none could have lived to tell the tale.

22 An invisible hand lit the bushes as it hurried towards them through the twilight.

23 Then the beam swung close over their heads, bringing down in crumbling ruin a portion of the gable of the house nearest the corner.

24 Suddenly a mounted policeman came galloping through the confusion with his hands clasped over his head, screaming. (**Complement of PG; Condition**)

✳ 25 Three persons were crushed and trampled there, and left to die amid the terror and the darkness.

Note: Suggested responses for the sentences marked by an asterisk (✳) are given at the back of the book. As a way of getting started on this activity, you might want to work first on those items. Some of the other items have a hint. The non*wh*- clause is underscored in some, and the non*wh*- clause type is provided for some others. Where your responses and the suggested ones differ, you will want to get advice from your instructor. Very often, several interpretations might be appropriate.

Text for Analysis

The following text (approximately 430 words) is taken from *The War of the Worlds*. Each sentence in the passage is numbered for your convenience. Analyze the text and report your results following the directions and the example in Sentences for Analysis.

This text was not selected to have a disproportionate number of subordinate non*wh*-clauses; in your analyses you will have to apply everything you have learned up to this point.

Note: Suggested responses for underscored items are given at the back of the book. Sentences 5 and 7 should look very familiar to you—see examples (33) and (34).

---

(1) And this Thing I saw! (2) How can I describe it? (3) A monstrous tripod, higher than many houses, striding over the young pine trees, and smashing them aside in its career; a walking engine of glittering metal, striding now across the heather, articulate ropes of steel dangling from it, and the clattering tumult of its passage mingling with the riot of the thunder. (4) A flash, and it came out vividly, heeling over one way with two feet in the air, to vanish and reappear almost instantly as it seemed, with the next flash, a hundred yards nearer. (5) Can you imagine a milking stool tilted and bowled violently along the ground? (6) That was the impression those instant flashes gave. (7) But instead of a milking stool imagine it a great body of machinery on a tripod stand.

(8) Then suddenly the trees in the pine wood ahead of me were parted, as brittle reeds are parted by a man thrusting through them; they were snapped off and driven headlong, and a second huge tripod appeared, rushing, as it seemed, headlong towards me. (9) And I was galloping hard to meet it! (10) At the sight of the second monster my nerve went altogether. (11) Not stopping to look again, I wrenched the horse's head hard round to the right and in another moment the dog cart had heeled over upon the horse; the shafts smashed noisily, and I was flung sideways and fell heavily into a shallow pool of water.

(12) I crawled out almost immediately, and crouched, my feet still in the water, under a clump of furze. (13) The horse lay motionless (his neck was broken, poor brute!) and by the lightning flashes I saw the black bulk of the overturned dog cart and the silhouette of the wheel still spinning slowly. (14) In another moment the colossal mechanism went striding by me, and passed uphill towards Pyrford.

(15) Seen nearer, the Thing was incredibly strange, for it was no mere insensate machine driving on its way. (16) Machine it was, with a ringing metallic pace, and long, flexible, glittering tentacles (one of which gripped a young pine tree) swinging and rattling about its strange body. (17) It picked its road as it went striding along, and the brazen hood that surmounted it moved to and fro with the inevitable suggestion of a head looking about.

[18] Behind the main body was a huge mass of white metal like a gigantic fisherman's basket, and puffs of green smoke squirted out from the joints of the limbs as the monster swept by me. [19] And in an instant it was gone.

Dialog for Analysis

What follows is another unedited excerpt (about 330 words) from *The War of the Worlds*. This excerpt differs from the one in the Text for Analysis activity in that it contains a significant amount of dialog. By using dialog, H. G. Wells tried to create a sense of interpersonal interaction to contrast with the narrative that carries most of the story.

Several parts of the excerpt have been numbered and underscored. See how far your skill at analyzing sentence structure takes you in the direction of understanding how dialog works. Be particularly alert to relationship and discourse elements. After all, written dialog is supposed to capture the tone of live interaction.

After a time we drew near the road, and as we did so we heard the clatter of hoofs and saw through the tree stems three cavalry soldiers riding slowly towards Woking. We hailed them, and they halted while we hurried towards them. It was a lieutenant and a couple of privates of the 8th Hussars, with a stand like a theodolite, which the artilleryman told me was a heliograph.

'You are the first men I've seen coming this way this morning,' said the lieutenant. [1] 'What's brewing?'

His voice and face were eager. The men behind him stared curiously. The artilleryman jumped down the bank into the road and saluted.

[2] 'Gun destroyed last night, sir. [3] Have been hiding. [4] Trying to rejoin battery, sir. You'll come in sight of the Martians, I expect, about half a mile along this road.'

[5] 'What the dickens are they like?' asked the lieutenant.

[6] 'Giants in armour, sir. [7] Hundred feet high. [8] Three legs and a body like 'luminium, with a mighty great head in a hood, sir.'

[9] 'Get out!' said the lieutenant. [10] 'What confounded nonsense!'

'You'll see, sir. They carry a kind of box, sir, that shoots fire and strikes you dead.'

[11] 'What d'ye mean—a gun?'

(12) 'No, sir,' and the artilleryman began a vivid account of the Heat-Ray. Halfway through, the lieutenant interrupted him and looked up at me. I was still standing on the bank by the side of the road.

'It's perfectly true,' I said.

(13) 'Well,' said the lieutenant, 'I suppose it's my business to see it too. Look here'—to the artilleryman—'we're detailed here clearing people out of their houses. You'd better go along and report yourself to Brigadier-General Marvin, and tell him all you know. He's at Weybridge. (14) Know the way?'

(15) 'I do,' I said; and he turned his horse southward again.

(16) 'Half a mile, you say?' said he.

(17) 'At most,' I answered, and pointed over the treetops southward. He thanked me and rode on, and we saw them no more.

Chapter 10

Non*wh*- Complementation, Apposition, Discontinuity; Nonfinite *Wh*- Clauses

Preliminaries

In the last chapter we saw that non*wh*- clauses could perform event-structure functions such as participant, attribute, and circumstance, and that they could also function as complements to preposition groups (*objects of the preposition*) to form prepositional phrases. This chapter shows that non*wh*- clauses can become embedded in noun groups and adjective groups, that they can co-perform an event-structure function with an ***appositive noun group*** as co-performer, and that they can participate in discontinuous extraposed structures. We will also consider briefly ***nonfinite*** *wh*- ***clause*** complexes, which possess the coreference characteristics of *wh*- clauses but are marked as non*wh*- clauses.

Non*wh*- Complement Clauses

The term *embedded* in Chapter 8 referred to word groups, prepositional phrases, and *wh*- clauses that are tucked into word groups, becoming constituents of those host word groups. In this chapter the term ***complement clause*** is applied to those non*wh*- clauses that are embedded in adjective groups and noun groups.

We want to introduce the term *complement clause* not just to make your life more complicated but rather because non*wh*- embedding (which we here call *complementation*) is a form of hypotactic relationship distinct from both *wh*-embedding and *nonwh*- subordination. Here is why we make the terminological distinction:

a ***Wh*- embedding** takes place only in noun groups and it always requires that a coreference relationship exist between the head of the noun group in the host clause and the missing element (the *wh*- information gap) in the embedded clause; moreover, the *wh*- marker must match up with these coreferent elements, forming a three-element set.

b **Non*wh*- subordination** substitutes a clause as participant, circumstance, or attribute, or as complement to a preposition group.

Like *wh*- embedding, non*wh*- complementation embeds a clause in a noun group or an adjective group; however, unlike *wh*- embedding, the head of the host group *cannot be coreferent* with any element in the embedded clause. That is, the essential feature of a *wh*- embedded clause complex—coreference—cannot apply. If there *is* group-internal coreference between an element in the host group and an element in the complement clause, it cannot directly involve the head of the host group.

Nonfinite Non*wh*- Complement Clauses

In (1), an infinitive clause (marked with *to* at the left-hand edge of the verb group) is an embedded complement in the adjective group headed by *ready*. This complement clause completes the sense of *ready* in such a way that *ready to follow* is unitary. This type of complement clause is called an ***adjective complement***.

(1)

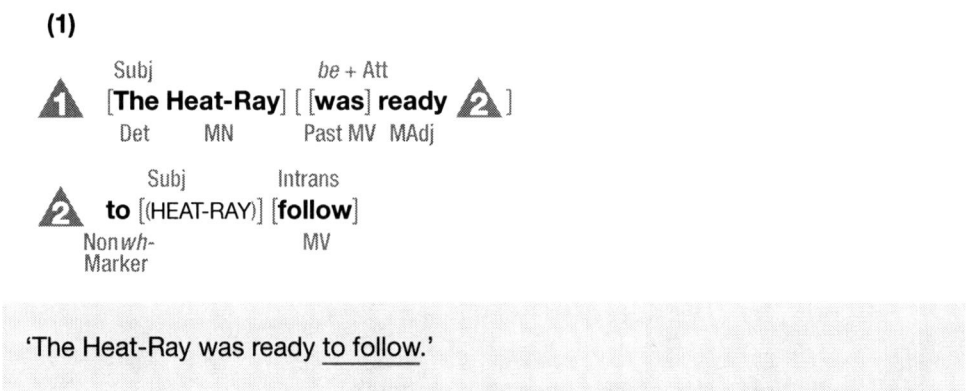

'The Heat-Ray was ready to follow.'

In (2), an infinitive clause (marked with *to* at the left-hand edge of the verb group) is an embedded complement in the noun group headed by *time*. As with example (1), the embedded clause completes the sense of the word group headed by *time* so that *no time to add a word of comment* is unitary. This complement clause is called a ***noun complement***.

(2)

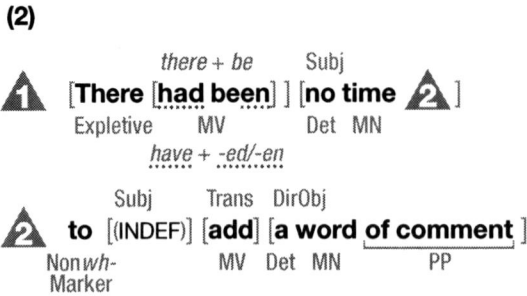

there + *be*   Subj
1 [There [had been]] [no time **2**]
Expletive   MV   Det MN
            have + *-ed/-en*

          Subj   Trans DirObj
2 to [(INDEF)] [add] [a word of comment]
     Non*wh-*   MV Det MN   PP
     Marker

'There had been no time <u>to add a word of comment</u>.'

ACTIVITY **10.1**

See what you make of example (3). One possible response is given at the back of the book.

(3) I had a momentary impulse <u>to go back</u> and <u>help him</u> that <u>my fears overruled</u>.

Non*wh*- *That* Complement Clauses

In (4) and (5), finite clauses (having either tense or modal at the left-hand edge of the verb group), marked with *that*, are embedded complements in the noun groups headed by *idea*. As with examples (1) and (2), the complement clauses in (4) and (5) complete the sense of their respective word groups so that *a fixed idea that these monsters must be sluggish* and *a vague idea that he might see something of me* are each unitary.

(4)

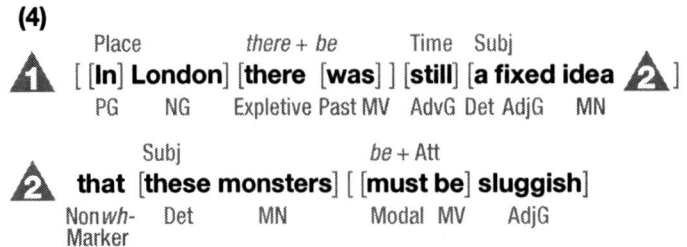

          Place   *there* + *be*   Time Subj
1 [[In] London] [there [was]] [still] [a fixed idea **2**]
     PG   NG   Expletive Past MV AdvG Det AdjG   MN

              Subj   *be* + Att
2 that [these monsters] [[must be] sluggish]
     Non*wh-* Det   MN   Modal MV   AdjG
     Marker

'In London there was still <u>a fixed idea that these monsters must be sluggish</u>.'

(5)

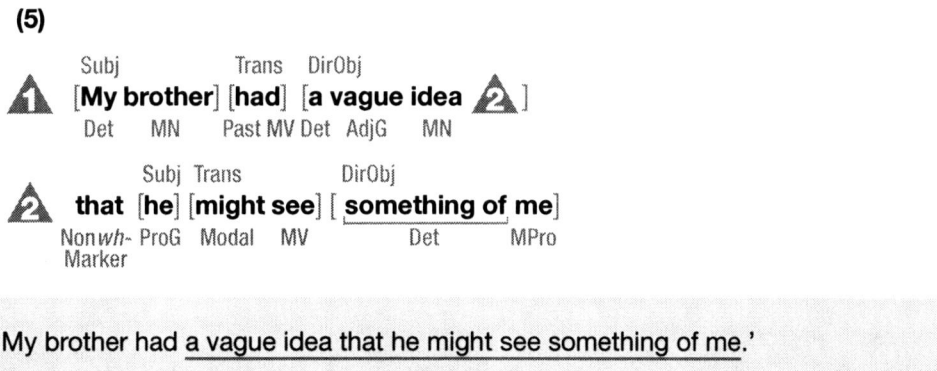

'My brother had a vague idea that he might see something of me.'

Appositive Non*wh*- *That* Clauses

Appositive non*wh*- clauses co-function with a noun group as participant, attribute, complement of a preposition group, or circumstance. Recall that, in a strict sense, apposition differs from conjoining and from embedding in two crucial ways. First, the elements in an appositive relationship refer to exactly the same elements of the event structure—that is, they are said to be strictly coreferential. And second, either of the members of the appositive pair must be substitutable for the other. Whereas *all of the elements* that share a conjoined relationship (Chapter 7), or an embedded *wh*- relationship (Chapter 8), or a non*wh*- complement relationship (immediately above) are needed to convey sense, in a **non*wh*- appositive** relationship, *either of the elements* could do the job; therefore, each of the appositive elements realizes *exactly the same function* in the clause.

In other words, non*wh*- appositive clauses differ from non*wh*- complement clauses in that the appositive clause, being of equal rank with its noun-group co-occupant, can normally stand alone in the function that it is co-performing. Indeed, it can often be seen to define the head word in its host noun group. By contrast, non*wh*- complement clauses are necessary to complete the meaning of the word group into which they are embedded and cannot therefore stand alone. Whereas all of the elements involved in a non*wh*- complementary relationship, for example, *ready to ride,* are needed to convey the intended sense, in an appositive non*wh*- relationship, either of the elements can do the job.

As can be seen in examples (6) and (7), either *the fact* or the appositive clauses themselves can stand alone in the place of the rest of their respective appositive noun groups.

(6)

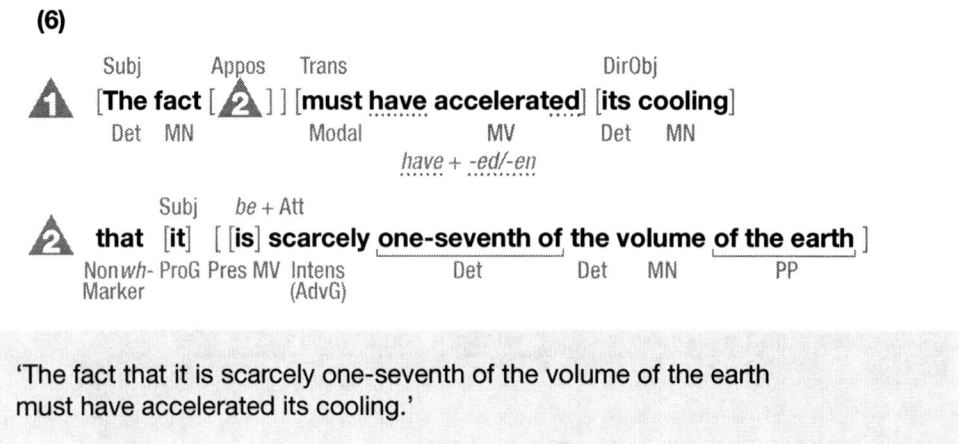

'The fact that it is scarcely one-seventh of the volume of the earth must have accelerated its cooling.'

In (6) either *This fact must have accelerated its cooling* or *That it is scarcely one-seventh of the volume of the earth must have accelerated its cooling* can express the sense of the entire sentence.

(7)

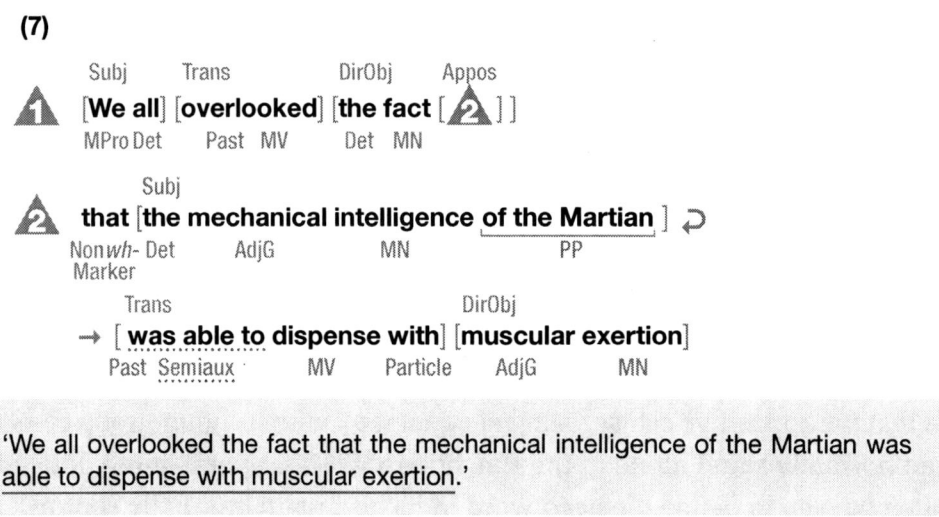

'We all overlooked the fact that the mechanical intelligence of the Martian was able to dispense with muscular exertion.'

Likewise in (7), either *We all overlooked the fact* or *We all overlooked that the mechanical intelligence of the Martian was able to dispense with muscular exertion* can express the sense of the entire sentence.

The head nouns that can share structural and functional space with appositive clauses are limited to a very small set: *fact*, *proposition*, and perhaps a few other neutral abstract terms such as these. In the Sentences for Analysis, at the end of the chapter, there are one or two examples of abstract nouns that might be candidates for an appositive relationship with a non*wh-* clause. For example, in Sentence for

Analysis (9), the word *impression* occurs in relationship with a non*wh*- clause, and in Sentence for Analysis (18) the word *idea* occurs. I have suggested that these are not appositive relationships because to me *impression* and *idea* as they are employed in these sentences are not neutral in the sense that they convey. In Sentence for Analysis (9) is it the case that the houses were still occupied? In Sentence for Analysis (18) what is the narrator warning against? Give it some thought.

Discontinuity: Extraposition

Consider the nature of the event structures in examples (8) to (10) below.

In example (8), what is curious? That is, what is the event-structure participant about which the quality of curiousness is being claimed? If your response was *It*, you get only partial credit. If your answer was *recalling some of the mental habits of those departed days,* you're right on target. Example (8) demonstrates an extraposed subject. The main-clause process has been underscored, and a partial paraphrase of the entire complex has been provided.

(8) **It is curious to recall some of the mental habits of those departed days.**
(To recall mental habits is curious.)

Extraposition in a clause, you will recall from Chapter 8, is the forward displacement of material from its expected location. We normally expect to see the subject of a clause before we see the process. In this case the spot at which we would normally see the subject is being occupied by a place-holding, nonreferential *it*. That is why the response of *it* to the question about what is curious in (8) earned only part credit. *It* in (8) does not refer to anything in particular. It only serves as a cue that the subject participant of the clause has been displaced, *extraposed*, to the right in the clause.

Examples (9) and (10) further demonstrate extraposition of a non*wh*- clause functioning as the subject participant. In example (9), the subject, *that it fell to earth about one hundred miles east of him,* has been extraposed not only around the process, but also around an oblique-object participant, *to him*. And in (10), the subject has been displaced around a circumstance of manner, *by approaching them with signals*. As was the case with (8), the main-clause processes in (9) and (10) have been underscored, and a partial paraphrase of the entire complex has been provided for each.

(9) **It seemed clear to him that it fell to earth about 100 miles east of him.**
(That it fell to earth seemed clear.)

(10) **. . . it had been resolved to show them, by approaching them with signals, that we too were intelligent.**

(To show them that we were intelligent <u>had been resolved</u>.)

Because the *it* of extraposition is structurally related to the actual subject participant of the clause, it is appropriate to treat them together as a discontinuous constituent. Here's what I mean:

(11)

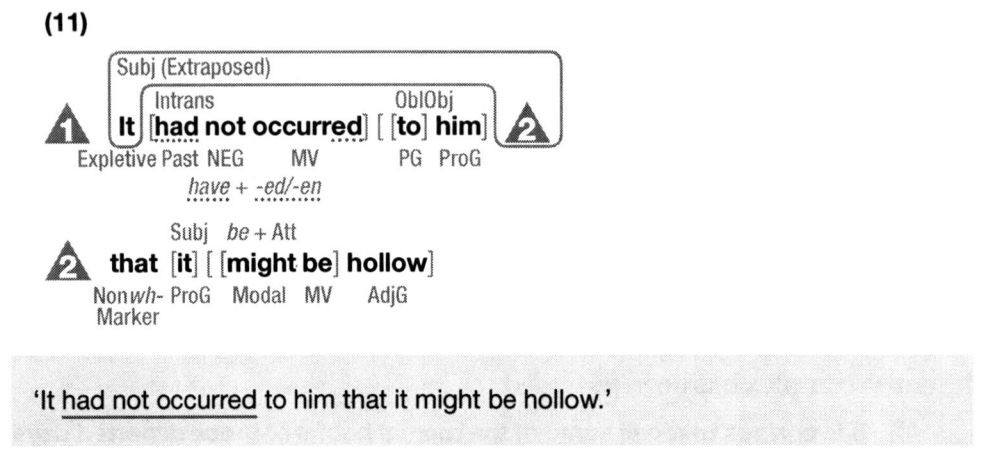

'It <u>had not occurred</u> to him that it might be hollow.'

Traditionally, the *it* of non*wh*- extraposition has been called ***anticipatory it*** and the extraposed subject has been called a ***delayed subject***. We'll use the term expletive to identify the *it* of non*wh*- extraposition, putting it in the same category as dummy *do* (in yes/no questions, for example) and *there* (in *there*-plus-*be* processes).

Discontinuity: Raising

Sometimes, in a process of displacement that is structurally analogous to extraposition, the entire non*wh*- clause that is the subject participant of a host clause is not displaced. In this process, called *raising*, one of the constituents of the subordinate clause is left to hold down the subject spot on its own. No expletive *it* is then required. Consider (12) and (13). Is the same thing not dangerous in both complexes?

(12) **For you to pet lions is dangerous.**

(13) **Lions are dangerous for you to pet.**

One way to capture this relationship is to say that the direct-object participant, *lions*, in the subordinate non*wh*- *pet* clause (*For you to pet lions*) has been **raised** to fill the subject-participant spot (as in 13). After all, the form of the verb changes from *is* in (12) to *are* in (13) so that it can match up with *lions*. The subject participant is discontinuous, as in extraposition; however, in raising, the part of the clause left behind (in this case *lions*) has to match up with the verb (in this case *are*) so that it sounds right. Compare the analyses for (12) and (13), given below at (14) and (15):

(14)

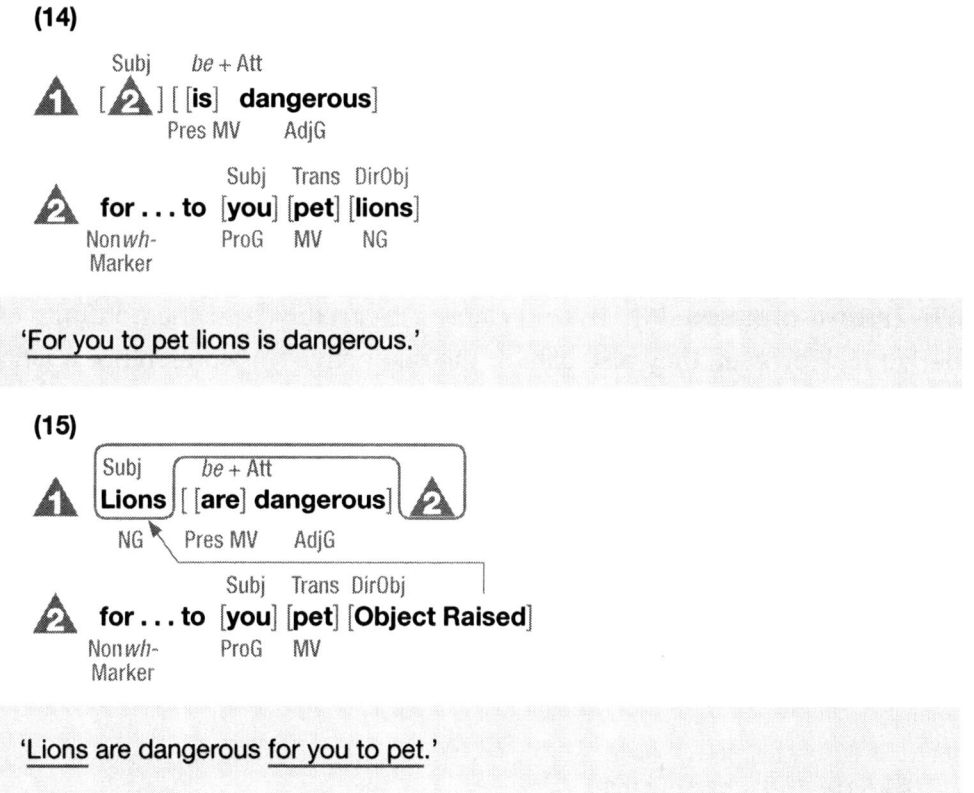

'For you to pet lions is dangerous.'

(15)

'Lions are dangerous for you to pet.'

Another sort of raising can be proposed to explain the inconsistency in the event structures represented in clause complexes such as, for example, *Ted wanted her to leave*. The event structures here are (a) *Ted wanted something* and (b) the thing Ted wants is that *she leave*. However, the pronoun in the example is *her*, not *she* (compare the *is* and *are* forms in (12) to (15)). *Her* is the form we would use for object participants, not subject participants. The complex does not imply that *Ted wanted her*, quite the opposite—he wanted her to be gone. If *she* is the subject of *leave* and not the object of *want*, then why the form *her*? One answer is to say that the subject participant in the subordinate clause has been raised to the host clause and therefore has to sound like an object instead of a subject. We made the same suggestion for *him* back in example (31) in Chapter 9, remember?

Nonfinite *Wh-* Clauses

This final segment is about clause complexes that appear to possess characteristics of both *wh-* and non*wh-* clauses simultaneously. On one hand, they all exhibit the distinguishing within-group coreference that unequivocally identifies a *wh-* relationship. In every instance of the clause types considered in this segment, there is coreference between the main noun of a host noun group and a missing element (the information gap) within the structure of the embedded clause.

On the other hand, however, the clauses are not clearly and unambiguously marked as either *wh-* or non*wh-* structures. We will consider two clause types: *wh-* hybrid and *wh-* double-marked.

***Wh-* hybrid clauses** *Wh-* hybrid clauses invariably bear the nonfinite non*wh-* marker *to*. However, they also exhibit the distinctive *wh-* coreference relationship between the head noun of the host noun group and an information gap (a missing element) in the embedded clause. A *wh-* hybrid is a *wh-* clause in this respect, but it is marked with a non*wh-* marker. An example is given at (16), and detail is provided in (17) for the *wh-* hybrid relationship.

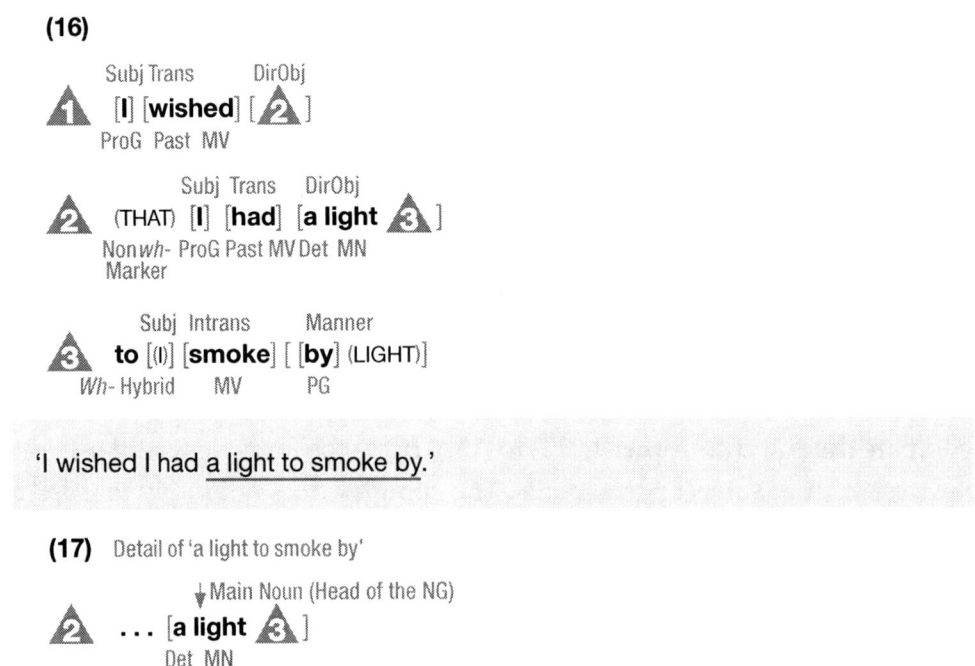

(16)

Subj Trans   DirObj
1 [**I**] [**wished**] [2]
ProG Past MV

Subj Trans   DirObj
2 (THAT) [**I**] [**had**] [**a light** 3]
Non*wh-* ProG Past MV Det MN
Marker

Subj Intrans   Manner
3 **to** [(I)] [**smoke**] [[**by**] (LIGHT)]
Wh- Hybrid   MV   PG

'I wished I had <u>a light to smoke by</u>.'

(17) Detail of 'a light to smoke by'

↓ Main Noun (Head of the NG)
2 ... [**a light** 3]
Det MN

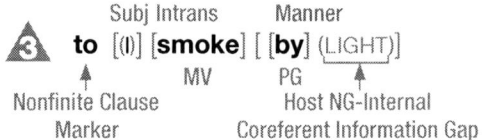

Subj Intrans   **Manner**

3️⃣ **to** [(I)] [**smoke**] [[**by**] (LIGHT)]

Nonfinite Clause Marker   MV   PG   Host NG-Internal Coreferent Information Gap

Wh- double-marked clauses On the other hand, *wh*- double-marked clauses are always signaled by both a *wh*- marker and a nonfinite non*wh*- marker (always nonfinite *to*) at the left-hand edge of the clause. This structure occurs far less frequently than normal *wh*- clauses, but the example at (18), detailed at (19), is fairly typical, in that the head of the host noun group is a missing element (it is a headless *wh*- clause).

(18)

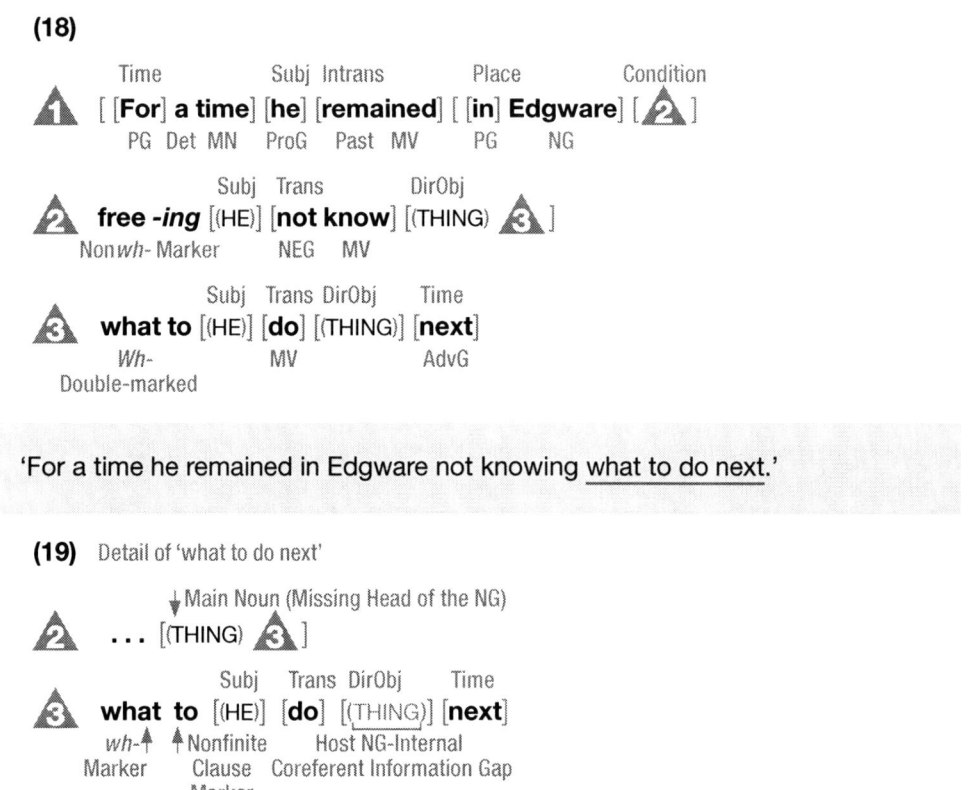

'For a time he remained in Edgware not knowing <u>what to do next</u>.'

(19) Detail of 'what to do next'

↓ Main Noun (Missing Head of the NG)

2️⃣ ... [(THING) 3️⃣]

Subj Trans DirObj Time

3️⃣ **what to** [(HE)] [**do**] [(THING)] [**next**]

wh-↑ ↑Nonfinite Host NG-Internal
Marker   Clause   Coreferent Information Gap
     Marker

Markers *Wh*- hybrid and *wh*- double-marked clauses draw into focus the question of how clause markers cue the status of the clause to follow. Among all of the markers that we have seen (List 9.1), all except five introduce clauses in which the verb group has tense or modal at the left-hand edge (finite clauses). The five that do not are the nonfinites (see list on next page).

Chart 10.1 *Wh- and Nonwh- Embedded Clause Types (a Decision-making Chart)*

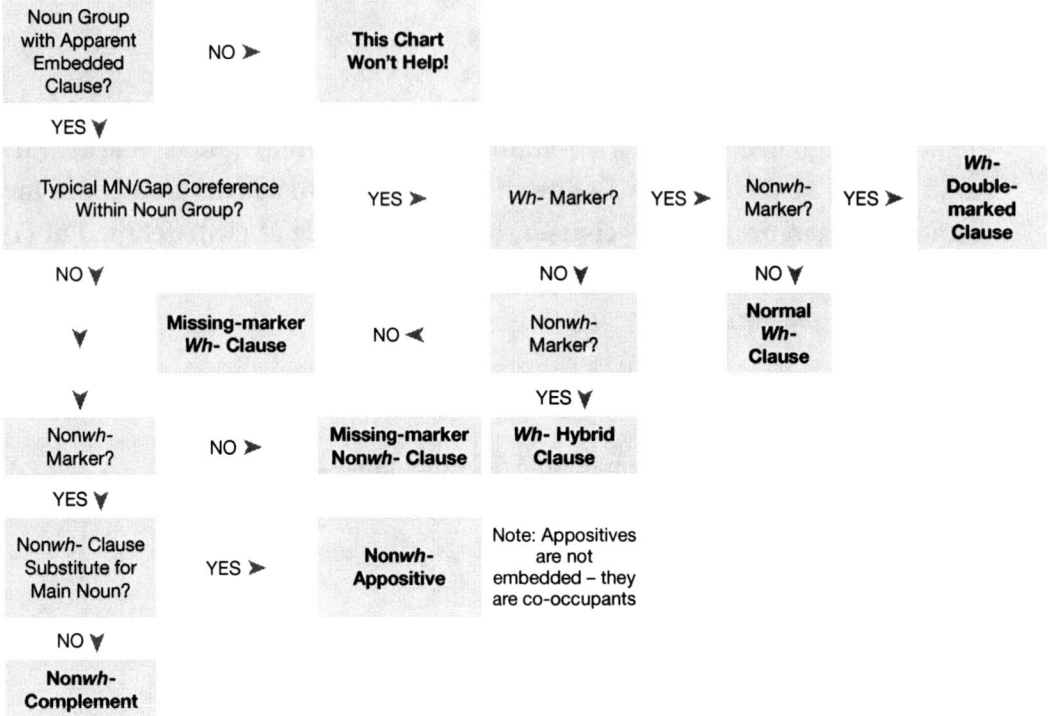

Three variants of the *to* nonfinite	Two variants of the free *-ing* nonfinite
to	free *-ing*
(to)	poss . . . free *-ing*
for . . . to	

Among markers, these five nonfinite markers are unusual in that they compete with verb-group elements for the place at the left-hand edge of the group. In this way, they are marginally clause markers and marginally verb-group elements. In the verb group they are also unusual in that they cannot serve as the operator (see Chapter 6). Moreover, among these five, only two, *to* and occasionally *for . . . to*, can function in *wh-* hybrids or double-markeds. Clearly, the nonfinite markers are exceptional among clause markers, and among the nonfinites the *to* infinitive is the most remarkable.

Chart 10.1 will help you distinguish among the various types of embedded clauses.

The safe course will be to assume that *wh*- and non*wh*- clauses form a continuum with basic *wh*- embedded clauses at one end and non*wh*- subordinate clauses at the other. In between fall the two types under consideration here, *wh*- hybrids and *wh*- double-markeds. We will pursue this safe course, treating *wh*- hybrids and *wh*-double-markeds as exceptional with respect to the much more frequently occurring *wh*- and non*wh*- clauses and as unrelated to one another in any other than the most obvious ways.

Conclusion

At the beginning of the book we set out to become proficient at doing ten things:

a Identifying the elements of event structure that are reflected in language: the things that happen and the claims that are made, the main characters and the essential props, and the elements of the scenarios

b Identifying those elements of language that are not related directly to the event structure but more clearly pertain to interpersonal relationships and discourses

c Identifying process types, participant roles, and circumstance details

d Identifying the edges and elements of word groups

e Recognizing and interpreting beginnings—the leading edge

f Recognizing and tracking coreference relationships

g Identifying markers

h Accounting for missing elements

i Recognizing and tracking discontinuity

j Analyzing subordination, embedding, complementation, and apposition

After you finish the activities at the end of this chapter, you will have been sent well on your way to attaining all of these goals. Look back now to all of the activities in Chapter 1. It will give you a sense of how your analytical skills have grown.

Practice with Terminology

What follows is a preview of the sentences that you will encounter in this chapter's Sentences for Analysis. Certain elements in the sentences have been underscored. Label each underscored element using one or more of the following terms or an applicable term from a previous chapter. Check the Glossary if you are not certain about the definition of any of the terms.

Adjective complement	Extraposition (anticipatory *it*	Raising
Appositive	and delayed subject)	*Wh-* double-marked clause
Expletive	Nonfinite clause	*Wh-* hybrid clause
	Noun complement	

1   My mind <u>was</u> occupied by my need to find my wife.

2   My cousin was not likely <u>to</u> realize danger quickly, <u>to</u> rise promptly.

3   My only consolation was the fact <u>that the Martians were moving Londonwards and away from her.</u>

4   I felt <u>an impatience to see it opened.</u>

5   <u>Finally</u> we were relieved of our fear that the Black Smoke might return.

6   The invigorating influences of this excess of oxygen upon the Martians indisputably did much to counterbalance the increased weight <u>of their bodies.</u>

7   <u>When</u> it was clear to him that I meant to go alone, he suddenly roused himself to join me.

8   At Hampton Court our eyes were relieved <u>to find a patch of green that had escaped the suffocating drift.</u>

9   I was misled by my impression that <u>many of</u> the houses here were still occupied by scared inhabitants.

10   Up the hill <u>it</u> appeared <u>that Richmond town was deserted.</u>

11   My need to reach Leatherhead <u>would</u> not let me rest.

12   <u>One officer from the Inkerman barracks, Major Eden,</u> was reported to be missing.

13   It was manifest the Martians were <u>about us.</u>

14   In a moment it was evident that a Martian <u>fighting-machine</u> pursued them.

15   I was <u>very glad to do what he asked.</u>

16   They wanted a light railing put up, and help <u>to keep the people back.</u>

17   <u>The mechanisms</u> were certain <u>to hold our attention for some time.</u>

18   I want <u>to warn the reader against the idea that they were inflexible.</u>

19   These Martians were repulsive <u>to view.</u>

20   <u>It</u> is worthy of remark that a certain speculative writer forecast for man a final structure not unlike the actual Martian condition.

21 To me it is quite credible that the Martians <u>may</u> be descended from beings not unlike ourselves.

22 I was struck <u>by the curious fact</u> that in all their machinery the *wheel* is absent.

23 <u>And in this connection</u> it is curious to remark that even on this earth Nature has never hit upon the wheel.

24 I did not know it, but that was the last civilized dinner <u>to be eaten for very many strange and terrible days.</u>

25 I <u>scarcely</u> know how to speak of it.

26 <u>These things</u> are disagreeable <u>for me</u> to recall and write.

27 Those who <u>have</u> <u>escaped</u> the dark aspects of life will find my brutality easy enough to blame.

28 It grew upon my mind that there was as yet <u>no</u> justification for absolute despair.

29 I thought that the length of its tentacle might be insufficient <u>to reach me.</u>

30 I was emboldened by the fact that no inquiring <u>tentacle</u> followed the noise.

31 We were astonished to see an unaccountable redness <u>mingling</u> with the black of the scorched meadows.

32 It was <u>nearly</u> eleven o'clock before we gathered courage to start again.

33 My neighbour <u>was</u> of the opinion that the troops would be able to capture or to destroy the Martians during the day.

34 Down the road towards Maybury Bridge <u>there were</u> voices and the sound of feet, but I had not the courage to shout or to go to them.

35 He promised to stay with them, at least until they could determine <u>what to do.</u>

> **Note:** You do not need to limit your choices to the new terms from this chapter. Where appropriate, use an applicable term from any previous chapter.

Analyzing and Reporting Multiclausal Sentences

As was noted at the end of Chapter 9, when clause complexes contain two or three clauses or even more, it can sometimes become a chore to keep up with the analysis— not because it is so difficult, but because it is so long. This is when following a charting procedure can help you keep track of the steps you have taken to analyze the complex. Here is another example:

> (20) **My immediate trouble was why we should dig this long tunnel, when it was possible to get into the drain at once down one of the manholes.**

Step 1: *Identifying processes* Start a chart by identifying processes and opening up the minimal number of functional spots for the requisite participant roles for each one. Label the process and participant functions. In the example there are four processes:

> **My immediate trouble was why we should dig this long tunnel, when it was possible to get into the drain at once down one of the manholes.**

The Chart

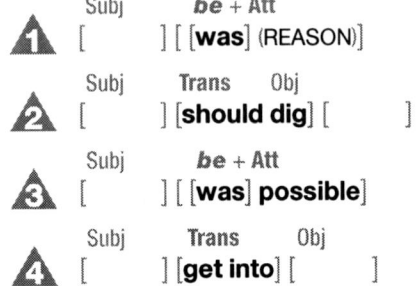

Subj   ***be*** + Att
1 [   ] [[**was**] (REASON)]

Subj   **Trans**   Obj
2 [   ] [**should dig**] [   ]

Subj   ***be*** + Att
3 [   ] [[**was**] **possible**]

Subj   **Trans**   Obj
4 [   ] [**get into**] [   ]

Was (REASON) requires one participant role, *dig* requires two, *was possible* requires one, and *get into* requires two. While you are identifying processes and opening up participant slots on the chart, take note of passive-voice verb groups (*be* + *-ed/-en*). Each is accompanied by a participant-function reversal: an active-voice object appears as the passive-voice subject, and the active-voice subject appears as an oblique object, usually introduced with *by*. In the example being developed, there are no passive-voice clauses.

Step 2: *Studying the complex and filling in the requisite participant slots on your chart* Using the logic of the event structure to do this step, seek out the role-players that are required for each process; they will usually be right in the neighborhood of the process. Remember that some participants might be missing elements and some might be clauses (even extraposed clauses). After this step, the only clause content left unaccounted for in the complex is either circumstances, clause markers, or relationship and discourse elements. Here the participants are underscored; I've underscored the *it* and the extraposed clause that is the subject of *was possible*, and within the extraposed clause I have used underscore to indicate a participant:

> **My immediate trouble was why we should dig this long tunnel, when it was possible to get into the drain at once down one of the manholes**

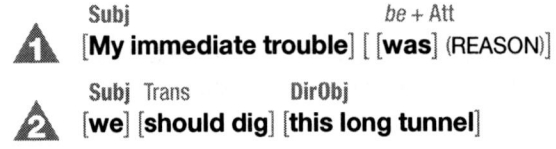

Subj   *be* + Att
1 [**My immediate trouble**] [[**was**] (REASON)]

Subj   Trans   DirObj
2 [**we**] [**should dig**] [**this long tunnel**]

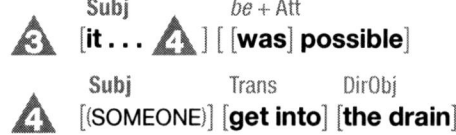

△3   [it ... △4] [[was] **possible**]   *Subj*   *be* + Att

△4   [(SOMEONE)] [**get into**] [**the drain**]   *Subj*   *Trans*   *DirObj*

Step 3: *Doing the math* Every complex has hypotactic and paratactic relationships among clauses, and all of these relationships are marked as either (1) conjoined, (2) *wh*-, or (3) non*wh*-. However, one of the clauses is the host clause and will not have a marker. Therefore, after you count the processes, you can subtract one (for the host clause), and the remainder will be the number of marked clauses, and therefore the number of markers, you will find. *Take care:* some *wh*- clauses could be double-marked, and it's always possible that a marker could be a missing element. Take your time at this step; it'll pay off.

Here's the math for our example:

> Four processes identified: 4
>
> *minus* One (for the host clause):   −1
>
> *yields* *Three* markers needed: 3

Step 4: *Finding markers and adding them to your chart* Remember that all markers (except the nonfinite clause markers, free *-ing* and *to*, which are at the far left-hand edge of the verb group—see Chapter 9) occur out in front of the clause. All markers (including free *-ing* and *to*) are charted and reported to the left of their clauses. Allow for the formal style in which preposition groups and determiners that might otherwise be inside the boundaries of a clause get pulled out to form a group with the marker. Our example has three overt markers, one *wh*- and two non*wh*- :*

**My immediate trouble was *why* we should dig this long tunnel,
when it was possible *to* get into the drain at once down one of the manholes**

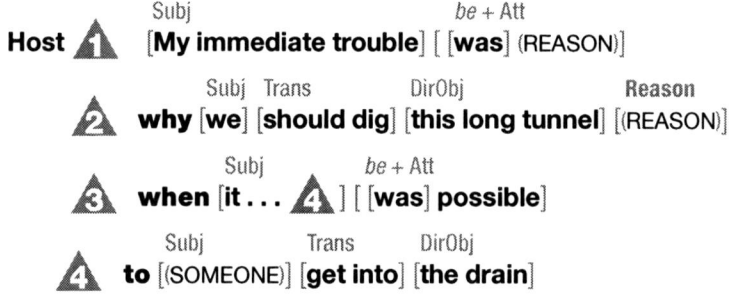

Host △1   [**My immediate trouble**] [[**was**] (REASON)]   *Subj*   *be* + Att

△2   **why** [**we**] [**should dig**] [**this long tunnel**] [(REASON)]   *Subj Trans*   *DirObj*   **Reason**

△3   **when** [it ... △4] [[was] **possible**]   *Subj*   *be* + Att

△4   **to** [(SOMEONE)] [**get into**] [**the drain**]   *Subj*   *Trans*   *DirObj*

*I analyze the *when* clause as non*wh*-, equivalent in meaning to *given that*, rather than as a time circumstance.

After this step, all that is left to account for in the clause complex will be either (a) circumstances or (b) relationship and discourse elements.

Step 5: *Taking stock* Locate circumstance, relationship, and discourse units. Here is the clause complex as it now stands after processes, participants, and markers have been transferred to your chart; the remaining units are underscored.

> **My immediate trouble was why we should dig this long tunnel,**
> **when it was possible to get into the drain <u>at once</u> <u>down one of the manholes</u>**

What do you make of what's left? Looks pretty straightforward, doesn't it?

At once is a manner circumstance (or perhaps you might see it as a time circumstance).

Down one of the manholes is a place circumstance (or perhaps you might see it as a means circumstance).

Step 6: *Adding circumstance, relationship, and discourse units to your chart* Amend participants as required. Fill in missing elements as required. You might have to refer to the context of the passage.

> **My immediate trouble was why we should dig this long tunnel,**
> **when it was possible to get into the drain <u>at once</u> <u>down one of the manholes</u>**

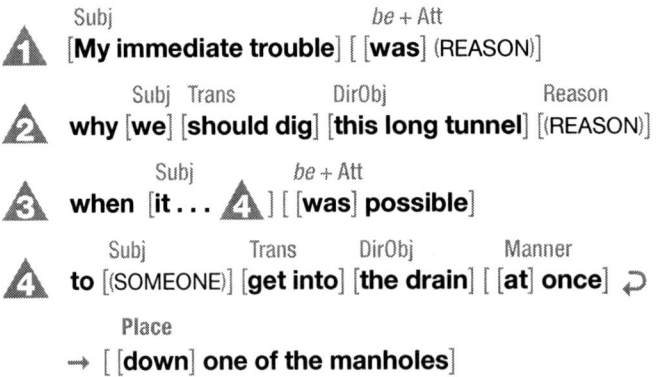

All that remains is to make sure that each embedded and subordinate clause (in addition to ▲4, which we have already identified as an extraposed subject and which we now locate in its extraposed spot) has a place to dock in its host clause.

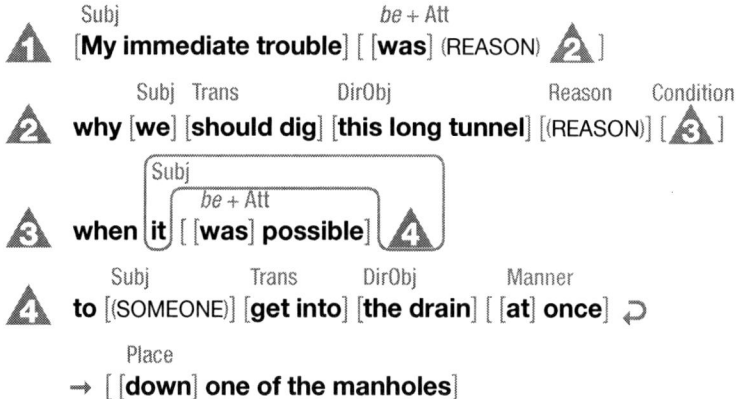

Step 7: *Making a triangle-convention report* The 'chart' has evolved into a triangle-convention report. All that remains is to observe minimal bracketing and labeling protocol.

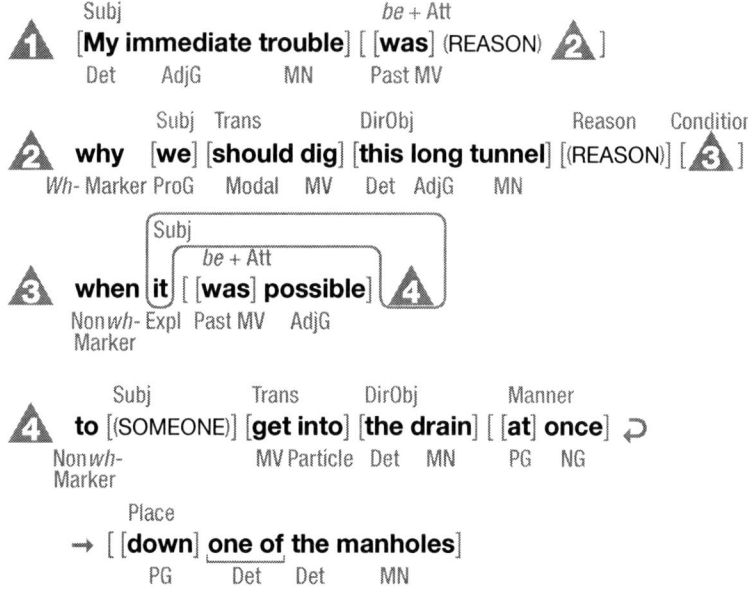

Sentences for Analysis

The following sentences are adapted from *The War of the Worlds*. Analyze them and report your results as shown in the example. Make certain that your analyses have the following features:

a Bracket processes, participants, and circumstances and label them by function at the top of the bracket.

b Sub-bracket as necessary, observing minimal bracketing conventions.

c Label elements in all word groups. One-element groups should be given a group label.

d Follow the triangle convention in reporting embedded and subordinate clauses.

(21)

'My immediate trouble was why we should dig this long tunnel,
when it was possible to get into the drain at once down one of the manholes.'

1   My mind was occupied by my need to find my wife.

2   My cousin was not likely to realize danger quickly, to rise promptly. (**Subject-to-subject raising**)

✱ 3   My only consolation was the fact that the Martians were moving Londonwards and away from her. (**Appositive**)

4   I felt an impatience to see it opened.

5   Finally we were relieved of our fear that the Black Smoke might return. (**Complement**)

6   The invigorating influences of this excess of oxygen upon the Martians indisputably did much to counterbalance the increased weight of their bodies. (**Wh- hybrid**)

7   When it was clear to him that I meant to go alone, he suddenly roused himself to join me.

✱ 8   At Hampton Court our eyes were relieved to find a patch of green that had escaped the suffocating drift. (**Nonwh- complement; normal wh-**)

9   I was misled by my impression that many of the houses here were still occupied by scared inhabitants. (**See pages 202–3**)

10   Up the hill it appeared that Richmond town was deserted. (**Extraposition**)

11   My need to reach Leatherhead would not let me rest.

✱ 12   One officer from the Inkerman barracks, Major Eden, was reported to be missing.

13   It was manifest the Martians were about us.

14   In a moment it was evident that a Martian fighting-machine pursued them. (**Extraposition**)

15   I was very glad to do what he asked.

✱ 16   They wanted a light railing put up, and help to keep the people back.

17   The mechanisms were certain to hold our attention for some time.

18   I want to warn the reader against the idea that they were inflexible. (**See comment, pages 202–3**)

19   These Martians were repulsive to view.

20   It is worthy of remark that a certain speculative writer forecast for man a final structure not unlike the actual Martian condition. (**Extraposition**)

✱ 21   To me it is quite credible that the Martians may be descended from beings not unlike ourselves.

22   I was struck by the curious fact that in all their machinery the *wheel* is absent.

23   And in this connection it is curious to remark that even on this earth Nature has never hit upon the wheel.

24   I did not know it, but that was the last civilized dinner to be eaten for very many strange and terrible days.

✱ 25   I scarcely know how to speak of it. (**Wh- double-marked**)

26   These things are disagreeable for me to recall and write. (**Object-to-subject raising**)

27   Those who have escaped the dark aspects of life will find my brutality easy enough to blame.

28   It grew upon my mind that there was as yet no justification for absolute despair.

29   I thought that the length of its tentacle might be insufficient to reach me.

30 I was emboldened by the fact that no inquiring tentacle followed the noise.

31 We were astonished to see an unaccountable redness mingling with the black of the scorched meadows.

✱ 32 It was nearly eleven o'clock before we gathered courage to start again. **(Time; Complement)**

33 My neighbour was of the opinion that the troops would be able to capture or to destroy the Martians during the day.

34 Down the road towards Maybury Bridge there were voices and the sound of feet, but I had not the courage to shout or to go to them.

35 He promised to stay with them, at least until they could determine what to do.

Note: Suggested responses for the sentences marked by an asterisk (✱) are given at the back of the book. As a way of getting started on this activity, you might want to work first on those items. Some of the other items have a hint. The non*wh*- clause is underscored in some, and the non*wh*- clause type is provided for some others. Where your responses and the suggested ones differ, you will want to get advice from your instructor. Very often, several interpretations might be appropriate.

Text for Analysis

The text that follows (approximately 430 words) is taken from *The War of the Worlds*. Each sentence in the passage is numbered for your convenience. Analyze the text and report your results following the directions and the example in Sentences for Analysis.

This text was not selected to have a disproportionate number of embedded, appositive, and discontinuous non*wh*- clauses; in your analyses you will have to apply everything you have learned up to this point.

---

(1) I sat up, strangely perplexed. (2) For a moment, perhaps, I could not clearly understand how I came there. (3) My terror had fallen from me like a garment. (4) My hat had gone, and my collar had burst away from its fastener. (5) A few minutes before, there had only been three real things before me—the immensity of the night and space and nature, my own feebleness and anguish, and the near approach of death. (6) Now it was as if something turned over, and the point of view altered abruptly. (7) There was no sensible transition from one state of mind to the other. (8) I was immediately the self

of every day again—a decent, ordinary citizen. (9) The silent common, the impulse of my flight, the starting flames, were as if they had been in a dream. (10) I asked myself had these latter things indeed happened? (11) I could not credit it.

(12) I rose and walked unsteadily up the steep incline of the bridge. (13) My mind was blank wonder. (14) My muscles and nerves seemed drained of their strength. (15) I dare say I staggered drunkenly. (16) A head rose over the arch, and the figure of a workman carrying a basket appeared. (17) Beside him ran a little boy. (18) He passed me, wishing me good night. (19) I was minded to speak to him, but did not. (20) I answered his greeting with a meaningless mumble and went on over the bridge.

(21) Over the Maybury arch a train, a billowing tumult of white, firelit smoke, and a long caterpillar of lighted windows, went flying south—clatter, clatter, clap, rap, and it had gone. (22) A dim group of people talked in the gate of one of the houses in the pretty little row of gables that was called Oriental Terrace. (23) It was all so real and so familiar. (24) And that behind me! (25) It was frantic, fantastic! (26) Such things, I told myself, could not be.

(27) Perhaps I am a man of exceptional moods. (28) I do not know how far my experience is common. (29) At times I suffer from the strangest sense of detachment from myself and the world about me. (30) I seem to watch it all from the outside, from somewhere inconceivably remote, out of time, out of space, out of the stress and tragedy of it all. (31) This feeling was very strong upon me that night. (32) Here was another side to my dream.

(33) But the trouble was the blank incongruity of this serenity and the swift death flying yonder, not two miles away. (34) There was a noise of business from the gasworks, and the electric lamps were all alight. (35) I stopped at the group of people.

> **Note:** Suggested responses for underscored items are given at the back of the book.

Dialog for Analysis

The following text is another unedited excerpt (about 325 words) from *The War of the Worlds*. This excerpt differs from the one in the Text for Analysis activity in that it contains a significant amount of dialog. By using dialog, H. G. Wells tries to create a sense of interpersonal interaction to contrast with the narrative that carries most of the story.

Several parts of the excerpt have been numbered and underscored. See how far your skill at analyzing sentence structure takes you in the direction of understanding how dialog works. Be particularly alert to relationship and discourse elements. After all, written dialog is supposed to capture the tone of live interactions.

But the trouble was the blank incongruity of this serenity and the swift death flying yonder, not two miles away. There was a noise of business from the gasworks, and the electric lamps were all alight. I stopped at the group of people.

(1) 'What news from the common?' said I.

There were two men and a woman at the gate.

(2) 'Eh?' said one of the men, turning.

(3) 'What news from the common?' I said.

(4) 'Ain't yer just *been* there?' asked the men.

'People seem fair silly about the common,' said the woman over the gate. 'What's it all abart?'

(5) 'Haven't you heard of the men from Mars?' said I; 'the creatures from Mars?'

(6) 'Quite enough,' said the woman over the gate. (7) 'Thenks'; and all three of them laughed.

I felt foolish and angry. I tried and found I could not tell them what I had seen. They laughed again at my broken sentences.

'You'll hear more yet,' I said, and went on to my home.

I startled my wife at the doorway, so haggard was I. I went into the dining room, sat down, drank some wine, and so soon as I could collect myself sufficiently I told her the things I had seen. The dinner, which was a cold one, had already been served, and remained neglected on the table while I told my story.

(8) 'There is one thing,' I said, to allay the fears I had aroused; 'they are the most sluggish things I ever saw crawl. They may keep the pit and kill people who come near them, but they cannot get out of it. . . . But the horror of them!'

(9) 'Don't, dear!' said my wife, knitting her brows and putting her hand on mine.

(10) 'Poor Ogilvy!' I said. (11) 'To think he may be lying dead there!'

My wife at least did not find my experience incredible. When I saw how deadly white her face was, I ceased abruptly.

SUGGESTED RESPONSES

Chapter 2

Selected Sentences for Analysis

              Intrans
(1) **The curate [talked] wildly to me under the hedge**

                      be + Att
(9) **The Ripley gunners [were unseasoned artillery volunteers]**

                be + Loc
(14) **The Martians [were very near to them]**

                   Trans
(20) **Both of his companions [aimed] their Heat-Rays on the men**

       LV + Att
(26) **He [resembled a speck of blight]**

               Intrans
(31) **A dozen rockets [sprang] out of the hills**

             be + Att
(36) **The night [was lit only by the slender moon]**

               Intrans
(42) **A hundred questions [struggled] together in my mind**

              Trans
(46) **In my excitement I [forgot] my personal safety**

     there + be
(50) **[There had been] no crash, no answering explosion**

Chapter 3

Activity 3.1

Participant	Participant role	Participant function
No one	believer	subject
this world	watchee	subject
by intelligences greater than man's . . .	watcher	oblique object
themselves	busyee	direct object
they	scrutinizee	subject
a man with a microscope	scrutinizer	subject
the transient creatures that swarm . . .	scrutinizee	direct object
the infusoria under the microscope	doer	subject
to the older worlds of space	thinkee	indirect object
of them	thinkee	oblique object
some of the mental habits of . . .	recallee	direct object
other men upon Mars . . .	exister	subject
this earth	regardee	direct object
with envious eyes	tool for regarding	oblique object
the great disillusionment	arriver	subject
the light and heat	attributee	subject
this earth	ceaser	subject
life upon its surface	beginner	subject
its course	beginnee	direct object
its cooling	acceleratee	direct object

Activity 3.2

Circumstance	Circumstance type
in the last years of the nineteenth century	time or place
keenly	manner
With infinite complacency	manner
to and fro	place or manner
across the gulf of space	place or time
slowly and surely	manner
early in the twentieth century	time or place
at a mean distance of 140,000,000 miles	place
if the nebular hypothesis has any truth	condition
up to the very end of the nineteenth century	time or place
far, or indeed at all, beyond its earthly level	manner
even in its equatorial region	place
about either pole	place
across space	place

Activity 3.3

(39) At once, <u>with a quick mental leap</u>, he linked the Thing <u>with the flash upon Mars.</u>

with a quick mental leap sounds like circumstance of manner to me, telling how he linked the Thing with the flash

with the flash upon Mars sounds like an oblique-object participant to me; it is one of the two link*ees* (the Thing and the flash)

Selected Sentences for Analysis

Subj   *be* + Att
(5) [They] [were serene]

Subj   Trans   DirObj   Manner
(8) [Other minds] [regarded] [this earth] [with envious eyes]

Time   Subj   Intrans   OblObj
(14) [Generation after generation] [the destruction] [creeps] [upon them]

      Subj   Trans   DirObj

(17) [European immigrants] [waged] [a war of extermination] ↺

         OblObj

→ [against the Tasmanians]

      Subj Trans   DirObj

(20) [We] [might have seen] [the gathering trouble] ↺

         Time

→ [far back in the nineteenth century]

      Subj   Trans   Place

(23) [A great light] [was seen] [on the illuminated part of the disk]

      Subj   LV + Att   Time

(32) [This jet of fire] [became invisible] [about a quarter past twelve]

      Subj   Trans   OblObj

(37) [Ogilvy, the well-known astronomer] [was immensely excited] [at the news]

      OblObj   Subj Trans DirObj

(41) [Through the telescope] [one] [saw] [a circle of deep blue]

      OblObj   Subj LV + Att

(47) [In a telescope] [it] [seems far profounder]

Chapter 4

Activity 4.1

The Martians seem to have calculated their descent with <u>amazing</u> subtlety—their <u>mathematical</u> learning is evidently far in excess of ours—and to have carried out their preparations with a <u>well-nigh perfect</u> unanimity. Had our instruments permitted it, we might have seen the <u>gathering</u> trouble far back in the nineteenth century. Men like Schiaparelli watched the <u>red</u> planet—it is <u>odd</u>, by-the-bye, that for countless centuries Mars has been the star of war—but failed to interpret the <u>fluctuating</u> appearances of the markings they mapped so well. All that time the Martians must have been getting <u>ready</u>.

During the opposition of 1894 a <u>great</u> light was seen on the <u>illuminated</u> part of the disk, first at the Lick Observatory, then by Perrotin of Nice, and then by other observers. <u>English</u> readers heard of it first in the issue of *Nature* dated August 2. I am inclined to think that this blaze may have been the casting of the <u>huge</u> gun, in the <u>vast</u> pit sunk into their planet, from which their shots were fired at us. <u>Peculiar</u> markings, as yet <u>unexplained</u>, were seen near the site of that outbreak during the next two oppositions.

The storm burst upon us six years ago now. As Mars approached opposition, Lavelle of Java set the wires of the <u>astronomical</u> exchange palpitating with the <u>amazing</u> intelligence of a <u>huge</u> outbreak of <u>incandescent</u> gas upon the planet. It had occurred towards midnight of the twelfth; and the spectroscope, to which he had at once resorted, indicated a mass of <u>flaming</u> gas, chiefly hydrogen, moving with an <u>enormous</u> velocity towards this earth. This jet of fire had become <u>invisible</u> about a quarter past twelve. He compared it to a <u>colossal</u> puff of flame suddenly and violently squirted out of the planet, 'as <u>flaming</u> gases rushed out of a gun'.

Activity 4.2

A <u>singularly</u> appropriate phrase it proved. Yet the next day there was nothing of this in the papers except a little note in the *Daily Telegraph*, and the world went in ignorance of one of the gravest dangers that <u>ever</u> threatened the human race. I might not have heard of the eruption <u>at all</u> had I not met Ogilvy, the well-known astronomer, at Ottershaw. He was <u>immensely</u> excited at the news, and in the excess of his feelings invited me up to take a turn with him that night in a scrutiny of the red planet.

In spite of all that has happened <u>since</u>, I <u>still</u> remember that vigil <u>very distinctly</u>: the black and silent observatory, the shadowed lantern throwing a feeble glow upon the floor in the corner, the steady ticking of the clockwork of the telescope, the little slit in the roof—an oblong profundity with the stardust streaked across it. Ogilvy moved <u>about</u>, invisible but audible. Looking through the telescope, one saw a circle of deep blue and the little round planet swimming in the field. It seemed <u>such</u> a little thing, <u>so</u> bright and small and still, <u>faintly</u> marked with transverse stripes, and <u>slightly</u> flattened from the perfect round. But <u>so</u> little it was, <u>so</u> silvery warm—a pin's-head of light! It was as if it quivered, but <u>really</u> this was the telescope vibrating with the activity of the clockwork that kept the planet in view.

As I watched, the planet seemed to grow larger and smaller and to advance and recede, but that was <u>simply</u> that my eye was tired. Forty millions of miles it was from us—more than forty millions of miles of void. Few people realize the immensity of vacancy in which the dust of the material universe swims.

Near it in the field, I remember, were three faint points of light, three telescopic stars infinitely remote, and all around it was the unfathomable darkness of empty space. You know how that blackness looks on a frosty starlight night. In a telescope it seems far profounder. And invisible to me because it was so remote and small, flying swiftly and steadily towards me across that incredible distance, drawing nearer every minute by so many thousands of miles, came the Thing they were sending us, the Thing that was to bring so much struggle and calamity and death to the earth. I never dreamed of it then as I watched; no one on earth dreamed of that unerring missile.

Selected Sentences for Analysis

be + Loc (Inverted order)   Subj
(6) [**Down below** in the darkness [were]] [Ottershaw and Chertsey]
     MAdv   PP   VG   NG   Conj   NG

Subj   *be* + Att
(12) [The chances against anything manlike on Mars] [[are] a million to one]
      MN   PP   VG   MN   PP

Subj   Intrans   Place
(16) [Popular notes] [appeared] [here, there, and everywhere]
     AdjG   MN   VG   AdvG   AdvG   Conj   AdvG

Subj   Trans
(20) [People in these latter times] [scarcely [realize]] ⊃
     MN   PP   Intens   VG
                            (AdvG)

          DirObj
    → [the abundance and enterprise of our nineteenth-century papers]
               MN   Conj   MN   PP

there + *be*   Subj   Place
(26) [There [were]] [lights] [[in] the upper windows of the houses]
    Expletive   VG   NG   PG   MN   PP

Subj LV + Att
(30) [It] [[seemed] so safe and tranquil]
    ProG   VG   Intens MAdj Conj   MAdj
                 (AdvG)

Subj *be* + Loc   Time
(35) [I] [[was] at home] [[at] that hour]
    ProG   VG   PP   PG   MN

```
         Subj                    Trans                OblObj
(40)  [An enormous hole] [had been made] [ [by] the impact of the projectile ]
         AdjG      MN           MV          PG        MN             PP
```

```
         Subj                 LV + Att
(44)  [The Thing itself] [lay [ almost entirely [buried in sand ] ] ]  ↻
         MN    ProG   VG        Intens          MAdj    PP
                                (AdvG)
```

```
              Place
  →  [ [amidst] the scattered splinters of a fir tree ]
           PG              AdjG          MN        PP
```

```
     Subj  Intrans      Place
(50)  [He] [remained] [ [at] the edge of the pit ]
     ProG    VG         PG       MN      PP
```

Chapter 5

Activity 5.1

(1) The fact that it is scarcely one-seventh of the volume of the earth must have accelerated its cooling to the temperature at which life could begin.

(2) The secular cooling that must someday overtake our planet has already gone far indeed with our neighbour.

(3) Its physical condition is still largely a mystery, but we know now that even in its equatorial region the midday temperature barely approaches that of our coldest winter.

(4) Its air is much more attenuated than ours, its oceans have shrunk until they cover but a third of its surface, and as its slow seasons change huge snowcaps gather and melt about either pole and periodically inundate its temperate zones.

Activity 5.2

```
              Trans
(36)  The dog [had been being given] free run of the house.

              Past                      MV
         have + -ed/-en   be + -ing   be + -ed/-en
```

Activity 5.3

(66) . . . no one on earth dreamed of that unerring missile.

Here we have to consider two possibilities: (a) dreamed, and (b) dreamed of. Would we get the same sense from . . . *no one on earth dreamed that unerring missile*? Doesn't *dreamed of* mean *imagined*, as in . . . *no one on earth could have imagined that unerring missile*? I think so. My guess is that *dreamed of* is a two-part verb that means something like *imagined*.

(67) I loved in those days to <u>look up at</u> the night sky . . .

Here, perhaps, three possibilities exist: (a) look, (b) look up, (c) look up at. Of the three, the only candidate for multiword verb status is (b) look up; however, this multiword verb usually means *search for*, and we don't have that sense here. My vote goes for *look* as process, *up* as circumstance of place, and *at the night sky* also as circumstance of place.

(68) He approached the mass, <u>surprised at</u> the size . . .

When I compare *surprised* with *surprised at*, I get no shift in the sense of *surprise*. For me, *surprise* is the process and *at the size* is an oblique object, playing the surpris*er* role.

(69) . . . the ashy encrustation that covered the meteorite, was <u>falling off</u> the circular edge of the end.

In this case, whether it *falls* or *falls off*, it still ends up on the ground. *Off* does not particularize *falls* such that *falls off* means something different from *falls* (but compare *buzz* and *buzz off*). Here, again, I would not vote for a multiword verb analysis.

(70) . . . then turned, <u>scrambled out of</u> the pit, and ↻

→ <u>set off</u> running wildly into Woking.

The *scramble* part of *scrambled*, *scrambled out*, and *scrambled out of* all mean the same thing to me. No multiword verb interpretation here. However, *set* and *set off* do contrast. The first, *set*, means *place*, and the other means *embark*, or *leave*, or *go*. This is a multiword verb.

Selected Sentences for Analysis

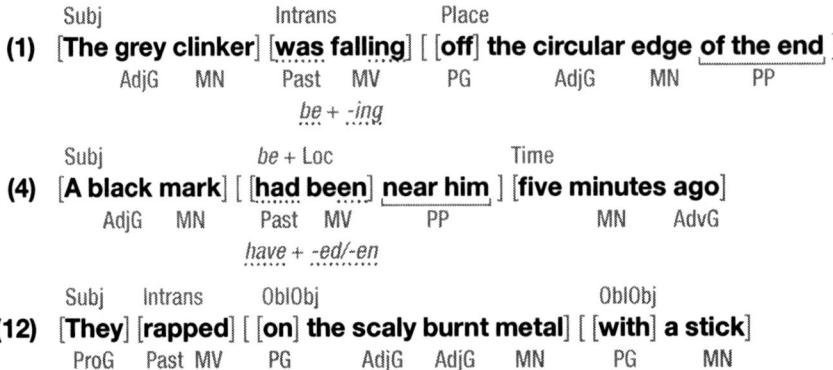

228

(19)
there + *be* — Subj — Place
[There [had been]] [four or five boys] [[at] the edge of the Pit]
Expletive Past MV — MN — PG — MN — PP
have + *-ed/-en*

(26)
Subj — Trans — DirObj
[Something] [seemed to have irritated] [him]
ProG — Past — MV — ProG
Semiaux — *have* + *-ed/-en*

(33)
Time — Subj — LV + Att
[[For] a moment] [that circular cavity] [[seemed] perfectly black]
PG — MN — AdjG — MN — Past MV — Intens — MAdj
(AdvG)

(39)
Time — Subj Trans — OblObj
[Even [[at] this first glimpse]] [I] [was overcome] [[with] disgust and dread]
Intens — PG — MN — ProG Past — MV — PG — NG — Conj — NG
(AdvG) — *be* + *-ed/-en*

(42)
Subj Trans — DirObj — OblObj
[I] [could not avert] [my face] [[from] these things]
ProG Modal NEG MV — MN — PG — MN

(47)
Subj Intrans — Time — Manner
[We] [continued watching] [[for] a time] [side by side]
ProG — Past — MV — PG — MN — MN — PP
continue + *-ing*
(Alternate Progressive Aspect)

(50)
Subj — Intrans — Manner — Place
[Some cabmen and others] [had walked] [boldly] [[into] the sand pits]
MN — Conj — MN — Past MV — AdvG — PG — MN
have + *-ed/-en*

Chapter 6

Activity 6.1

(26) Where's your shells [(LOCATION)] **?**
Missing Element

The missing element is the Location of the discontinuous *be* + Location process: Your shells is [(LOCATION)]. *Over there* would be a fine reply to the question.

(27) How are we to get to Leatherhead [(MANNER)]**?**
Missing Element

The missing element is a Manner circumstance: We are to get to Leatherhead [(MANNER)]. *In a horse and dog cart* might be the reply.

Selected Sentences for Analysis

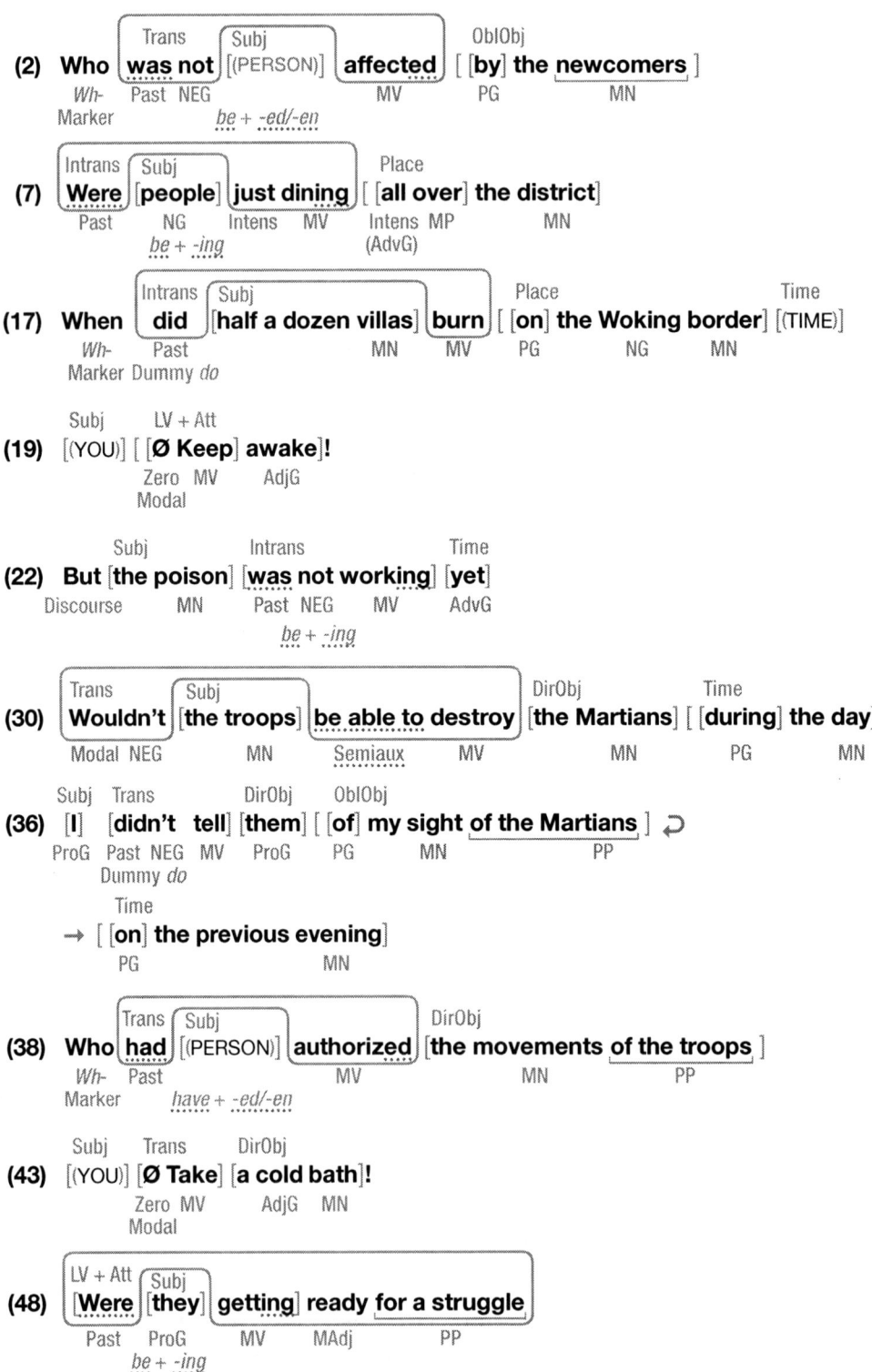

(2) Who was not [(PERSON)] affected [[by] the newcomers]
   Wh- Past NEG *be* + *-ed/-en* MV PG MN
   Marker
   Trans Subj OblObj
   PG MN

(7) Were [people] just dining [[all over] the district]
   Past NG Intens MV Intens MP MN
   be + *-ing* (AdvG)
   Intrans Subj Place

(17) When did [half a dozen villas] burn [[on] the Woking border] [(TIME)]
   Wh- Past MN MV PG NG MN
   Marker Dummy *do*
   Intrans Subj Place Time

(19) [(YOU)] [[Ø Keep] awake]!
   Zero MV AdjG
   Modal
   Subj LV + Att

(22) But [the poison] [was not working] [yet]
   Discourse MN Past NEG MV AdvG
   be + *-ing*
   Subj Intrans Time

(30) Wouldn't [the troops] be able to destroy [the Martians] [[during] the day]
   Modal NEG MN Semiaux MV MN PG MN
   Trans Subj DirObj Time

(36) [I] [didn't tell] [them] [[of] my sight of the Martians]
   ProG Past NEG MV ProG PG MN PP
   Dummy *do*
   Subj Trans DirObj OblObj
   → [[on] the previous evening]
   PG MN
   Time

(38) Who had [(PERSON)] authorized [the movements of the troops]
   Wh- Past MV MN PP
   Marker *have* + *-ed/-en*
   Trans Subj DirObj

(43) [(YOU)] [Ø Take] [a cold bath]!
   Zero MV AdjG MN
   Modal
   Subj Trans DirObj

(48) [Were] [they] getting] ready for a struggle
   Past ProG MV MAdj PP
   be + *-ing*
   LV + Att Subj

Chapter 7

Activity 7.1

(8) **That night nearly forty people lay under the starlight about the pit, charred and distorted beyond recognition, and all night long the common from Horsell to Maybury was deserted and brightly ablaze.**

Here *that night* is a circumstance of time, *nearly forty people* is a participant, *the starlight* is the complement of a preposition group in a circumstance of place, *the pit* is the complement of a preposition group in another circumstance of place, *recognition* is the complement of a preposition group in a circumstance of condition, *all night long* is a circumstance of time, and *the common from Horsell to Maybury* is a participant.

(9) **The news of the massacre probably reached Chobham, Woking, and Ottershaw about the same time.**

Here *the news of the massacre* is a participant; *Chobham, Woking* and *Ottershaw* are the direct objects of *reached*; *about the same time* is a noun group that is a circumstance of time (I take *about* to be an intensifier here, not a preposition group).

(10) **As yet, of course, few people in Woking even knew that the cylinder had opened, though poor Henderson had sent a messenger on a bicycle to the post office with a special wire to an evening paper.**

Here *few people in Woking* is a participant; so are *the cylinder, poor Henderson*, and *a messenger*. *A bicycle* is the complement of a preposition group in a circumstance of manner. *The post office* is the complement of a preposition group in a circumstance of place. *With a special wire to an evening paper* is an oblique object participant in the *sent* process, and *a special wire to an evening paper* is the complement of the preposition group *with*.

(11) **Stent and Ogilvy, anticipating some possibilities of a collision, had telegraphed from Horsell to the barracks as soon as the Martians emerged, for the help of a company of soldiers to protect these strange creatures from violence.**

Here *Stent* and *Ogilvy* are participants; so is *some possibilities of a collision*, although in a different process. *Horsell* and *the barracks* are the complements of preposition groups in circumstances of place. *The Martians* is a participant; *the help of a company of soldiers* is the complement of a preposition group in an oblique object participant in the *telegraphed* process. *These strange creatures* and *violence* are both participants in the *protect* process, with *violence* being expressed in an oblique object as the complement of a preposition group.

Selected Sentences for Analysis

```
        Subj                      be + Loc
(1)  [My younger brother] [ [was]  in London ]
      Det   Det      MN    Past MV      PP
```

```
        Subj                       Trans         DirObj
(5)  [The papers on Saturday ] [contained] [a brief and vague telegram]
      Det    MN       PP         Past MV    Det AdjG  Conj  AdjG     MN
```

```
       Subj    Trans  DirObj
(12) [They] [told] [nothing beyond the movements of troops about the common ]
      ProG  Past MV    MN                          PP
```

```
       DirObj                        Subj         Trans
(18) [The nature of the accident ] [my brother] [could not ascertain]
      Det    MN         PP          Det    MN     Modal NEG    MV
```

```
       Subj                         Trans       DirObj
(20) [A nocturnal newspaper reporter] [mistook] [my brother] ⟳
      Det    AdjG         NG            Past MV   Det   MN
```

```
              OblObj
       → [ [for] the traffic manager]
              PG   Det   NG      MN
```

```
       Subj                 Trans     DirObj              Subj       Trans     DirObj
(26) [The newspapers] [made] [startling reports] but [Londoners] [ignored] [them]
      Det      MN     Past MV   AdjG      MN     Conj    NG       Past MV    ProG
```

```
       Subj               be + Att                        OblObj
(31) [The field guns ] [ [have been] absolutely useless] [ [against] their armour]
      Det     MN         Pres MV      Intens     MAdj       PG     Det    MN
                         have + -ed/-en  (AdvG)
```

```
       Subj            be + Att  Time
(37) [The train service] [was] [now] very much disorganized
      Det   NG     MN    Past MV AdvG   Intens       MAdj
                                        (AdvG)
```

```
       Subj                       Trans       DirObj
(40) [A man in a blue and white blazer ] [addressed] [my brother]
      Det MN          PP                   Past   MV   Det   MN
```

```
       Subj                 Intrans            Place
(46) [ Five of the machines] [had been moving] [ [towards] the Thames]
       Det   Det   MN        Past      MV        PG    Det    MN
                             have + -ed/-en be + -ing
```

Chapter 8

Activity 8.1

(11)

'The reason why the Martians should come to Earth was not at first clear.'

(12)

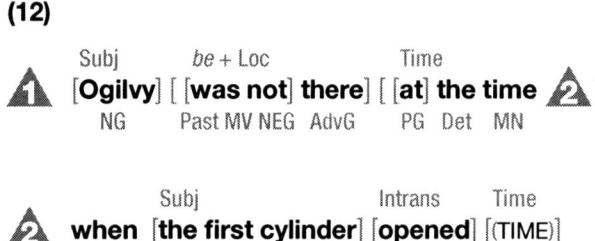

'Ogilvy was not there at the time when the first cylinder opened.'

(13)

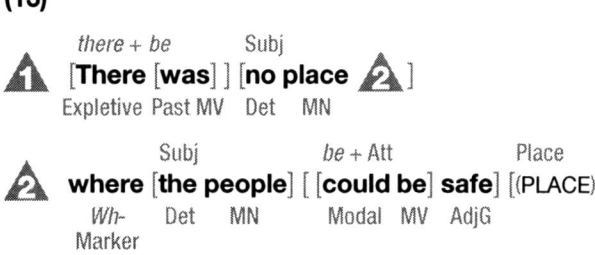

'There was no place where the people could be safe.'

Selected Sentences for Analysis

Normal version wh- *clause with formal preposing*

(2)

'This blaze may have been the casting of the huge gun from which their shots were fired at us.'

Whiz version wh- *clause; missing-marker version* wh- *clause*

(9)

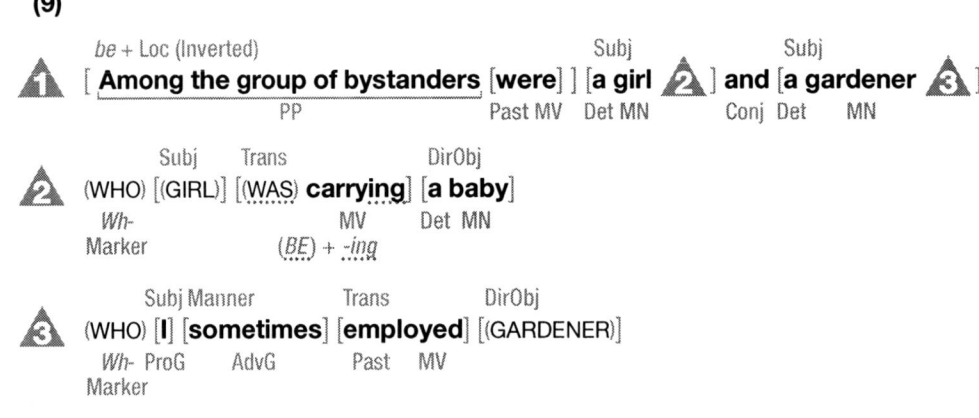

'Among the group of bystanders were a girl carrying a baby and a gardener I sometimes employed.'

Normal version wh- *clause with formal preposing*

(14)

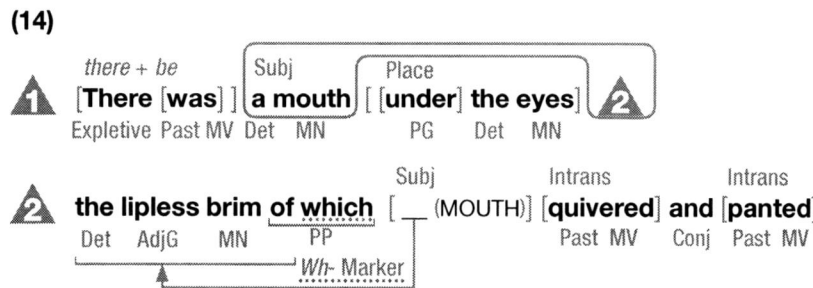

'There was a mouth under the eyes, the lipless brim of which quivered and panted.'

Normal version wh- *clause*

(21)

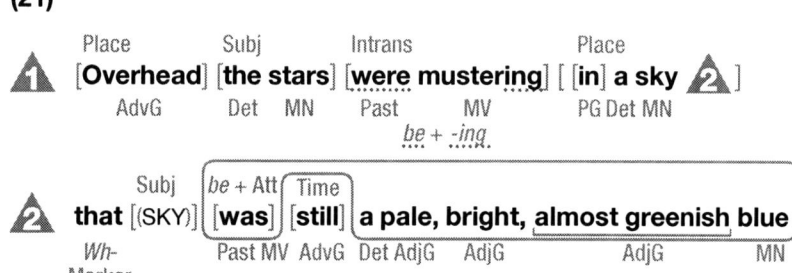

'Overhead the stars were mustering in a sky that was still a pale, bright, almost greenish blue.'

Normal version extraposed wh- *clause with formal preposing*

(29)

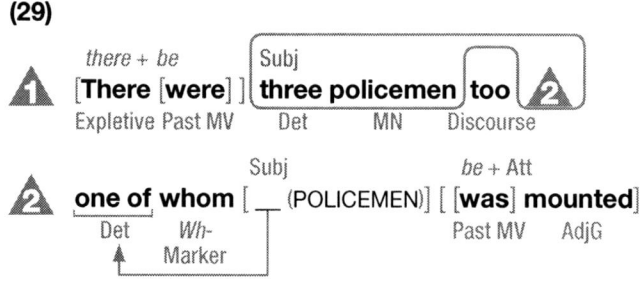

'There were three policemen too, one of whom was mounted.'

Normal version wh- *clause with determiner gap*

(38)

Subj   Trans   DirObj

[You] [could not have found] [one human being 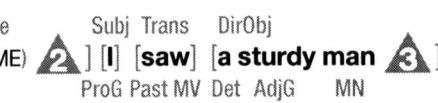]

ProG   Modal NEG   MV   Det   MN

have + -ed/-en

Subj   Trans   OblObj

whose [(HUMAN BEING'S) **emotions] [were not affected]** [[by the newcomers]

Wh-   MN   Past NEG   MV   PG   Det   MN

Marker   *be + -ed/-en*

'You could not have found one human being whose emotions were not affected by the newcomers.'

Headless version and whiz *version*

(44)

Time   Subj Trans DirObj

[(TIME) 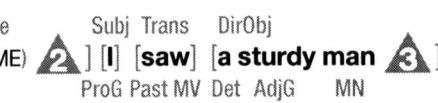] [I] [saw] [a sturdy man** 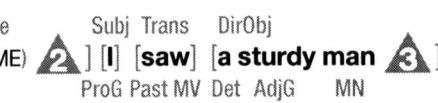]

ProG Past MV Det AdjG   MN

Subj   Intrans Time

When [the next flash] [came] [(TIME)]

Wh-   Det   Det   MN   Past MV

Marker

Subj   *be + Att*

(WHO) [(MAN)] [[(BE)] **cheaply but not shabbily dressed]**

Wh-   AdvG Conj   AdvG   MAdj

Marker

'When the next flash came, I saw a sturdy man, cheaply but not shabbily dressed.'

Normal version wh- *clause with determiner gap*

(49)

Subj *be + Att*

[It] [[was] the landlord of the Spotted Dog 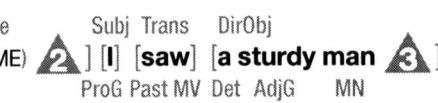]

ProG Past MV Det   MN   PP

DirObj   Subj Trans

whose [(LANDLORD'S) **conveyance] [I] [had taken]**

Wh-   MN   ProG Past   MV

Marker   *have + -ed/-en*

'It was the landlord of the Spotted Dog, whose conveyance I had taken.'

Chapter 9

Activity 9.1

(16)   The secular cooling that must someday overtake our planet has already gone far indeed with our neighbour. Its physical condition is still largely a mystery, but we know now <u>that even in its equatorial region the midday temperature barely approaches that of our coldest winter.</u> Its air is much more attenuated than ours, its oceans have shrunk <u>until they cover but a third of its surface</u>, and <u>as its slow seasons change</u> huge snowcaps gather and melt about either pole and periodically inundate its temperate zones. That last stage of exhaustion, which to us is still incredibly remote, has become a present-day problem for the inhabitants of Mars. The immediate pressure of necessity has brightened their intellects, enlarged their powers, and hardened their hearts. And <u>looking across space with instruments, and intelligences such as we have scarcely dreamed of</u>, they see, at its nearest distance only 35,000,000 of miles sunward of them, a morning star of hope, our own warmer planet, green with vegetation and grey with water, with a cloudy atmosphere eloquent of fertility, with glimpses through its drifting cloud wisps of broad stretches of populous country and narrow, navy-crowded seas.

---

that even in its equatorial region the midday temperature barely approaches that of our coldest winter

This non*wh*- subordinate clause, marked with *that*, is functioning as a participant. It is the direct object of the *know* process.

---

until they cover but a third of its surface

This non*wh*- subordinate clause, marked with *until*, is functioning as a circumstance of manner (or time), telling how badly the Martian oceans have shrunk.

---

as its slow seasons change

This non*wh*- subordinate clause, marked with *as*, is functioning as a circumstance of time (or manner), giving the timeframe for the gathering and melting of the Martian polar snowcaps.

> looking across space with instruments, and intelligences such as we have scarcely dreamed of

This non*wh*-subordinate clause, marked with free *-ing*, is functioning as a circumstance of means, telling how the Martians are conducting their surveillance of Earth.

---

(17) I remember how I sat on the table there in the blackness, with patches of green and crimson swimming before my eyes.

The underscored non*wh*-subordinate clause, marked with free *-ing*, is the complement of the preposition group *with*. (See the discussion of 'Absolute clauses' later in this chapter.)

---

(18) He was full of speculation that night about the condition of Mars, and scoffed at the vulgar idea of its having inhabitants who were signalling us.

The underscored non*wh*-subordinate clause is also a free *-ing* clause. This one is the complement of the preposition group *of*.

Activity 9.2

(33)

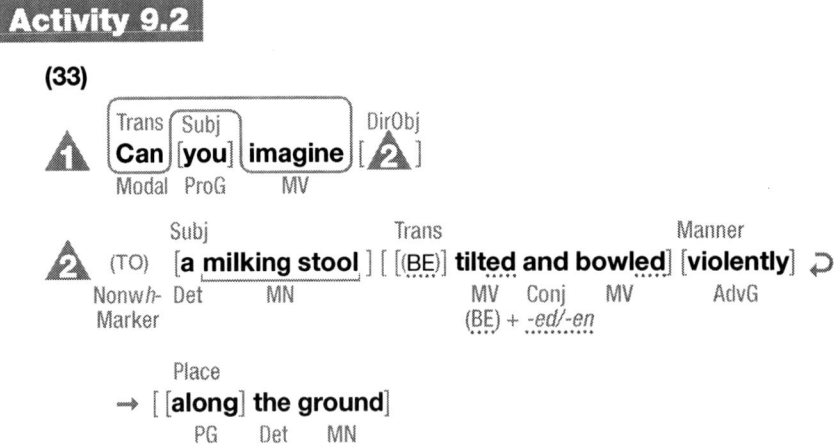

'Can you imagine a milking stool tilted and bowled violently along the ground?'

(34)

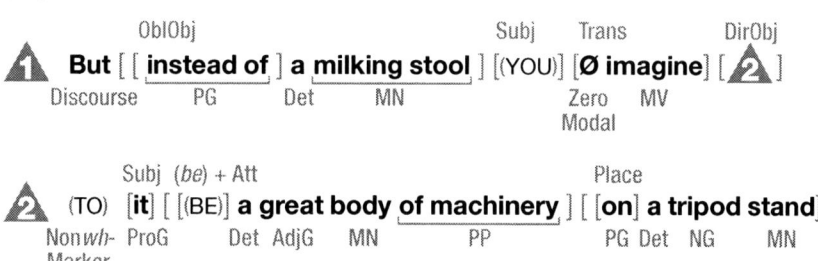

              OblObj   Subj   Trans   DirObj

1   But [[**instead of**] a **milking stool**] [(YOU)] [**Ø imagine**] [**2**]

    Discourse   PG   Det   MN   Zero MV
                                                               Modal

               Subj *(be)* + Att   Place

2   (TO) [**it**] [[(BE)] **a great body of machinery**] [[**on**] **a tripod stand**]

   Non*wh*- ProG   Det AdjG MN   PP   PG Det NG   MN
   Marker

'But instead of a milking stool imagine it a great body of machinery on a tripod stand.'

Selected Sentences for Analysis

Nonwh- clause as condition circumstance

(4)

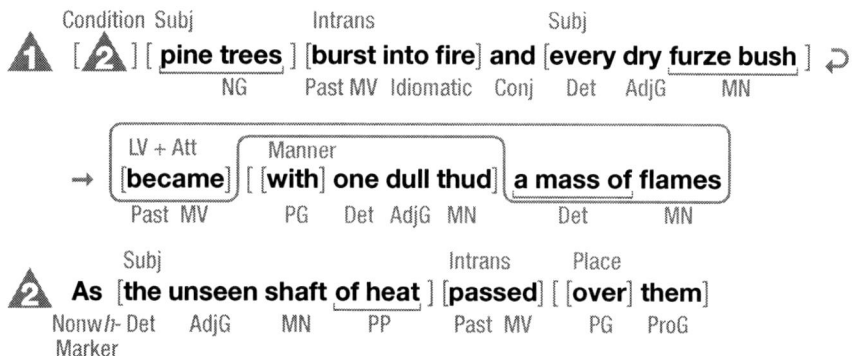

   Condition Subj   Intrans   Subj

1   [**2**] [**pine trees**] [**burst into fire**] and [**every dry furze bush**]

                    NG   Past MV Idiomatic Conj   Det AdjG   MN

          LV + Att   Manner

 → [**became**] [[**with**] **one dull thud**] **a mass of flames**

        Past MV   PG   Det AdjG MN   Det   MN

       Subj   Intrans   Place

2   As [**the unseen shaft of heat**] [**passed**] [[**over**] **them**]

  Non*wh*- Det   AdjG   MN   PP   Past MV   PG ProG
  Marker

'As the unseen shaft of heat passed over them, pine trees burst into fire, and every dry furze bush became with one dull thud a mass of flames.'

Nonwh- clause as complement of preposition group

(10)

            Subj   Trans DirObj   Condition

△1 [**It**] [**had**] [**an extraordinary effect**] [[**in**] **△2**]

         ProG Past MV Det   AdjG   MN   PG

                     Subj Trans   DirObj

△2 free **-ing** [(IT)] [**unman**] [**me**]

      Nonwh-   MV   ProG
      Marker

'It had an extraordinary effect in unmanning me.'

Nonwh- clause as direct object

(15)

         Subj Trans   DirObj

△1 [**I**] [**thought**] [**△2**]

      ProG Past MV

              Subj   Trans   DirObj

△2 (THAT) [**the news of the massacre**] probably [**reached**] [**C, W, and O**] ↻

      Nonwh- Det   MN   PP   Relationship Past MV   NG NG Conj NG
      Marker   (AdvG)

               Time

 → [**about** [**the same time**]]

        Intens Det Det   MN
        (AdvG)

'I thought the news of the massacre probably reached Chobham, Woking, and Ottershaw about the same time.'

Nonwh- clause as reason circumstance

(19)

'To protect the strange creatures from violence, Stent and Ogilvy had telegraphed from Horsell to the barracks for the help of a company of soldiers.'

Nonwh- clause as condition circumstance

(25)

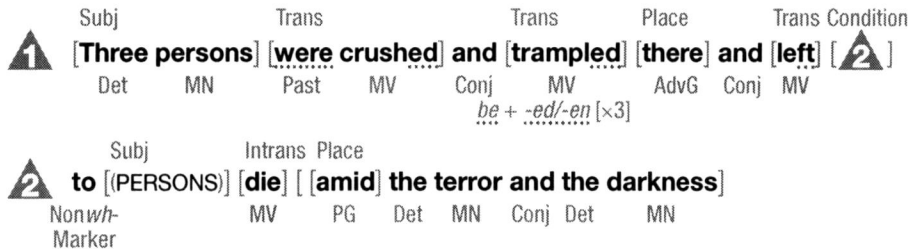

'Three persons were crushed and trampled there, and left to die amid the terror and the darkness.'

Selected Sentences from the Text for Analysis

(3)

'A monstrous tripod, higher than many houses, striding over the young pine trees, and smashing them aside in its career; a walking engine of glittering metal, striding now across the heather, articulate ropes of steel dangling from it, and the clattering tumult of its passage mingling with the riot of the thunder.'

(6)

△1
Subj   *be* + Att
[**That**] [[**was**] the impression **△2**]
ProG   Past MV Det   MN

△2
     Subj   Trans   DirObj
(THAT) [**those instant flashes**] [**gave**] [(IMPRESSION)]
Wh-   Det   AdjG   MN   Past MV
Marker

'That was the impression those instant flashes gave.'

(8)

△1
        Manner   Subj
Then [suddenly] [**the trees** in the pine wood ahead of me] ↺
Discourse   AdvG   Det   MN   PP

     Trans   Manner
→ [**were parted**] [**△2**] ➤ **△4**
    Past   MV
    be + *-ed/-en*

△2
      Subj   Trans   OblObj
as [**brittle reeds**] [**are parted**] [[by] **△3**]
Non*wh-* AdjG   MN   Pres   MV   PG
Marker   *be* + *-ed/-en*

△3
        Subj   Intrans   Place
free *-ing* [a man] [**thrust**] [[**through**] them]
Non*wh-*   Det MN   MV   PG   ProG
Marker

△4
       Subj   Trans
(AND) [**they**] [**were snapped off**] ➤ **△5**
Conj   ProG   Past   MV   Particle
        be + *-ed/-en*

△5
       Subj   Trans   Manner
and [(THEY)] [(WERE) driven] [**headlong**] ➤ **△6**
Conj   MV   AdvG
      (BE) + *-ed/-en*

△6
       Subj   Intrans
and [a second huge tripod] [**appeared**] **△7**
Conj Det   Det   AdjG   MN   Past MV

△7
       Subj   Intrans   Manner   Place
(THAT) [(TRIPOD)] [(WAS) **rushing**] **△8** [**headlong**] [[**towards**] me]
Wh-   MV   Relationship   AdvG   PG   ProG
Marker   (BE) + *-ing*

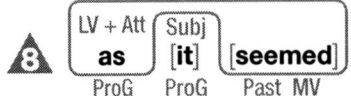

    LV + Att   Subj

⑧   **as**   **[it]**   **[seemed]**

    ProG   ProG   Past MV

'Then suddenly the trees in the pine wood ahead of me were parted, as brittle reeds are parted by a man thrusting through them; they were snapped off and driven headlong, and a second huge tripod appeared, rushing, as it seemed, headlong towards me.'

(12)

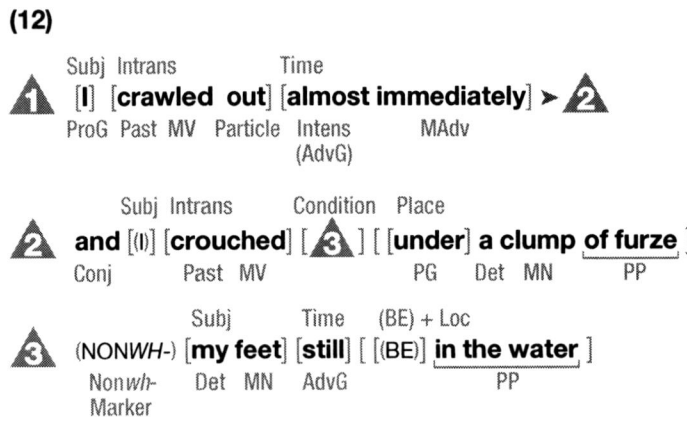

Subj Intrans   Time

▲1   **[I] [crawled out] [almost immediately]** ➤ **▲2**

ProG Past MV   Particle   Intens   MAdv

                     (AdvG)

     Subj Intrans   Condition   Place

▲2   **and [(I)] [crouched] [▲3] [[under] a clump of furze]**

   Conj   Past MV   PG   Det   MN   PP

        Subj   Time   (BE) + Loc

▲3   **(NONWH-) [my feet] [still] [[(BE)] in the water]**

  Nonwh-   Det   MN   AdvG   PP

  Marker

'I crawled out almost immediately, and crouched, my feet still in the water, under a clump of furze.'

(17)

Subj Trans   DirObj   Time

▲1   **[It] [picked] [its road] [▲2]** ➤ **▲3**

ProG Past MV   Det   MN

     Subj Intrans   Manner

▲2   **as   [it] [went striding] [along]**

Nonwh- ProG   Past   MV   AdvG

Marker   *go + -ing*

       (Alternate Progressive Aspect)

      Subj   Intrans   Manner

▲3   **and [the brazen hood ▲4] [moved] [to and fro]** ↻

   Conj   Det   AdjG   MN   Past MV   AdvG

      Manner

→ **[[with] the inevitable suggestion of ▲5]**

      PG   Det   AdjG   MN   PP

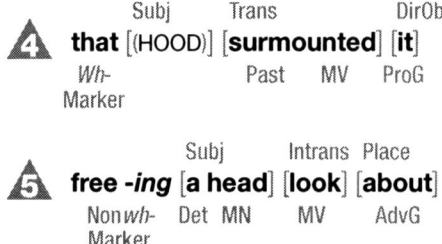

Subj   Trans   DirObj
4 **that** [(HOOD)] [**surmounted**] [**it**]
   Wh-   Past   MV   ProG
   Marker

              Subj   Intrans Place
5 **free -*ing*** [**a head**] [**look**] [**about**]
   Non*wh-*   Det MN   MV   AdvG
   Marker

'It picked its road as it went striding along, and the brazen hood that surmounted it moved to and fro with the inevitable suggestion of a head looking about.'

Chapter 10

Activity 10.1

In this example, two infinitive clauses (one marked with *to* at the left-hand edge of the verb group and the other marked with (TO)) are complements in the noun group headed by *impulse*. The noun group also has a *wh-* embedded clause marked with *that*. A total of three clauses are embedded in the same noun group.

(3)

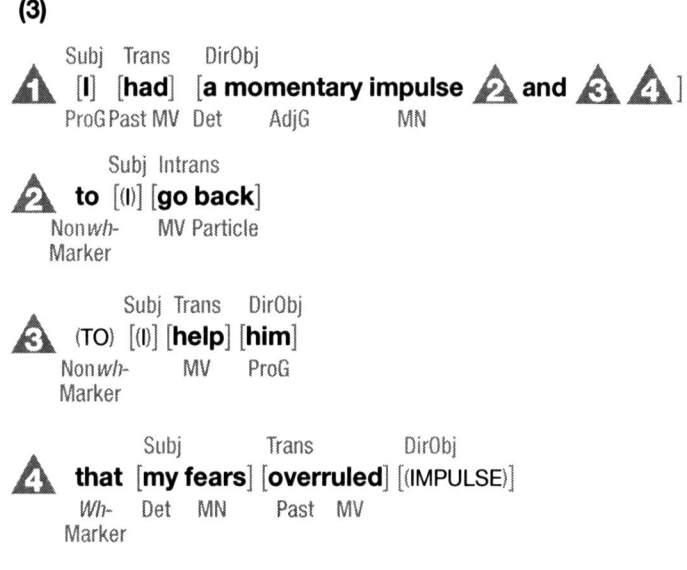

Subj Trans   DirObj
1 [**I**] [**had**] [**a momentary impulse** 2 and 3 4]
  ProG Past MV Det   AdjG   MN

         Subj Intrans
2 **to** [(I)] [**go back**]
  Non*wh-*   MV Particle
  Marker

        Subj Trans   DirObj
3 (TO) [(I)] [**help**] [**him**]
  Non*wh-*   MV   ProG
  Marker

        Subj   Trans   DirObj
4 **that** [**my fears**] [**overruled**] [(IMPULSE)]
  Wh-   Det   MN   Past MV
  Marker

'I had a momentary impulse to go back and help him that my fears overruled.'

Selected Sentences for Analysis

Nonwh- clause as appositive

(3)

'My only consolation was the fact that the Martians were moving Londonwards and away from her.'

Nonwh- clause as complement to main adjective (or as direct object)

(8)

As complement

As direct object

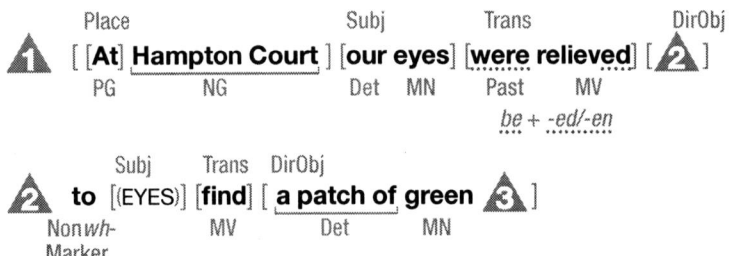

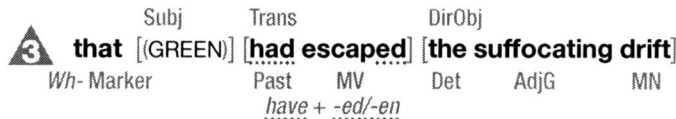

	Subj	Trans	DirObj
3	**that** [(GREEN)]	[**had escaped**]	[**the suffocating drift**]
Wh- Marker		Past MV	Det AdjG MN
		have + *-ed/-en*	

'At Hampton Court our eyes were relieved to find a patch of green that had escaped the suffocating drift.'

Subject-to-subject raising

(12)

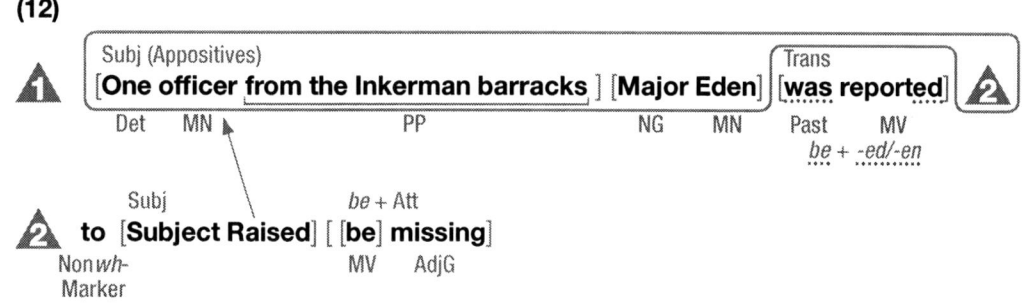

'One officer from the Inkerman barracks, Major Eden, was reported to be missing.'

Non*wh-* *clause as direct object;* wh- *hybrid*

(16)

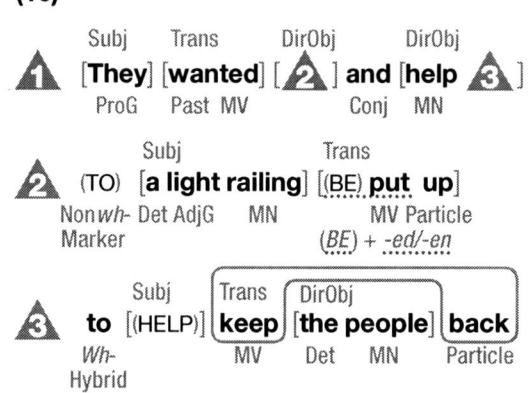

'They wanted a light railing put up, and help to keep the people back.'

Nonwh- *clause as extraposed subject*

(21)

▲1   OblObj   Subj   *be* + Att
[[To] me]   it   [[is]   quite credible]   ▲2
PG ProG   Expl   Pres MV Intens   MAdj
                          (AdvG)

▲2   Subj   *be* + Att
    that [the Martians] [[may be] descended from beings not unlike ourselves]
    Nonwh- Det   MN   Modal MV   MAdj   PP
    Marker

'To me it is quite credible that the Martians may be descended from beings not unlike ourselves.'

Wh- *double-marked*

(25)

▲1   Subj Trans   DirObj
    [I] [scarcely [know]] [(MANNER) ▲2]
    ProG   Intens   Pres MV
    (AdvG)

▲2   Subj   Intrans   OblObj   Manner
    how to [(I)] [speak] [[of] it] [(MANNER)]
    Wh-   MV   PG ProG
    Double-marked

'I scarcely know how to speak of it.'

Nonwh- *time clause with* nonwh- *clause as complement to main noun*

(32)

▲1   Subj   Zero-participant Process   Time
    [It] [[was] nearly eleven o'clock] [▲2]
    Expletive Past MV Intens   MN   AdvG
                   (AdvG)

▲2   Subj   Trans   DirObj
    before [we] [gathered] [courage ▲3]
    Nonwh- ProG   Past MV   MN
    Marker

        Subj   Intrans Time
3 **to** [(WE)] [**start**] [**again**]
  Non*wh*-   MV   AdvG
  Marker

'It was nearly eleven o'clock before we gathered courage to start again.'

Selected Sentences from the Text for Analysis

(8)

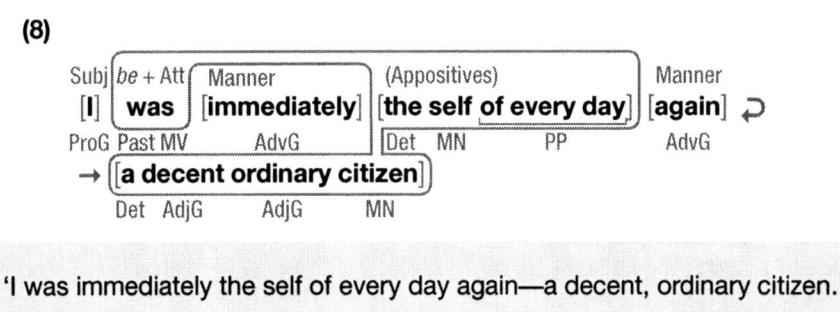

'I was immediately the self of every day again—a decent, ordinary citizen.'

(10)

In addition to the transitive analysis suggested below, in which the arrangement of the VG signals subordination, this clause complex could also be seen as involving a discourse element and a reportative clause. See also sentences 15 and 26.

As direct object

     Subj Trans   IndObj   DirObj
1 [I] [**asked**] [**myself**] [**2**]
  ProG Past MV   ProG

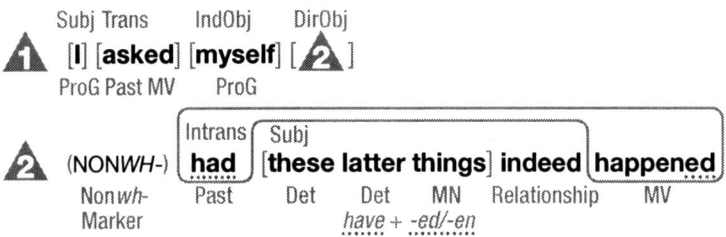

As reportative

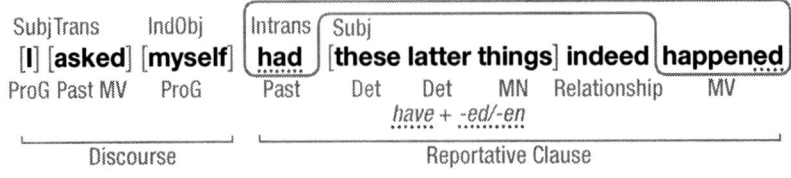

'I asked myself had these latter things indeed happened?'

(19)

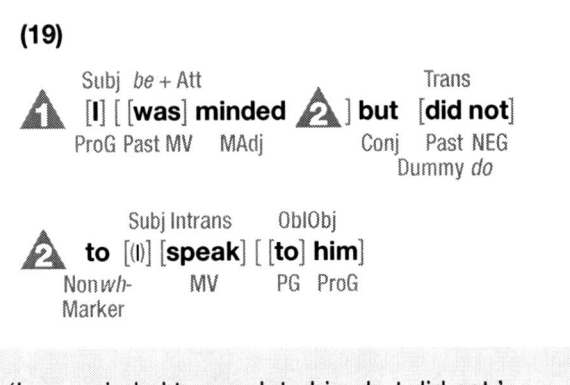

'I was minded to speak to him, but did not.'

(26)

In addition to the transitive analysis suggested below, in which the clause marker is a missing element, this clause complex could also be seen as involving a discourse element and a 'reportative' clause. See also sentences 10 and 15.

As direct object

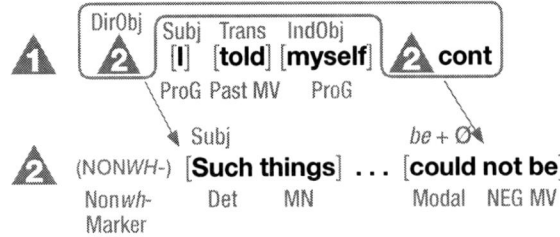

As reportative

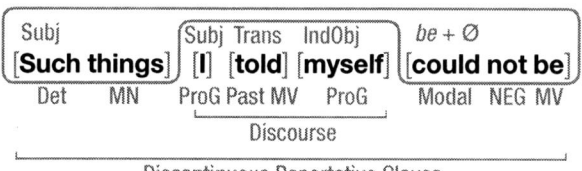

Subj	Subj	Trans	IndObj	*be* + Ø
[**Such things**]	[**I**]	[**told**]	[**myself**]	[**could not be**]
Det MN	ProG Past MV	ProG	Modal NEG MV

Discourse

Discontinuous Reportative Clause

'Such things, I told myself, could not be.'

(28)

	Subj	Trans		DirObj	
1	[**I**]	[**do not know**]	[(EXTENT) **2**]

ProG Pres NEG MV
  Dummy *do*

	Manner	Subj	*be* + Att
2	**how** [(EXTENT) **far**]	[**my experience**]	[[**is**] **common**]

Wh-   MAdv   Det   MN   Pres MV   AdjG
Marker

'I do not know how far my experience is common.'

Frequently Used Charts and Lists (Grouped by Related Topic)

Chart 4.2 *Identifying Word Types*

Nouns

Inflections	Nouns can often be made plural. Noun groups can be made possessive.
Derivational endings	-(i)an, -age, -al, -ant, -ation, -dom, -ee, -er, -ery, -ese, -ess, -ette, -ful, -hood, -ing, -ism, -ist, -ite, -ity, -ment, -ness, -or, -ship, -ster
Syntax	Nouns fit into the main noun position in a noun group; therefore, they can be preceded by a determiner.

Verbs

Inflections	Verbs can be inflected for present tense, past tense, progressive, perfect, and passive participles.
Derivational endings	-ate, -en, -ify (-fy), ize
Syntax	Verbs fit into the main verb position in a verb group; therefore, they can be preceded by a modal, a semiauxiliary, or a core auxiliary.

Adjectives

Inflections	Adjectives often have comparative and superlative forms.
Derivational endings	-able, -al, -ed, -esque, -ful, -ic, -ish, -ive, -less, -like, -ly, -ous, -y
Syntax	Adjectives can appear in processes as attributes (but so can nouns). Adjectives can often be compared, using *more/most* or *less/least*, and emphasized, using *very* (but so can adverbs).

Adverbs

Inflections	None
Derivational endings	-ly (if the part to which -ly is added is an adjective), -ward, -wise
Syntax	Adverbs can appear alone as circumstance (but so can nouns). Adverbs can often be compared, using *more/most* or *less/least*, and emphasized, using *very* (but so can adjectives).

Other categories Determiners, modals, markers, prepositions, and pronouns are in **closed classes**, that is, they do not easily admit new members. Since they are in closed classes, they can be gathered into lists, as has been done throughout this book.

List 2.1 *Six Process Types*

Transitive	Other-than-transitive
a Any process that entails at least two directly expressible participant roles is a transitive process (Trans)	**b** *be* plus attribute (*be* + Att) **c** *be* plus location (*be* + Loc) **d** *there* plus *be* (*there* + *be*) (and certain other verbs of existence) **e** linking verb plus attribute (LV + Att) **f** intransitive (Intrans) (including *be* + Ø)

List 3.2 *Participant Functions*

Subject	The first-named participant of a clause is called the subject.
Object	All participants other than the subject are called objects.
Direct object	A direct object is never introduced by a preposition group.
Oblique object	An oblique object is always introduced by a preposition group.
Indirect object	An indirect object must be capable of appearing both with and without a preposition group; an indirect object usually plays the role of recipient (to whom things are transferred), or beneficiary (for whose benefit an action is undertaken), or client (at whose behest an action is undertaken).

List 3.3 *Circumstance Types*

Circumstance of Time
Sets the timeframe, frequency, or duration of a process

Circumstance of Place
Tells the locations, positions, directions, or distances at which
a process occurs

Circumstance of Reason
Gives the reasons, contingencies, or the purposes for which
a process occurs

Circumstance of Means
Tells about the resources through which a process occurs

Circumstance of Manner
Specifies the way in which a process occurs or the degree or extent to which it occurs

Circumstance of Condition
Specifies the qualifying factors under which a process occurs
or the outcomes or results of a process

Chart 5.1 *The Verb Group*

		Central Word	
Left-hand edge	**Precentral space**		**Right-hand edge**
Tense (either present or past) or Modal or Nonfinite clause marker	Semiauxiliaries and core auxiliaries or The periphrastic auxiliary verb (dummy *do*) for Q or NEG if no modal or other auxiliary is present (see Chapter 6)	**Main verb**	Postposed particles (verb particles) Idiomatic elements

Note: Intensifiers can fit in almost anywhere.

Modals (can't be tensed)	can, could, dare, had best, had better, may, might, must, need, ought (to), shall, should, used to, will, would, would rather, would sooner, Ø (zero)	**Nonfinite clause markers**	infinitive to; infinitive (to); free *-ing*; poss . . . free *-ing*
Semiauxiliaries (can be tensed)	appear to, be (un)able to, be about to, be (dis)inclined to, be liable to, be supposed to, be bound to, be fixin' to, be going to, be to, be (un)willing to, come to, dare (to), fail to, get to, happen to, have (got) to, need to, seem to, tend to, turn out to . . .	**Core auxiliaries**	*have* + *-ed/-en* (perfective aspect); *be* + *-ing* (progressive aspect); *be* + *-ed/-en* (passive voice) *Note:* Occasionally *get* substitutes for *be* to form either progressive aspect or passive voice.
		Periphrastic auxiliary	dummy *do*

Chart 7.1 *The Noun Group*

Left-hand edge	Precentral space	Central Word	Right-hand edge
Determiners (Det)	Adjective group Noun group Prepositional phrase Clause Adverb group	Main noun	Prepositional phrase Clause Adjective group Noun group Adverb group

Note: Entire noun groups can be within the scope of an intensifier.

Three types of determiners (These are listed in the order in which they generally appear with respect to each other. These are not intended to be exhaustive lists.)

Predeterminers:	all (of), half (of), most (of), both (of), some (of), a cup of, double, such, one-third, three times, what, . . .
Primary determiners:	the, a(n), this, that, these, those, each (of), no, enough (of), every, either (of), neither (of), my, our, his, her, its, their, Possessive NG's, whose, which, . . .
Postdeterminers:	cardinal and ordinal numbers, additional, further, last, next, older, younger, . . .

Chart 4.3 *The Adjective Group*

Left-hand edge	Precentral space	Central Word	Postcentral space	Right-hand edge
Intensifier*	Adverb group Adjective group Noun group	Main adjective	*indeed*	Prepositional phrase Clause

* Some common intensifiers for adjective groups (same as adverb group intensifiers): a bit, a little, absolutely, all, almost, at all, barely, completely, extremely, fully, hardly, kind of, mildly, nearly, quite, really, scarcely, slightly, so, sort of, such, totally, utterly, very

Chart 4.4 *The Adverb Group*

Left-hand edge	Central Word	Right-hand edge
Intensifiers*	Main adverb	*indeed* Prepositional phrase

*Some common intensifiers for adverb groups (same as for adjective groups): a bit, a little, absolutely, all, almost, at all, barely, completely, extremely, fully, hardly, kind of, mildly, nearly, quite, really, scarcely, slightly, so, sort of, such, totally, utterly, very

Adverb groups are capable of carrying information at several levels: (a) they can be used to express clause-level circumstance, (b) they can be relationship-level comment—usually on the content of an entire clause, or (c) they can be discourse organizers.

Note: The words that we are calling intensifiers are themselves usually classified as adverbs.

Chart 4.5 *The Prepositional Phrase (a Preposition Group and Its Complement)*

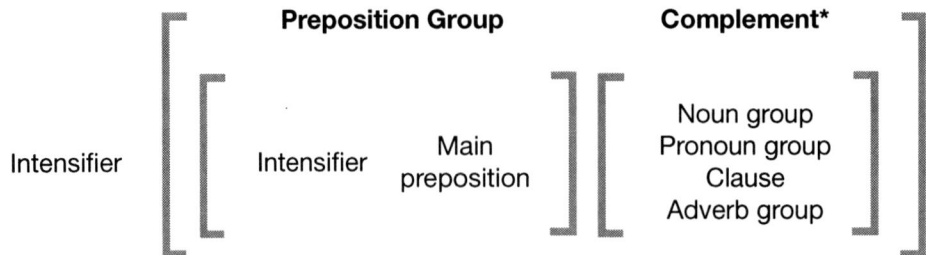

*The complement of the preposition group in a prepositional phrase is often called the *object of the preposition*.

Some common intensifiers for prepositional phrases (the same ones can be found with the preposition group itself): all, almost, close, completely, directly, exactly, far, just, more or less, nearly, only, partly, really, right, somewhat, soon, straight, very, way, well, . . .

Some preposition groups that can be followed by an adverb group: after (after today), at (at last), before (before long), by (by tomorrow), for (for later), from (from now on), since (since then), until (until tonight)

List 4.1 *Some Common (and Not-So-Common) Prepositions*

Single-word Prepositions: about, above, across, after, against, along, among, around, as, at, atop, barring, before, behind, below, beneath, beside, between, beyond, but, by, concerning, considering, despite, down, during, except, excepting, excluding, following, for, from, given, granted, in, including, inside, into, less, like, minus, near (to), notwithstanding, of, off, on, onto, opposite, out, outside, over, past, pending, plus, regarding, respecting, save, since, through, throughout, times, to, toward(s), under, underneath, unlike, until, up, upon, versus, with, within, without, . . .

Multiple-word Prepositions: according to, ahead of, along with, as far as, as for, as to, away from, because of, but for, by means of, by way of, close to, contrary to, due to, except for, followed by, for the sake of, in addition to, in back of, in case of, in common with, in contact with, in favor of, in front of, in line with, in place of, in return for, in spite of, inside of, instead of, near to, next to, on account of, on behalf of, on top of, out of, outside of, owing to, prior to, regardless of, thanks to, up against, up to, with the exception of, . . .

List 5.1 *The Many Unusual Forms of Be (Am, Are, Is, Was, Were, Been)*

Present tense	I **am** you **are** he **is**, she **is**, it **is**	we **are** you (all) **are** they **are**
Past tense	I **was** you **were** he **was**, she **was**, it **was**	we **were** you (all) **were**
-ed/-en	**been**	they **were**

List 6.1 Wh- *Markers for Content Questions*

In a **content question,** if the *wh-* marker is:	The **information gap** will be a **missing element** related to:
Where (-ever)	➡ a **Place**
Why (-ever)	➡ a **Reason**
Who (-ever) or *Whom* (-ever)	➡ a **Person**
When (-ever)	➡ a **Time**
What (-ever)	➡ a **Thing**
How (-ever)	➡ a **Manner**, a **Means**, or a **Condition**; also a **Quantifying determiner** (see Chapter 7) or **Intensifier**
Whose (-ever)	➡ a **Possessive determiner** (see Chapter 7)
Which	➡ a **Determiner** (see Chapter 7)

List 8.1 Wh- *Markers for Embedded Clauses*

In an embedded clause, if the *wh-* marker is:	The *wh-* gap will be a missing element coreferent with:
Where (-ever, -soever)	➡ a **Place** heading the host noun group
Why (-ever)	➡ a **Reason** heading the host noun group
Who (-ever, -soever) or *Whom* (-ever, -soever)	➡ a **Person** heading the host noun group
When (-ever)	➡ a **Time** heading the host noun group
What (-ever, -soever)	➡ a **Thing** heading the host noun group
How (-ever, -soever)	➡ a **Manner, a Means, or a Condition** heading the host noun group; also a **Quantifier**
Whose (-ver, -soever)	➡ a **Possessive determiner** related to the head of the noun group
Which (-ever) and *That*	➡ a **range of items** that could be heads in the host noun group, including places, reasons, persons, times, things, manners, means, or conditions; also a determiner (*which* only)

List 9.1 *Some Common (and Not-So-Common) Clause Markers*

For *wh-* clauses (Chapter 8)	how, however, howsoever, that, what, whatever, whatsoever, when, whenever, where, wherever, wheresoever, which, whichever, who, whoever, whosoever, whom, whomever, whomsoever, whose, whosesoever, why, whyever
For non*wh-* clauses (Chapter 9)	after, although, as, as far as, as if, as long as, as soon as, as though, assuming (that), because, before, but that, considering (that), even if, excepting (that), for, for . . . to, free *-ing*, given (that), granted (that), granting (that), if, in that, in order that, in order to, in the event that, like, now (that), once, poss . . . free *-ing*, provided (that), providing (that), seeing (that), since, so (that), such that, supposing (that), that, (that), though, till, to, (to), unless, until, when, whereas, whereupon, whether (to), while, . . .

Chart 9.1 *A Comparison of Wh- Clause Embedding with Nonwh- Clause Subordination*

Embedded *wh-* clause

Main Noun Embedded Clause

Wh- ... **(Wh- Gap)** ...
Word   Information Gap
Marker

Wh- clauses are always embedded in a host noun group.
Wh- clauses always exhibit a three-part coreference relationship among (1) an element in the host noun group, (2) the *wh-* marker, and (3) the gap in the *wh-* clause.

Subordinate non*wh-* clause

 ...[]...
Subordinate Clause

 Nonwh- ...
   Marker
   Marker

Subordinate non*wh-* clauses appear within host clauses at just those locations where you might otherwise be able to put a noun group: participant, attribute, circumstance, and complement of preposition group. They can also serve appositive functions.

Embedded Wh- Clause Types (Summarized from Chapter 8)

The normal version

The headless version

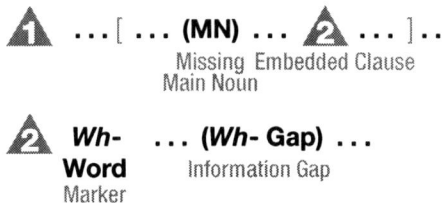

The missing-marker version

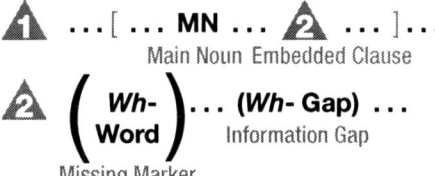

The whiz version

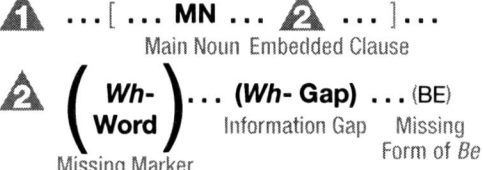

Glossary

> **Note:** The glossary defines the terms employed in this book; additionally, it defines several traditional terms in a manner compatible with the terminology used in the book, even though they may not occur in the book.

Absolute clause Free *-ing* or missing-marker *be*-deleted circumstance clauses with an overt subject not strictly coreferent with the subject of the host clause, sometimes the complement of the preposition *with*; note the terminological distinction between contemporary *absolute clause* and traditional *absolute phrase*.

Active voice (clause) The canonical (default) order for participant roles with respect to the process; the verb group cannot contain the element *be + ed/en*. Compare *Passive voice (clause)*.

Adjective Loosely, a word having an attributive relationship with a main noun or noun group, expressing qualities, features, or characteristics of that main noun or noun group.

Adjective clause A *wh-* clause that serves as a modifying constituent within a noun group the main noun of which is not a missing element. Compare *Adverb clause, Noun clause*.

Adjective complement Generally, any completer of an adjective group; often applied to a non*wh-* clause that is embedded in an adjective group and that completes the sense of the group.

Adjective group A word group headed by an adjective.

Adverb Adverbs generally function as circumstance in a clause but can also serve relationship (e.g. *hopefully*) and discourse (e.g. *next*) functions; *Intensifiers* are often, although not necessarily, adverbs.

Adverb clause Usually, a non*wh-* clause functioning as circumstance; however, also frequently applied to a headless *wh-* clause embedded in a noun group that is functioning as circumstance. Compare *Adjective clause, Noun clause*.

Adverb group A word group headed by an adverb.

Affected The role played by the participant affected by or undergoing the process.

Agent The role played by the participant performing an action.

Ambiguity The quality of language whereby constituents at all levels, both singly and in functional combinations, are subject to various interpretations across and within individual language users.

Anticipatory it In clauses with extraposed subjects, the expletive placeholder for the subject. See *Expletive*.

Apposition Two constituents together performing a function that might otherwise be performed by only one member of the set, not usually signaled by a conjunction; either member of an appositive set can substitute for the other without modifying the sense of the set. Compare *Conjunction*.

Appositive adjective (group) Infrequent. Used to label an adjective group that appears to the right of rather than the left of the main noun in a noun group.

Appositive noun (group) A word group (or, sometimes, clause) that is a co-constituent in a paratactic equivalence relationship with a co-occupant in a grammatical unit. See *Apposition*.

Article The determiners *the* and *a(n)*.

Aspect Perfective (*have* + *-ed/-en*) or progressive (*be* + *-ing*); in verb groups, two optional discontinuous core auxiliaries that interact with tense and with each other to express time orientation and complete (perfective)

or incomplete (progressive) realization of the process.

Associate The role played by the participant with whom an action is carried out.

Attribute A characteristic, quality, trait, or property; more specifically, the complement of the verb in *be*-plus-attribute or linking-verb-plus-attribute processes.

Attributive See *Attribute*.

Bare infinitive A verb group with the missing-element nonfinite clause marker (TO) at the left-hand edge. Also *Zero infinitive*.

Basic form The uninflected, neutral form.

Be The main verb in the verb group of a *be*-plus-attribute, *be*-plus-location or *there*-plus-*be* process. Also, the primary auxiliary verb involved in expressing progressive aspect (*be* + *-ing*) and passive voice (*be* + *-ed/-en*). Also, infrequently, the verb used to express *exist* (intransitive *be* or *be* + Ø).

Beneficiary The role played by the participant for whose benefit an action is undertaken. Compare *Client* and *Recipient*.

Canonical Of or pertaining to the simplest or most basic form; the default structure.

Catenative Elements formed into a chain; usually said of multiword elements. See *Multiword verb*.

Causer The role played by the participant causing an *Affected* to undergo a process.

Circumstance Event-structure (clause) constituents that limit the event with respect to time, place, reason, means, manner, and condition.

Circumstance of condition Specifies the state of affairs under which an event occurs or indicates the outcomes of an event.

Circumstance of manner Specifies the way in which an event occurs, or the degree or extent to which it occurs.

Circumstance of means Specifies the resources or mechanisms through which an event occurs.

Circumstance of place Specifies the locations, positions, directions, or distances at which an event occurs.

Circumstance of reason Gives the reasons, contingencies, or the purposes for which an event occurs.

Circumstance of time Sets the timeframe, frequency, or duration of an event.

Clause A phrase comprised of a process and its entailed and optional participants as well as its entailed and optional circumstances.

Clause complex A grammatical unit comprised of more than one clause; a host clause and all of the clauses that modify or combine with it to form a sentence.

Client The role played by the participant on whose behalf an action is undertaken. Compare *Beneficiary* and *Recipient*.

Closed class Word types (determiners, modals, markers, prepositions, and pronouns) that belong to sets that do not easily admit new members.

Comitative adverb A prepositional phrase introduced by the word *with* in which that word has the sense of *in the company of* or *together with*. Compare *Oblique object*.

Common noun Pertains to a class of referents larger than one. Compare *Proper noun*.

Comparative Extent expression in which comparison involves only two entities. Compare *Superlative*.

Complement Generally, any completer; often, instead of *postmodifier* for any constituent that follows the main word within a group. Also, the noun group, clause, or adverb group that together with a preposition group forms a prepositional phrase. Also, the attribute in attributive processes.

Complement clause Finite or nonfinite non*wh*- clause embedded in a noun group or an adjective group. Compare *Subordination*.

Compound (compounding) Linear (paratactic) joining of elements as structural equivalents, in which one element initiates the relationship and the other continues it; often marked with coordinate conjunctions. See *Conjunction*.

Condition (circumstance) Specifies the state of affairs under which an event occurs or indicates the outcomes of an event.

Conditional (mood) The grammatical meaning expressed by any modal auxiliary in a verb group.

Conjunction (conjoining) Linear (paratactic) joining of elements as structural equivalents, in which one element initiates the relationship, and the other continues it; often marked with coordinate conjunctions. Also, a marker of conjunction. See *Compound*.

Constituent Any grammatical unit that is itself a component of a larger grammatical unit.

Content question See *Wh- question*.

Convention Those normal and customary practices and procedures employed in developing and reporting grammatical analyses.

Coordinate conjunction Markers of a compound or conjoined relationship between elements: most commonly *and, or, nor, but,* and *but not*; also, rarely, *for, so, yet*.

Core auxiliary Perfective aspect, progressive aspect, and passive voice.

Coreferent; coreferential Distinct constituents that refer to the identical event-structure elements.

Correlative conjunction Coordinate conjunctions appearing in discontinuous pairs such as *both . . . and, either . . . or, neither . . . nor, not only . . . but also*.

Delayed subject See *Extraposition*.

Demonstrative The determiners *this, that, these, those*.

Dependent clause In a clause complex, the embedded or subordinate clause; a dependent clause can be a non*wh-* constituent of a superordinate clause, or a non*wh-* constituent within a noun group, or a *wh-* constituent within a noun group.

Derivational ending One of two types of suffix (compare *Inflection*); derivational endings have the potential to change the word to which they are affixed from one lexical class to another; note that some derivational elements can be prefixed rather than suffixed.

Determiner A prenominal element in noun groups the function of which is to point out, particularize, specify, quantify, enumerate, and so forth.

Dialog Written or oral conversation involving two or more interactants.

Direct object For transitive processes, an entailed participant, other than the subject, that cannot be expressed in a prepositional phrase. Compare *Indirect object, Oblique object*.

Discontinuous constituent Any syntactic constituent whose elements are interrupted by the constituents of another structure; for example, question-order auxiliaries, extraposed *wh-* and non*wh-* clauses, raised subjects and objects, particles separated from their main verbs in multiword verbs, complements separated from main adjectives, or even prepositions separated from their complement noun groups.

Discourse The aggregate of the coherent spoken or written language that accompanies and comments on the events comprising ordinary experience; a connected series of spoken or written utterances.

Discourse unit An element adjoined to a clause, external to the event structure represented in the clause, with the primary function of organizing the flow of discourse.

(Dummy) do The periphrastic (stand-in) auxiliary verb; in this periphrastic use called an *Expletive*. Also, the omnibus intransitive or transitive process.

Edge (left-hand, right-hand) The frontmost and rearmost elements in word groups are at the left-hand and right-hand edges of the group; similarly applied to clauses, especially to the left-hand edge.

Embedded The term describing a word group, a phrase, or a clause functioning as a constituent within a word group. Compare *Apposition*, *Conjunction*, *Subordination*.

Entailed Included in the sense of; used with respect to the number and role-type(s) of participants (and, infrequently, circumstances) inherent in the sense of a process.

Event structure The processes, participants, and circumstances that comprise ordinary everyday experience.

Existential there clause A clause in which the process is *there + be*; in this structure the word *there* is an expletive.

Experiencer The role played by the participant who is affected by mental phenomena such as feeling, liking, thinking, wanting.

Expletive Nonreferential or grammatical *do* (as periphrastic auxiliary); also, *it* (anticipatory in clauses with extraposed subjects or otherwise nonreferential in time and weather expressions); also, *there* (in *there + be*). See *Nonreferential*.

Extent Degree, quantity, level, amount, amplitude, proportion, number, scope, size, range, mass, magnitude, and so forth.

Extent expression An embedded grammatical unit that expresses, with respect to a head word, its degree, quantity, level, amount, amplitude, proportion, number, scope, size, range, mass, magnitude, and so forth. See *Intensifier*.

Extraposition (extraposed) Any discontinuous constituent in which one part is displaced to the right. More frequently, a subordinate clause functioning as subject and appearing to the right of the verb group, having its canonical position filled with expletive *it*.

Finite A verb group that contains either past or present tense or a modal auxiliary is said to be finite because of its participation in establishing timeframe. Compare *Nonfinite*.

Formal preposing In *wh-* embedding: clause elements, primarily prepositions or determiners, displaced to the left of the clause to a position preceding the *wh-* marker, usually in formal settings. Compare *Extraposition*.

Free -ing The nonfinite non*wh-* clause marker comprised of the suffix *-ing* appended to the basic form of the verb; sometimes accompanied by possessive marking on the subject of the clause. See *Infinitive*.

Function Any constituent's grammatical contribution to the larger structure of which it forms a part. Often, the use of a clause, whether that use be assertion, question, or request.

Functional An approach to the study of language that focuses on the way language works, the purpose of which to gain insight into the way language is organized to do its work.

Gap See *Wh- gap*.

Genitive See *Possessive*.

Gerund A non*wh-* clause marked with *Free -ing* or *poss . . . free -ing* (see *Gerund with genitive*).

Gerund with genitive A non*wh-* clause marked with *poss . . . free -ing*.

Goal The role played by the participant toward whom an action is directed. Compare *Patient*.

Group The syntactic unit that is the elaboration of a word (the head) by premodifiers and complements (postmodifiers); a group might contain only one word (usually the head). Compare *Phrase*.

Head (word) The core word of a group; a group takes its name from the head. Also *Main word*.

Headless version wh- clause Those *wh-* clauses that are embedded in noun groups the heads of which are missing elements. Compare *Missing-marker version wh- clause, Normal version wh- clause, Whiz version wh-clause*.

Hierarchy In general, multilevel systems in which superordinance and subordinance relationships obtain; more specifically, in syntax, the constituency system by which sentences are made up of one or more clauses that are in turn made up of one or more word groups (or phrases) that are themselves made up of one or more words (or word groups) that are themselves made up of one or more morphemes, and so forth down to the component elements of sounds.

Host clause A clause into which another clause is embedded or to which another clause is subordinate. Also *Superordinate clause*.

Hypotactic Used with respect to subordinate or embedded

relationships between clauses in a clause complex (*hypo-* means 'at a lower level' and *tactic* means 'arranged'). Compare *Paratactic*.

Idiomatic (expression) An assemblage of words, established by common usage, the meaning of which cannot usually be determined by aggregating the meanings of the individual words.

Imperative (mood) A request or demand; a clause of direct address in which the second-person subject (*you*, or *you all*, or *you guys*) is missing, the basic form of the verb appears in the verb group, and the auxiliary in the verb group contains a *zero modal* (affirmative clauses) or dummy *do* (negative clauses). Compare *Indicative (mood)* and *Interrogative (mood)*.

Independent clause A clause that is syntactically capable of standing by itself as a complete sentence. Also, a clause, other than a *wh-* question, that cannot be introduced by a marker (whether missing or explicit) of *wh-* or non*wh-* dependency. In a clause complex, a superordinate (host) clause or a conjoined clause.

Indicative (mood) An assertion or statement; the neutral or *unmarked* grammatical meaning expressed in finite, tensed verb groups. Compare *Imperative (mood)* and *Interrogative (mood)*.

Indirect object For transitive processes, an entailed participant that may be expressed *either* obliquely by a prepositional phrase

or directly by a simple noun group. Compare *Direct object*, *Oblique object*.

Infinitive A verb group containing one of the nonfinite clause markers (*to* or *free -ing*) at the leading edge. Also a non*wh-* clause marked with *to*, *for . . . to*, *(to)*, *free -ing* or *poss . . . free -ing*.

Inflection Word-level elements that create comparative (*-er*), participle (*-ing* or *-ed/-en*), plural (*-s*), possessive (*-'s*), superlative (*-est*), past tense (*-ed*), or present tense (*-s*).

Information gap See *Wh- gap*.

Instrument The role played by the participant (usually a tool or implement) with which an actor accomplishes an action.

Intensifier A specifying constituent, usually within verb groups, adjective groups and adverb groups, but with a much broader potential range of distribution, the function of which is to fine-tune the sense of the main word or, sometimes, the entire group (or phrase or clause), by amplifying, boosting, or maximizing on the one hand or by compromising, diminishing, downtoning, or minimizing on the other. See *Extent expression*.

Intensive relationship Close relationship in sense, as between subject and complement in attributive processes. Also, often applied to the relationship between the main noun and a complementary prepositional phrase introduced by *of*.

Interrogative (mood) A question. Signaled by the preposing of the *Operator* to the front of a clause. Compare *Indicative (mood)* and *Imperative (mood)*.

Intransitive be The word *be* (and its variants, *am, is, are, was,* and *were*) when employed to express existence as an omnibus process (*be* + Ø).

Intransitive process All other-than-transitive processes not employing either *be* or a linking verb as main verb. Intransitive processes entail only one directly expressible role.

Intransitive verb Main verb expressing an intransitive process.

Irregular verb A main verb whose tense and/or perfective aspect inflections are other than canonical. Compare *Regular verb.*

Lexical Of or pertaining to the items stored individually or in meaningful combinations in one's mental dictionary.

Linking verb Main verb, other than *be*, in the verb group of an attributive (and, infrequently, locative or *there-*existential) process.

Location The specified site or time in a *be* + location process. Also, the role played by the participant that designates the place of the state or action.

Locative Expressing location in space or time.

Main word The core word of a word group; a group takes its name

from the main word. Also *Head (word).*

Manner (circumstance) Specifies the way in which an event occurs, or the degree or extent to which it occurs.

Marker The word or word-set that signals the relationship between two clauses in a clause complex: conjoined, *wh-*, or non*wh-*.

Means (circumstance) Specifies the resources or mechanisms through which an event occurs.

Missing element Any structural element that can be omitted from its grammatical context (and nearly all can be), leaving an understood or implied element; the meaning of every missing element can be recovered in some considerable detail from the discourse context, and its implicit form can be estimated.

Missing-marker version wh-clause Those embedded *wh-* clauses for which both the *wh-* marker and the *wh-* information gap are missing elements. Compare *Headless version wh- clause, Normal version wh- clause, Whiz version wh- clause.*

Modal (auxiliary) A finite auxiliary expressing mood in verb groups other than those containing tense (or a nonfinite clause marker). See *Modality.*

Modal idiom Used with respect to those *Semiauxiliaries* that most closely approximate the *Modals* in sense (i.e.

probability, possibility, obligation, and so forth). See *Idiomatic expression*.

Modality Mood. Also, that grammatical meaning expressed in a modal auxiliary, for example, certainty, necessity, obligation, permission, possibility, potential, prediction, probability, prohibition, volition, and so forth. See *Modal (auxiliary)*.

Modify In a word group, modifiers add descriptive information to the head word; note that *modify* contrasts with *determine*: Determiners in a noun group specify the kind of reference a main noun has (for example, definite, indefinite, numerative, partitive, universal, and so forth); modifiers that precede a head are premodifiers and those that follow are complements (postmodifiers).

Morphology The study of the form and constituency of words. Word parts are often called *morphemes*.

Multiword verb Grammatical constituent formed from the combination of a main verb and the postposed particles required to complete its meaning; functions much as does a single-item lexical verb. See *Idiomatic expression*, *Phrasal verb*, *Verb particle*.

Negative clause A clause whose verb group contains the constituents *not*, *n't*, or *never*.

Nominal clause See *Noun clause*.

Nonfinite Incapable of establishing a timeframe. Compare *Finite*.

Nonfinite clause marker For non*wh*- clauses, *to, for . . . to, (to), free -ing* and *poss . . . free -ing*. For *wh*-clauses, *to*.

Nonfinite wh- clause An embedded clause that exhibits the distinctive *wh*- coreference relationship between the head noun of the host noun group and a missing element in the embedded clause but that is marked with the non*wh*-marker *to* or with both a non*wh*-marker and a *wh*- marker.

Nonreferential A grammatical unit that does not refer (or corefer) to some aspect of an event structure. See *Expletive*.

Nonrestrictive (modifier) A nonessential or nondefining modifier; the head of the word group being modified can be identified other than through the modification. Compare *Restrictive (modifier)*.

Nonwh- appositive Non*wh*-clauses that are co-constituents in a paratactic equivalence relationship with a co-occupant in a functional unit, generally a noun group. See *Apposition*, *Appositive noun*.

Nonwh- marker Any member of the set of markers that signal embedded and subordinate non*wh*-clauses. Includes the two nonfinite markers, *to* and *Free -ing* and their variants. Compare *Wh- marker*.

Nonwh- subordination A clause functioning as participant, circumstance, or attribute, or as complement to a preposition group.

Normal version wh- clause Those embedded *wh-* clauses for which only the *wh-* information gap is a missing element. Compare *Headless version wh- clause, Missing-marker version wh- clause, Whiz version wh- clause.*

Noun A word that can be made plural.

Noun clause A headless *wh-* clause embedded in a noun group that is functioning as participant, attribute, or complement of a preposition group. Also, subordinate finite and nonfinite non*wh-* clauses serving the same functions. Also *Nominal clause.* Compare *Adjective clause, Adverb clause.*

Noun complement Generally, any completer of a noun group; applied to a non*wh-* clause that is embedded in a noun group and that completes the sense of the group; contrasts with *appositive* in that an appositive is a co-occupant rather than a completer.

Noun group A word group headed by a noun; participants in English are normally noun groups or noun-group substitutes (such as pronouns or clauses).

Object In a canonical (SVO) clause, any participant other than the first-named participant. Compare *Subject.*

Object complement Following the direct object in some transitive processes, an attribute of that direct object; traditionally treated as an attributive word group or phrase in the predicate of the host clause

but analyzed here as a subordinate non*wh-* clause with an attributive process.

Object of the preposition The word-group (usually noun-group, but also adverb-group and clause) complement of the preposition group in a prepositional phrase. See *Complement.*

Object of a prepositional verb The oblique object in those processes that require one entailed participant to be introduced by a preposition group.

Oblique object A participant introduced by a preposition group. For transitive processes, those entailed participants that can be expressed both directly and obliquely are traditionally termed *indirect objects.* Compare *Direct object, Indirect object.*

Operator The verb-group element that appears to the left of (precedes) the subject in questions, usually an auxiliary element, but main verb *be* and sometimes *have* also function in this capacity; the operator also serves to attract clause-level negation. See *Periphrastic auxiliary.*

Other-than-transitive All process types that strictly entail only one participant role.

Paratactic Used with respect to the juxtaposed (strung together) or equivalence relationship that is characteristic, for example, of conjoined or appositive elements (*para-* means 'on the same level' and *tactic* means 'arranged'). Compare *Hypotactic*.

Participant The role-players and the essential props involved in an event; many participants are strictly *Entailed* by processes, some are optional.

Participant function The grammatical functions *Subject*, *Direct object*, *Oblique object*, and *Indirect object*.

Participant role The experiential relationship between a process and a participant; the nature of the participant's involvement in the process; the part played in the narrative event specified by the process.

Participial phrase See *Past participial phrase* and *Present participial phrase*.

Participle The *-ing* and *-ed/-en* verb forms.

Particle Word or words, morphologically similar to prepositions or spatial adverbs, that follow the main verb in multiword verbs. Also *Postposed particle*, *Verb particle*.

Passive participle See *Past participle*.

Passive voice (clause) A clause in which the verb group contains the element *be + -ed/-en*; in a clause with a passive verb group, the participant roles that are normally expressed by the subject are expressed by an oblique object, and the roles

normally expressed by direct or oblique objects are expressed by the subject. Compare *Active voice (clause)*.

Past participial phrase Generally, a *wh-* clause with a missing *Wh-marker* and missing form of *be* (from *be + -ed/-en*) in the verb group; the *-ed/-en* form involved is here termed *Passive participle* rather than the more traditional *Past participle*. Also *Whiz version wh- clause*.

Past participle The *ed/-en* form that in partnership with *have* expresses the perfective aspect and that in partnership with *be* expresses the passive voice; because this form is not marked for tense, it is here called either *perfect participle* or *passive participle* rather than *past participle*.

Patient The role played by the participant that undergoes an action. Compare *Goal*.

Perfective aspect Discontinuous core auxiliary in the precentral position of the verb group, formed with *have + -ed/-en*. See *Aspect*.

Perfect participle See *Past participle*.

Periphrastic auxiliary When a clause requires an operator but none is available, *do* substitutes. See *(Dummy) do*.

Phrasal verb Another label for a unit composed of a main verb and the particle that completes its meaning. See *Multiword verb*.

Phrase A syntactic unit made up of at least two word groups, neither of which is embedded in the other. Compare *Group*.

Place (circumstance) Specifies the locations, positions, directions, or distances at which an event occurs.

Possessive The determiners *my, our, your, his, her, its, their, whose*. Also, the pronouns *mine, ours, yours, his, hers, theirs*. Also, loosely, the *'s* marker for possession, origin, description, measure, and so forth; sometimes expressed in *of-* constructions. See *Genitive*.

Postmodifier In a word group, the modifiers that follow the head. See *Complement*.

Postnominal Elements appearing to the right of or following the main noun in a noun group.

Postposed particle Word or words, morphologically similar to prepositions or spatial adverbs, that follow the main verb in multiword verbs. Also *Particle, Verb particle*.

Predeterminer Any determiner that can occur to the left (in front) of the articles *a(n)* and *the*.

Predicate Loosely, all clause elements other than the *Subject*.

Predicate adjective The main adjective in a *be*-plus-attribute or linking-verb-plus-attribute process of which the attribute is an adjective group.

Predicate noun The main noun in a *be*-plus-attribute or linking-verb-plus-attribute process of which the attribute is a noun group.

Premodifier In a word group, the modifiers that precede the head. Compare *Postmodifier*.

Prenominal Elements appearing to the left of or prior to the main noun in a noun group.

Preposition Words that mark oblique or indirect objects, specifying the participant role of their complement, which can be either a noun group, a clause, or an adverb group. Also, words that in combination with their complements are capable of functioning as complements to main nouns within noun groups. Also, words that with their complements are capable of functioning as circumstances, relationship units, discourse units, or as attributes or locations in attributive or locative processes. See *Prepositional phrase, Intensive relationship*.

Prepositional phrase A phrase comprised of a preposition group and its complement, which can be either a noun group, a clause, or an adverb group.

Prepositional verb Any verb that requires an oblique object.

Present participial phrase Generally, a *wh-* clause with a missing *wh-* marker and missing form of *be* (from *be* + *-ing*) in the verb group; the *-ing* form involved is here termed *progressive participle* rather than the more traditional *present participle*. Also *Whiz version wh- clause*.

Present participle The *-ing* participle; because this form is not marked for tense, it is here called the *progressive participle* rather than the *present participle*.

Primary auxiliary (verb) *Be* in *be + -ing* (progressive aspect) and *be + -ed/-en* (passive voice), or *have* in *have + -ed/-en* (perfective aspect).

Process The core constituent of a clause; determines participant roles of entailed and optional participants; occasionally entails circumstance.

Proform A word that stands for another word, word group, phrase, or clause.

Progressive aspect Discontinuous core auxiliary in the precentral position of the verb group, formed with *be + -ing*. See *Aspect*.

Progressive participle See *Present participle*.

Pronoun A proform standing for a noun group.

Proper noun Name of specific person, institution, place, and so forth, for which reference is typically unique and that therefore properly forms a set of only one member. Compare *Common noun*.

Raising Any syntactic structure in which an element that is part of the event structure of a dependent clause functions as an element in the superordinate clause.

Reason (circumstance) Gives the reasons, contingencies, or the purposes for which an event occurs.

Recipient The role played by the participant to whom a *Patient* is transferred.

Recursion The process whereby groups, phrases, and clauses appear within constituents of like or smaller rank in the structural hierarchy.

Reduced relative Embedded *wh-* clauses in which both the *wh-* marker and a form of *be* are missing. See *Whiz version wh- clause*.

Regular verb A regular verb has five distinct forms: basic, *-s* present, *-ed* past, *-ed/-en* participle, and *-ing* participle. Compare *Irregular verb*.

Relationship function The facility of language whereby speakers can represent, organize, effect, and comment upon interpersonal relationships.

Relationship unit An element adjoined to a clause, external to the event structure, that reflects the relationships among speakers or comments on those relationships.

Relative clause An embedded *wh-* clause.

Relative pronoun The set of *wh-* markers. Sometimes subdivided into *relative pronouns* (who, what, which, . . .) and *relative adverbs* (when, where, why, how, . . .). Also *Wh-marker*.

Representational function The process by which language organizes the mental record of ordinary experience into units that stand for (*represent*) the events in experience.

Restrictive (modifier) Essential or defining modifiers; the head of the word group being modified can be identified through the modification alone. Compare *Nonrestrictive (modifier)*.

Result The role played by the participant that is the outcome of a process.

Semiauxiliary (verb) That set of elements of the verb group (other than the modal and the core auxiliaries, all of which express mood) that are comprised of more than one word, terminate with the particle *to*, and can be inflected with tense.

Sentence The structural unit that is the largest unit of analysis in the grammar, composed of clauses or clause complexes and functioning as assertions, questions, and requests/demands.

Structural Approaches to the study of language that focus on the way language is organized.

Subject The first-named participant in a canonical (SVO) clause. Compare *Object*.

Subject complement The attribute in a *be*-plus-attribute or linking-verb-plus-attribute process.

Subordination The grammatical configuration in which one clause functions as process (i.e. attribute), participant, or circumstance in another clause; also, the grammatical configuration in which a clause functions as complement to a preposition group in a prepositional phrase.

Superlative Extent expression in which comparison involves more than two entities. Compare *Comparative*.

Superordinate clause A clause into which another clause is embedded or to which another clause is subordinate. Also *Host clause*.

SVO The Subject-Verb-Object order of the canonical English clause; the expected or default order of English clauses.

Syntactic Of or pertaining to *Syntax*.

Syntax The regularities that govern the spatial or temporal sequences of elements in the grammar of words, word groups, phrases, clauses, and clause complexes.

Tense A bound grammatical unit (an *Inflection*), designating either present or past, appearing only in verb groups that contain neither a modal nor a nonfinite clause marker.

Time (circumstance) Sets the timeframe, frequency, or duration of an event.

Transitive process A process that entails at least two directly expressible participant roles.

Transitive verb The main verb (or, in multiword verbs, the main verb plus postposed particles) expressing a process that entails at least two directly expressible participant roles.

Triangle convention The reporting convention wherein an embedded or subordinate structure, normally a clause, is represented in an arrowhead shape that resembles a triangle.

Uninflected Any lexical item that is not inflected. Also *Basic form*.

Verb A word that can be inflected for tense.

Verb group A word group headed by a verb; all processes in English include at least one verb group in their structure.

Verb particle Word or words, morphologically similar to prepositions or spatial adverbs, that follow the main verb in multiword verbs. Also *Particle, Postposed particle*.

Wh- clause A clause with a *wh-* marker to the left of its left-hand edge and a missing-element coreferential information gap (*wh-*gap) within the clause proper.

Wh- double-marked clause A nonfinite *wh-* clause that is marked with both a *wh-* marker and the non*wh-* marker *to*.

Wh- gap The missing-element coreferential information gap in a *wh-*clause; may occur at any location in the clause where a noun group might otherwise be located; the *wh-* gap always corefers with the *wh-* marker.

Wh- hybrid clause A nonfinite *wh-*clause that is marked only with the non*wh-* marker *to*.

Wh- marker A member of one of the two sets of markers that signal content questions (*where, why,*

who(m), when, what, how, which, and *whose,* as well as their *-ever* forms) or *wh-* embedded clauses (*where, why, who(m), when, what, how, which, whose,* and *that,* as well as their *-ever* and *-soever* forms). Compare *Nonwh-marker*.

Wh- question Content question; the verb group is discontinuously structured such that its left-hand edge precedes the subject of the clause, exactly as in a *yes/no question*; however, unlike a yes/no question, a *wh-* question clause is preceded by a *wh-* question marker and contains a related *wh-* information gap to focus content; *wh-* question markers are *who(m), whose, what, which, when, where, how,* and *why,* as well as their *-ever* forms.

Wh- relationship The connection between a *wh-* word and its related information gap.

Whiz version wh- clause Those embedded *wh-* clauses for which three elements are missing: (1) the *wh-* marker itself, (2) any form of *be,* except the one in a *there*-plus-*be* process, and (3) the *wh-* information gap. Compare *Headless version wh-clause, Missing-marker version wh-clause, Normal version wh- clause*.

Word group See *Group*.

Yes/no question A clause in which the verb group is discontinuous and its left-hand edge (or main verb *be*) precedes the subject, so as to appear at the left-hand edge of the clause.

You understood The second-person missing-element subject in imperative (direct requests and demands) clauses.

Zero infinitive A verb group with the missing-element nonfinite clause marker (TO) at the left-hand edge. Also *Bare infinitive*.

Zero modal The element postulated to occupy the left-hand edge of the verb group in English-language imperative (direct-request) clauses.

References

Aarts, Flor, and Jan Aarts. *English Syntactic Structures: Functions and Categories in Sentence Analysis.* Oxford: Pergamon, 1982.

Baker, C. L. *English Syntax.* 2nd ed. Cambridge, MA: MIT Press, 1995.

Bloor, Thomas, and Meriel Bloor. *The Functional Analysis of English: A Hallidayan Approach.* London: Arnold, 1995.

Burton-Roberts, Noel. *Analysing Sentences: An Introduction to English Syntax.* 2nd ed. London: Longman, 1997.

Bybee, Joan, Revere Perkins, and William Pagliuca. *The Evolution of Grammar: Tense, Aspect, and Modality in the Languages of the World.* Chicago: University of Chicago Press, 1994.

Celce-Murcia, M., and D. Larsen-Freeman. *The Grammar Book: An ESL/ EFL Teacher's Course.* Rowley, MA: Newbury House, 1983.

Crystal, David. *A Dictionary of Linguistics and Phonetics.* 3rd ed. Oxford: Blackwell, 1991.

Dik, Simon C. *The Theory of Functional Grammar. Part 1: The Structure of the Clause.* Dordrecht: Foris, 1989.

Givón, T. *English Grammar: A Function-based Introduction.* 2 vols. Amsterdam: Benjamins, 1993.

Halliday, M. A. K., and Ruqaiya Hasan. *Cohesion in English.* London: Longman, 1976.

Halliday, M. A. K., and Christian M. I. M. Matthiessen. *An Introduction to Functional Grammar.* 3rd ed. London: Arnold, 2004.

Heine, Bernd. *Cognitive Foundations of Grammar.* New York: Oxford University Press, 1997.

Huddleston, Rodney. *Introduction to the Grammar of English.* Cambridge: Cambridge University Press, 1984.

Huddleston, Rodney, and Geoffrey K. Pullum. *The Cambridge Grammar of the English Language.* Cambridge: Cambridge University Press, 2002.

Hurford, James R. *Grammar: A Student's Guide.* Cambridge: Cambridge University Press, 1994.

Jackson, Howard. *Grammar and Meaning: A Semantic Approach to English Grammar*. London: Longman, 1990.

Lock, Graham. *Functional English Grammar: An Introduction for Second-language Teachers*. Cambridge: Cambridge University Press, 1996.

McCawley, James D. *The Syntactic Phenomena of English*. 2nd ed. Chicago: University of Chicago Press, 1998.

Postal, Paul. *On Raising: One Rule of English Grammar and Its Theoretical Implications*. Cambridge, MA: MIT Press, 1974.

Quirk, Randolph, Sidney Greenbaum, Geoffrey Leech, and Jan Svartvik. *A Comprehensive Grammar of the English Language*. London: Longman, 1985.

Rudanko, Juhani. *Prepositions and Complement Clauses*. Albany, NY: SUNY Press, 1996.

Thompson, Geoff. *Introducing Functional Grammar*. London: Arnold, 1996.

Index

Note: This index cites *charts and lists* in italic and **main discussion(s)** in bold.